650 net

D1256031

Date Due			

The Literature of Liberal Adult Education 1945 - 1957

Compiled By

J. D. Mezirow

and

Dorothea Berry

for

The Center for the Study of Liberal Education for Adults

The Scarecrow Press, Inc.

New York   1960

Table of Contents

Preface

Several years ago Jack Mezirow approached the Center about the publication of a bibliography describing adult education work carried on by public libraries. In view of the Center's major concern with university adult education we could not take the opportunity to publish that document, but we immediately suggested a bibliography dealing with university liberal education for adults.

This publication - which grew out of that discussion - is proof that high quality work can be produced despite a variety of logistic and geographical obstacles. Shortly after Mezirow, Assistant Professor of Education, and Dorothea Berry, Assistant Reference Librarian, at the University of California at Riverside, were commissioned to undertake the preparation of this bibliography, Mezirow accepted an assignment in Pakistan for two years and left the country - but he continued active participation in the preparation of the bibliography. At about the same time, the Center established its Clearinghouse; and Roger DeCrow, with his library background and interest in the bibliography, took responsibility for the Center's participation in the project.

For the next year a very salubrious and productive three-cornered editorial team with axes in Chicago, Riverside, California and Karachi, Pakistan went into action. Early in 1959 this experiment in world-wide collaboration was enlarged. We were delighted when Ralph R. Shaw, ingenious inventor of the Scarecrow Press, agreed to publish the document. As a result he was brought into the editing circle, a fact which thus included the east coast. As is the wont of publishers, Shaw decided that the bibliography was a masterpiece - but that the notes had to be cut in half. At this point - aware of Solomon's prior research on the attitude of parents toward the mutilation of their children - we asked Coolie Verner at Florida State University to help out on some of the surgery. This he did expertly and ruthlessly.

After his excisions were cleared in Riverside, Karachi, Chicago and finally New Brunswick, N.J., with several limbs and a few other vital organs restored, the manuscript was ready for publication.

The net result of this long-distance operation is one which we at the Center are proud to sponsor. We feel that it will fill an unmet need in the field. We believe that it is well done and expertly produced. We salute Miss Berry and the other members of our far-flung team and thank them for their diligence, patience and forebearance in completing this task. We are happy also to announce that the Center will keep their work up to date through biennial supplements to the bibliography.

A. A. Liveright, Director
Center for the Study of Liberal
Education for Adults

Introduction

This book is designed to provide readers of the professional literature of adult education a comprehensive guide to journal articles, government publications, pamphlets and books published in certain major segments of the field since World War II in the United States, Great Britain and Canada.

The period 1945-1957 has witnessed the most spectacular growth in the history of the adult education movement in the United States, both in numbers participating and in development toward professionalization. Estimated participation has been reported to have increased nearly 59 per cent during the five year period 1950-1955 alone. C. Hartley Grattan attributes the dynamism of the period to the social disturbance and national insecurity resulting from World War II and the Cold War. He cites the stimulus of the experiments in adult education in the armed forces as a contingent factor. The G.I. Bill and its counterparts on the state level also introduced thousands of adults to educational programs. A national conviction that crucial decisions will have to be made by the adults of this generation or not at all is documented by the concern over the need for and direction of adult education by a succession of high level committees and commissions in the post-war and Cold War periods from the President's Commission on Higher Education in 1947 to the President's Committee on Education Beyond the High School a decade later.

The thirteen year period saw the establishment of UNESCO and its significant contributions to adult education through field work, publications and the sponsorship of three international conferences. The National Training Laboratory for Group Development was established in 1947 by the National Education Association and stimulated the development of an international movement through research, publications and regional training laboratories. Three major educational institutions were created in 1951, the Adult Education Association of the U.S.A., the Fund for Adult Education, and the Center for the Study of Liberal Education for Adults, which together sparked the most intensive professional activity ever

vii

experienced in American adult education with publications, conferences, research, program experimentation and training programs. Every phase of adult education has shared in this awakened interest, and whole new vistas have been discovered in educational television, group process education, community development, education for the aging and liberal adult education. With this renaissance the literature of the field has proliferated beyond the point where it is manageable even for the scholar. The average adult educator is hard put to keep abreast of professional developments in his particular area of specialization because of the valuable overlapping implications of advances in other parts of the field.

Within the scope defined below we have attempted in this publication to compile as all-inclusive a bibliography as possible drawing upon the body of references organized in the standard indexes of periodical literature as the core of our work and supplementing this with additional references which came to our attention. Every index listed in the section on Bibliography was utilized in our effort to achieve as comprehensive a coverage as possible. We have hoped to enhance the utility of the bibliography by the liberal use of annotations. Indeed, in most instances, we have exceeded the usual scope of annotation and have written abstracts or precis of each entry in what we have considered the most relevant categories of our taxonomy so that the reader can briefly judge the appropriateness of a publication for his purposes and direct his further research or reading as economically as possible.

The ambiguity of the relatively recent term "liberal adult education" and the skirmishes which have resulted when adult educators of widely divergent philosophical orientations have appropriated it to interpret their familiar positions in more fashionable terms have made the task of delimiting the subject to workable proportions difficult. The limitations of space have required that we attempt this in operational terms. Publications have been subsumed under the following five areas:

    I.   Direction Finding: Philosophy and Trends
    II. Research and Bibliography - reviews of research, adult learning, student needs and interests, student characteristics, program planning and evaluation, research needs and methods, training of teachers of adults, historical studies and other research; bibliographies
    III. The Roles of Universities and Colleges - United States, Canada and Great Britain

IV.   The Roles of Other Agencies - public schools; libraries; business, industry and labor; specialized agencies.

V.   Courses and Curricula

All publications included in Sections I, II and III are abstracted or annotated; those in Sections IV and V are not. Doctoral dissertations have not been annotated.

While we have preferred to err in the direction of breadth in interpreting the scope of liberal adult education, especially in Sections I and II, publications included in Sections III, IV and V have either been specifically designated as treating liberal adult education by their authors or are, in the compilers' judgment, wholly or in part concerned with the subject matter of the liberal arts, broadly defined to include the humanities, sciences and social science, organized in any of the varied forms and taught by any of the rich repertoire of methods of adult education. Thus the number of publications dealing with the roles of certain agencies are unfamiliarly small.

Descriptions of programs in the following fields of adult education are not included: vocational education; literacy and fundamental education; education in recreation, crafts and hobbies; guidance and counseling of adults; education in the armed forces; Americanization education; religious education; workers' education when confined to union operation and development; industrial and management training when confined to company operation and development and technical skills; audio-visual education; community development as such; group process education and human relations; professional training in adult education.

Also excluded are reports of research in personality, attitude formation and change, group dynamics, inter-group relations, leadership, discussion methods, communication and the mass media, participation, decision making and the sociology of the community.

Publications dealing primarily with methods, materials, financing and administration of adult education have been excluded as have annual reports of public school adult education.   The section on Bibliography does not list film and filmstrip bibliographies. Articles appearing in popular magazines and newspapers and foreign language publications have not been selected for inclusion nor has unpublished material with the exception of doctoral disserations and some of the publications of the Center for the Study of Liberal Education for Adults.   We trust these value judgments have not done violence to the spirit of liberal adult education.

This publication was made possible by the interest, encouragement and financial assistance of the Center for the Study of Liberal Education for Adults.   We are especially grateful to A. A. Liveright, Director of the Center, and to Roger De Crow, Director of the Center's Clearinghouse, for their personal interest, cooperation, and assistance in arranging publication; also to R. Philip Chamberlin of University Extension at UCLA, for his assistance on the section on Direction Finding, to Arlene Polanchek and Doris Major for their help in typing and proofreading, and to Ruth Phelps for her assistance in indexing.

J. D. Mezirow
Dorothea Berry

I. Direction Finding: Philosophy and Trends

Adam, Thomas R. Popular Understanding for Survival, In
  Adult Education Journal, 6 (July, 1947) 125-128.
    The great organizing test for the adult education move-
ment is to help people learn what they must know to live
free and at peace. The challenge to adult educators is
the problem of linking world policies to personal affairs
of ordinary people and so make them the subject of continuous discussion, study and practical judgment. The
adult education movement will become representative when
it is based upon community life and is made the instrument by which people translate their local and group purposes into the wider field of the nation and the world.
Media of predigested discussion and opinion such as press
and radio cannot be entrusted to supply information to a
free people. There are organizations for gathering and
distributing unbiased information on world affairs, but
channels of communication are blocked. Minimum requirements for proper use of such material are: (1) establishment in communities throughout the country of a
working system of discussion meetings to allow individuals
to relate personal needs and views to public affairs; (2)
a method by which needs of community groups can be com-
municated to regional or national organizations dispensing
informational material and discussion aids; (3) a capacity
on the part of regional and national bodies to prepare material on world affairs so it can be applied by users in
terms of local problems.   1

Adler, Mortimer J. Adult Education, In Journal of Higher
  Education, 23 (February, 1952) 59-67, 115.
    Many professional educators and laymen hold the false
view that it is the purpose of schools, from kindergarten
through college, to give a complete education. Many also
hold a false view of adult education as remedial education,
or an avocation or hobby. Young people are more train-
able but mature adults are more educable if education is
conceived of as growth of understanding, insight and wisdom. Liberal education is education for freedom, respon-

sibilities of citizenship, and good use of leisure. Children should be given the skills of learning and the wish to
learn so they will continue learning in adult life. To keep
the mind alive and growing and to seek wisdom, there
must be a program of adult education that will sustain
learning through many years, that treats adults as adults,
that can be done voluntarily and is in every way proper
for the mind. The writer proposes the Great Books program as the one program fulfilling these requirements because the Great Books are inexhaustible, written for a-
dults, and deal with basic issues that confront mankind. 2

Adult Education Association of U.S.A. "Education Throughout Life: the Need, the Trends, the Demand, Problems
and Issues." Chicago: A.E.A., 1957. 15pp.
    Documents the need for continuous learning as evi-
denced by the number of adults whose education is obso-
lete, the demand for trained workers, and by enrollment
in various kinds of educational institutions for adults.
Prepared for the President's Committee on Education Beyond the High School by the A.E.A. Liaison Committee. 3

Adult Education for a New World, an Interrogation, In Adult
Leadership, 1 (April, 1953) 24-28.
    In answer to the questions "What do you think should
be the basic goals of the adult education movement in the
United States today?" and "Which social factors and conditions help us and which hinder us in formulating and a-
chieving these goals?" Lawrence K. Frank states that
the aim of adult education is "to help people learn how to
see themselves and their society more clearly, to think a-
bout problems more critically, and try to cope with them
more intelligently and creatively." Hindering conditions
include social lag, need for learning to think in terms of
a world community, urbanized living, lack of social control by the individual, increase in number of problems and
proposed solutions, and fear of change. Helping conditions are more leisure time, education, literacy, inclination to look to science for solving traditional problems,
and constructive efforts to solve anxieties. Herbert Thelen
adds that adult education must help people join to set
standards of thought and action in keeping with the realities of an industrial society. Social problems require
learning about how to participate in groups and relearning
beliefs and attitudes. Leadership must assist groups to
function effectively and democratically in facing and con-
trolling social and personal realities as part of the prob-

lem solving process. Kenneth Benne cites the conflict in
America over defining and applying democratic values in
inter-personal relations and social control. He identifies
two non-democratic ideologies of leadership in our tradition: (1) an individualistic conception of man and society, and (2) the idea of leadership by the elect, ordained
by aristocratic birth, native endowment or special access
to truth.   4

Alexander, W. P. Challenge and Response in Adult Education,
In Adult Education (London), 27 (Winter, 1954) 166-172.
    There is danger that adult education may become a
thing apart from the main structure of education and conceived in a narrow sense which would limit the service to
a few people. Three basic principles in the light of which
work in adult education and in all other branches of education must be judged are: (1) There is almost no correlation between provision of higher education and the economic and social stability of the nation. (2) There is a
very high correlation between the amount of education
which all of the people get and national and social health.
(3) The greatest current problem in modern society is the
widening gap between leaders and followers. Over-em-
phasis on tutorial courses of high academic quality has
limited adult education to a small proportion of the adult
population. This contributes to widening the gap between
leaders and followers and to disunity within the nation.
Adult education is a permanent national necessity, an inseparable aspect of citizenship, and should be universal
and lifelong. An immediate task is to get the full virtues
of liberal adult education embodied in the work of further
education. Residential colleges have a contribution to
make, as do voluntary bodies. The present pattern in
which sections of adult education tend to be divorced from
the general pattern of the educational system is a restrictive influence. A first requirement in finding the answer
to the real challenge in adult education is clarity on relevant basic principles. Emphasis must be on development
of a wide variety of opportunities which help people better
to interpret experience, based on the principle that the
economic and social strength of the nation rests on the
education which all of the people get. The National Institute of Adult Education has a great opportunity to make
suggestions how best to meet the real challenge which re-
mains so largely unanswered.   5

Benne, Kenneth D. John Dewey and Adult Education, In

Adult Education Bulletin, 14 (October, 1949) 7-12.
  Although John Dewey, in his writings, devoted a small
amount of discussion to adult education problems as such,
many of his theories are applicable. "The Public and
Its Problems" offers the most suggestions concerning the
central problem of adult education today. According to
this work, the task of converting the "Great Society,"
characterized by impersonal and mechanical modes of behavior, into the "Great Community" is no different from
democratizing industrial and national societies. The
conditions for democratizing modern life to bring adequately shared and genuinely "public" control are equally
the conditions of adequate adult education. Three of the
means Dewey suggests for building toward the "Great
Community" suggest more definite direction for adult education today: (1) Social science directed toward discovery of genuinely public facts and meanings must be put
to work in furnishing bases of knowledge for public policy and decision making. (2) Conditions of full and free
public expression with respect to social problems and to
investigations and thinking concerning them must be established and maintained. (3) The rebuilding of a healthy
public requires restoration of effective local communities
providing centers of effective identification and devotion
within the mass public.   6

Benne, Kenneth D. Some Philosophic Issues in Adult Education, In Adult Education, 7 (Winter, 1957) 67-82.
  States that the basic issues in adult education differ
little, if any, from basic issues in education generally,
and identifies a few of the issues which currently divide
educators of adults. Discusses three clusters of assumptions: (1) the nature of man--man as continuous with nature, man as discontinuous with nature, individual and social man, man as discontinuous with society, man as do-
er or thinker; (2) the nature of learning--the method of
authority, the method of induction, the method of experimentation; (3) the nature, source, and limits of pedagogical authority.   7

Benne, Kenneth D. Why I Ran for President of AEA, In
  Adult Leadership, 4 (January, 1956) 6-8.
  In our generation the social and moral environment has
undergone radical changes. Education for transmitting a
fixed cultural heritage is inadequate. Educational leadership is charged with the task of organizing an environment
in which people may engage in joint inquiry to solve per-

sonal, group and community problems. We need to develop a conception of education that includes adult education as an integral part. Our society leads to a continuous alienation of persons and groups from full participation in their communities and society. The major task of
adult education is reduction of alienation and resulting in-
ability to participate constructively in the social process.
This transcends personal therapy to include social factors
of disorganization. An important task of adult education
is rigorous self-appraisal of success as measured against
these criteria. The Adult Education Association can help
with the process of this self-appraisal and the self-train-
ing and reeducation by which adult educators must equip
themselves to achieve progress.   8

Bethel, Lawrence L. The Satisfaction of Needs in Adult
Education, In Junior College Journal, 16 (December,
1945) 169-176.
        Satisfaction of needs in adult education must start with
the satisfaction of wants. In adult education wants become especially significant because of their scope and
variation. A knowledge of specific needs must grow out
of local study and planning. In general adult needs are of
three types: (1) vocational competence, (2) social con-
sciousness, and (3) competence in group activity. Five
points of generalization concerning what adults want are:
(1) Subject matter must be functional to the lives of
people. (2) Methods of instruction must be varied. (3)
Adult education must be designed for the level of intellectual, social, and physical maturity of the adult. (4) It
must be flexible in tern s of individual needs, which vary
in terms of aptitude, ability, and previous achievement.
(5) It should provide opportunity for the individual to build a
systematic and coordinated program of education. Since
adult education is different from other types of education
in organizational operation, there is a trend toward separate administration and faculty. A program of adult education requires an unusual amount of flexibility which is
often difficult to procure when the administration of the
college is removed from needs of the adult community.
A good adult education faculty might well include specially
selected representatives of the regular faculty of the institution, representatives from industry, and people who
would devote full time to the adult program and provide
the necessary continuity and leadership. Separation of
organization and operation does not exclude necessity for
integration of the adult education program with regular

programs of the institution, but affords greater opportunity
for recognition and cooperation with the parent institution.
The junior college is particularly adaptable to the work
of adult education because it is in most cases a community
college with purposes established in terms of needs of its
community, and it is flexible.   9

Birnbaum, Max.   Mind and Emotion in Adult Education, In
Adult Education, 7 (Spring, 1957) 144-151.

The central issues in the philosophy of adult education
are: (1) the role of cognition; (2) the role of emotion
and the irrational; (3) the problem of values and attitudes;
(4) the role of the individual and the group; (5) the role
of the teacher.   Two functional problems are: Method
versus Content, and the Individual versus the Community.
These issues are discussed with two objectives in mind:
first, to state what appears to be the rationale for each
of the positions of the two major schools of adult education, the "Traditionalist" and the "Psychological," and
second, to attempt to harmonize the two positions where
possible.   The writer concludes that the distinction between the two approaches is often artificial.   The process
of education is almost always two-dimensional with inter-
weaving of the cognitive and emotional make up of man.
The two conflicting goals in adult education, development
of the mature individual or improvement of total communities, are interrelated and a collaborative relationship
between the two schools is the   solution.   10

Blakely, Robert J.   Adult Education and Civil Liberties, In
Food for Thought, 15 (November, 1954) 6-9.

The only real protection of freedom is in the responsible exercise of the freedom of education.   Education for
most young people ends with formal education with an increase of narrowly practical concerns and neglect of that
which is enduring and prevailing in significance.   Adult
education is inherent in the nature of man, in the nature
of life, and in the nature of social authority.   Liberal a-
dult education is the education of free man for freedom.
In our industrial democracy we have still to discover the
means to educate all adults to become free men.   To
strive toward the ideal we must regard all experience as
educative and treat and direct it as such, and regard ourselves as educators and all our influence over others as
educative.   The goal is to create not just good schools,
but a total environment conducive to self-realization.   11

Blakely, Robert J. Adult Education Needs a Philosophy and
a Goal, In Adult Education, 3 (November, 1952) 2-10.
Same under title Adult Education in and for a Free Society, In Adult Education (London), 25 (Spring, 1953) 286-
296.
    Blakely observes that in every period of vast social
change both compulsion and human aspiration are forces.
In our society compulsion is seen as "the consequences
of the application of science to the physical world" and
aspiration as democracy. Adult educators need and are
ready for a common cause and direction in whatever problem areas or programs they may work. The adult education movement must make a direct major approach to
general education, and address itself to the "over-arching
issues of personal and social life." Capricious and ill
considered wants should not dictate the adult educator's
role but he must help individuals find and fulfill values
beyond themselves. The idea of inducing behavior change
through increased sensitivity to and skill with emotional
factors has been overstated. Experimental situations have
subordinated objectives to methods and intellectual processes to emotional. Such priorities would be calamitous
in general practice. Skill in problem solving is a need
of major importance to groups since problems are the essence of life. Professional adult educators should form
a cadre to train "recruits," to insist on significance and
excellence in their education, and to make "persuasive
and moving statements of purpose and aims, not in one
standardized situation, but in a host of varied situations."
                                                        12

Blakely, Robert J. Adult Education: Stalk or Flower? In
National Education Association Journal, 42 (April, 1953)
232-233.
    An imaginary conversation between an adult educator
and a child prodigy, in which the relationship between a-
dult education and formal education is compared to that
between the stalk and the flower. Education should aim at
producing persons who trust and exemplify reason, with
freedom of speech and freedom to test the correctness of
their own and others' opinions. Education must be continuing. Formal schooling should concentrate on basic
skills to be exercised throughout life. Not enough adult
education is devoted to exercise and improvement of a-
bility to think, to the acquisition of knowledge indispensable to understanding and ability to cope with what is new.
Neither formal nor adult education has learned how to give

a liberal education to the many instead of the few. The
school cannot meet all educational needs of citizens but
one responsibility which it cannot sacrifice is its responsibility for providing intellectual training in every field
where systematic thinking is an important component of
success. Intellectual thinking is more essential than ever
before in the history of mankind. In one sense adult education is the stalk supporting the flower of formal education; in another sense the stalk of formal education is
supporting the flower of adult education.   13

Blakely, Robert J.   The Free Individual and the Free Society, In Fund for Adult Education, Liberal Adult Education.   White Plains, N.Y.: F.A.E., 1956. Pp. 69-78.
    In nature there are contrary tendencies, in one direc-
tion toward disorganization, in the other direction toward
order.   Life has purpose--purpose to live, grow, repro-
duce, and fulfill itself, and it advances to more complex
organization through evolution.   The mature human being
holds in his hands and mind the direction of his future evolution.   Culture is the individual's ecology because the human being is almost bereft of instinct.   Society is the individual's most important environment because for fulfillment of his purposes he needs cooperation of other human
beings.   The forces of dissolution work constantly upon
the physical organism.   Whether they work also upon the
mind and personality depends upon whether the individual
takes command of the development of awareness which depends upon his vigilance, self-discipline, affirmation and
effort, and upon possibilities within the cultural ecology
and social environment.   Man is conditioned by his physical and social environment, but his awareness of being
conditioned is the embryo of freedom.   A responsible
person acts with regard to the wholeness and complexity
of his own nature and the nature of everything.   "A free
society relates freedom and responsibility; a society which
is not free tries to separate them and destroys both." A
free society does not require conformity. We should resist efforts to make us conform against our sense of individuality and also resist the temptation to force others to
conform against theirs.   A free society has shared purposes, shared power and shared respect. It is an open or
"opening" society.   Liberal education is education for responsible use of freedom.   Liberal education has relevance for all of man's special functions, but, in itself, it
is a   return to or an advancement to our common humanity.   It is the effort to discover the larger purposes which

distinguish man and the effort to prepare him to fulfill
the'se larger purposes. Liberal education is not con=
cerned with thinkers or books as such, but with important issues. These issues concern the purpose of human
life which is to fulfill itself both as a unique individual
and as a unique species. The difficulty does not lie in
the issues but in how they are put and in the lack of education or miseducation of individuals to grapple with them.
                                                          14

Blakely, Robert J. Freedom, the University, and Adult Education. See No. 487.   15

Blakely, Robert J. The Path and the Goal, In Adult Education, 7 (Winter, 1957) 93-98.
      Education is more than the transmission and advance-
   ment of culture. It is central to the essence of our hu-
   manness and to the future of human freedom, and human
   survival. Adult education is the test of elementary, secondary and higher education, of whether the process of
   growth has really begun. Adult education is the foundation of the responsible exercise of authority, a means for
   successful self-government of human affairs. Adult education has among all of its forms more than a concern for
   techniques; it has a concern and relevance for the meaning of American and human life. Education is the means
   by which life is fulfilled and the end of life. A clear vision and sincere expression of ends are essential contexts
   within which means and techniques are utilized. The
   writer reproduces Vachel Lindsay's ''On the Building of
   Springfield'' to illustrate the goal he envisions for adult
   education.   16

Bowersox, John M. The Importance of Adult Education, In
   Sierra Educational News, 42 (December, 1946) 23.
      Discusses the importance of adult education classes for
   learning skills, family education, raising the level of educational attainment through courses not previously studied,
   learning use of leisure, human relations, understanding of
   other cultures for world peace.   17

Bradford, Leland P. Report of the Division of Adult Education Services of the N.E.A., In Adult Education Bulletin,
   11 (August, 1947) 164-178.
      Part 1 analyzes five trends in adult education: (1) hope
   for adult education to provide solution to world problems,
   (2) community development and growth, (3) importance of

adult education to the education of youth, (4) increase in
adult participancy, (5) cooperation among agencies concerned with adult education; and five problems: (1) educating adults for group work, (2) developing identification
of the participant with other individuals and groups, (3)
lack of leadership, (4) need for different methods in educating adults, (5) lack of basic materials and adequate
physical facilities. Part 2 discusses efforts of the Division of Adult Education toward developing a comprehensive
program especially in the areas of veterans' education,
conference planning and procedure, leadership and in-service training, methods, and basic materials. Part 3 discusses major areas for concentration in the future: community activity, national and international problems of the
atomic age, use of mass media, leadership training, increasing membership in national and state organizations.
                                                        18

Bradford, Leland P.   Toward a Philosophy of Adult Educa-
    tion, In Adult Education, 7 (Winter, 1957) 83-93.
    Discusses three areas with which adult education must
be concerned: the internal dynamic balance of the individual; his behavior in external situations; and his ability
to take membership in his societal units. Given goals of
growth and change, an approach to adult education should
be concerned with problems of the sources of learning
(content); of organization of learning (method); of conditions of learning; encouragement of the learner (involvement); and of the role and relationship of the teacher.
Six basic conditions for realizing learning goals are: (1)
exposure of thoughts and behavior and involvement of the
individual in the process of growth and change; (2) a system of feedback; (3) emotional climate conducive to change;
(4) directional forces for change; (5) opportunities for experimentation and practice; (6) application of learning.19

Bradford, Leland P.   Will Education Win the Race With
    Catastrophe? In Adult Leadership, 2 (December, 1953) 28.
    A comment on H. L. Keenleyside's (see No. 84) theme
of "education or catastrophe." In spite of more schooling and more knowledge than ever before, individual and
social problems have vastly increased. In face of dangers
and threat of catastrophe, apathy mixed with hysteria,
rather than effective action results. The task of education is to aid people to understand and operate successfully in the changing world. Education should be concerned with all problems of developing and changing knowl-

Brigham, Harold F.   11

edge, values, and behavior. Educators must not be concerned only with creating change but with seeing that desirable or necessary changes have a chance to be maintained.   20

Brigham, Harold F. Indiana Sets Goals, In Adult Education
Journal, 6 (July, 1947) 154.
    An excerpt from a statement of goals for adult educa-
tion adopted by the Indiana Association for Adult Education. "Adult education, in the broad acceptance of the
term, comprehends all educational activities engaged in by
persons who have terminated their basic formal schooling
and assumed the responsibilities of adulthood... Its ultimate end is that individual growth may become synonymous with community, national, and world progress."
Ten objectives of adult education are listed: That every
adult may (1) recognize his potentialities and evolve a
plan of development in keeping with his capacities, needs
and interests; (2) make use of his mental powers through
broad, deep, clear thinking, and through exercise of his
creative abilities; (3) develop maximum facility in use of
language and in understanding and interpretation of basic
areas of knowledge; (4) enjoy good health, proper posture
and physical fitness through developing and maintaining
them at a high level; (5) equip himself through general
and special education for earning a satisfactory living in a
vocation for which he is naturally well fitted; (6) develop
an understanding of basic tenets of Christian ideals and
apply them to daily living; (7) prepare himself for use of
leisure time through appreciation of literature, music, and
art, and through skill in recreational activities; (8) develop his personality for harmonious living with himself
and others; (9) prepare himself for the responsibilities
and privileges of family life and for contribution to the welfare of the community; (10) strive toward the ideals of
American citizenship and develop a feeling of responsibility
as a world citizen.   21

Brown, Muriel W. "Adapting Adult-Education Programs to
Postwar Needs," In National Society for the Study of Education, Forty-Fourth Yearbook, American Education in the
Postwar Period, Part I, Curriculum Reconstruction.
Chicago: University of Chicago Press, 1945. Pp. 57-79.
    Tasks of postwar reconstruction are to: (1) re-estab-
lish a sound peacetime economy; (2) reorganize communities for peacetime living; (3) stabilize and strengthen family life; (4) deal more effectively with serious social prob-

lems such as juvenile delinquency, crime, disease, etc;
(5) make better application of the principles of democracy
in the solution of domestic problems and in international
relationships. Adult education cannot supply all that is
needed for the solution of these problems, but it can be a
powerful and rich resource. Adult education presents
both opportunities and difficulties in curriculum development which are unique. A survey of present trends in a-
dult education helps to answer the question of how principles and procedures of curriculum development apply in
this complicated situation. Trends that represent significant observable tendencies are: (1) broadening of the
scope of organized programs; (2) coordination and cooperation among agencies and organizations offering educational
services to adults; (3) increasingly better provision for
systematic and continuous study of community needs as a
basis for program planning; (4) integration of programs
of study with programs of action and service, so that students may "learn by doing," and community improvement
can be facilitated; (5) a more democratic type of teacher-
student relationship in which learning experiences are
jointly planned; (6) seeking out and using a wide variety of
leadership; (7) freer and better planned use of the newer
media of instruction; (8) planning programs in relation to
ultimate values and purposes, as well as immediate goals.
Implications of these trends for curriculum-making in a-
dult education are summarized with respect to: (1) determination of goals and planning of programs; (2) development of curriculum experiences; (3) evaluation; (4) materials and working conditions; and (5) training of personnel.   22

Bryson, Lyman. "The Drive Toward Reason, in the Service
of a Free People." New York: Harper [c1954]. 148 pp.
    Based on three lectures sponsored by the Ford Founda-
tion Fund for Adult Education (See No. 24). Bryson re-
affirms faith in reason which he describes as "the untram-
meled power of the mind to examine all things." Only
reason can overcome the pessimism that seems to be en-
gulfing the nation, and to strengthen reason there must be
continuous learning of the kind that liberates the mind.
Through this process men can learn to be free by learning
to use reason in making the choices that face them. This
reason will be backed by a breadth of knowledge that will
free the mind to make rational selections. In order that
reason can be the driving force in our civilization men
must be "driven by motives stronger than mere survival

and material success." Through the advancement of communication, America is developing a community of ideas
but this needs to be strengthened by continuous liberal
studies.   This will provide the moral basis of decisions
and strengthen the effectiveness and courage of adults in
exercising reason as free citizens of democracy.   23

Bryson, Lyman. "Reason and Discontent: the Task of Liberal Adult Education." Pasadena: Fund for Adult Education, 1954. 48 pp.
    The first annual Fund for Adult Education Lectures on
the importance, significance and implications of liberal a-
dult education.   The first lecture, "Teaching Ourselves to
be Free," deals with the relationship of freedom and ra-
tionality in modern America.   In the second lecture, "The
Community of Ideas," Bryson analyzes what he considers
the most hopeful elements in our prsent situation and indicates forces to help us better ourselves in our communities with special reference to the mass media of communication.   The final lecture, "The Achievement of
Standards," considers the problem of determining moral
standards to measure progress.   24

Burch, Glen, ed.   Trends in Postwar Adult Education, In
Adult Education Journal, 5 (January, 1946) 1-55.
    Presents materials in a number of aspects of the field,
collected mainly from local or community level of adult
education activity, in a survey to assess and appraise a-
dult education trends in terms of the postwar era.   The
most significant finding is the evidence of a heavy upsurge
in enrollments.   While there is no diminution of demand
for vocational education, shifts in program offerings show
a balance with liberal education, especially social sciences
and humanities.   One lack in adult education offerings is
in the field of science.   The survey shows a growth in
the use of the discussion method as a principal technique.
The way is pointed toward careful study of the use of educational films, and toward the need for studies designed
to facilitate production in many forms of materials at every level of educational preparation.   Paucity of offerings
in some fields is the result of unwillingness of the public
to force adequate provision of funds.   The survey also indicates inadequate leadership both in amount and degree of
training.   Summaries are presented in the following fields:
Adult Education Councils, Alumni, Arts and Crafts, Correspondence Courses, Family Life Education, Films, Housing, Libraries, Museums, Naturalization and Citizenship,

Public Affairs, Public Schools, Radio, Rural Adult Educa-
tion, Safety Education, Social Work Agencies, Special
Schools, U.S. Armed Forces, Universities and Colleges,
Veterans, Vocational Education, and Workers Education.
                                                        25

Caliver, Ambrose. Continuous Learning for a Changing
    World, In Adult Leadership, 6 (September, 1957) 73-75,
    80.
        Adult education has become a necessity because of
    changes in size, mobility, and age of population, growth
    in mass media, increase in leisure, increase in produc-
    tion, and change in family life. It is possible to educate
    adults more effectively today because of the discovery of
    certain psychological insights.   Young adults especially
    need adult education to meet the problems of the modern
    world.   26

Caliver, Ambrose.   The National Concern for Adult Educa-
    tion, In School, Life, 39 (May, 1957) 5-6, 10-12.
        Adult education can aid in correcting the lag in intellec-
    tual, social, and moral advancement which have not kept
    pace with material advancement. It can aid in identifying
    and explaining underlying forces causing changes and re-
    late them to individuals' activities so they may understand
    effects and adjust and give direction to these forces, and
    it can help the nation make effective use of its human re-
    sources.   To achieve its potentialities adult education
    must be accepted as an integral part of educational pro-
    grams.   Certain agencies have   particular obligations,
    such as universities for research and preparation of
    teachers and leaders, and professional and voluntary or-
    ganizations for interpreting technological progress for the
    average citizen.   One of the greatest needs adult educa-
    tion can help meet is the need for diffusion of knowledge,
    methods, and spirit underlying advances of the new world
    and translating results of science and technology into the
    thought, language, and behavior of the average citizen.
    Needs within the adult education field itself are: better
    articulation between adult education and other areas of ed-
    ucation; improvement of teaching and supervision; develop-
    ment of programs, materials and methods better suited to
    adults; more cooperation of groups and agencies conduct-
    ing programs.   Overarching all these needs is the need
    for complete and fundamental educational reorientation re-
    quiring revision of ideas about the nature and purposes of
    education, administration and financing and a new approach

to materials and methods.   Each program should have the
benefit of an overall coordinating and guiding agency.
Where such an agency does   not exist, public school systems could take the lead on the local level, several
school systems or universities on the regional level, and
on the national level, the U.S. Office of Education coop-
erating with other federal and national agencies.   27

Carney, Francis W.   Catholics and Adult Education, In National Catholic Educational Association Bulletin, 53 (May,
   1957) 18-25.
      Catholic educators need to take a greater part in the a-
   dult education movement.   Catholic lay organizations
   should extend the scope of their educational programs and
   should relate themselves to other adult education agencies
   in the community to prevent a secularistic educational situation.   The Catholic parish should give consideration to
   adult education as well as to elementary and high school
   programs.   A deeper realization of community obligation
   and community influence ought to prompt many Catholic
   colleges to enter wholeheartedly into this field.   All levels
   of Catholic education are based upon the same educational
   philosophy: (1) The Catholic adult educator views man according to the totality of his being.   (2) The purpose of a-
   dult education is to assist in the formation of the super-
   natural man.   (3) The Catholic adult educator believes
   these purposes can be accomplished by a substantially
   Catholic pattern of education.   28

Carney, Francis W.   Philosophy and Purposes of Adult Education, In National Catholic Educational Association Bulletin, 53 (August, 1956) 358-361.
      Points out the controversy and confusion existing as to
   the philosophy and purposes of adult education, and the
   fact that the Catholic Church, with a basic and fundamental
   philosophy, is in position to formulate a more definite
   philosophy of adult education.   States purposes of adult education as: (1) development of general   and particular capacities of the adult as an individual in terms of his total
   nature; (2) development of the adult as a social being related to family life, economic and political society, and
   international society; (3) development of the adult Catholic
   as a member of the Mystical Body; and discusses how
   those purposes may be accomplished.   29

Carpenter, J.E.   For Civic Efficiency: Some Objectives for
   an Adult Citizenship Project, In Adult Education Journal,

6 (January, 1947) 14-18.

Education for civic efficiency is defined as education
for responsibility in the prevailing social order which is of
world wide scope and significance.   The reasons why a-
dult education has a responsibility in this area are: (1)
The need for civic efficiency is urgent; in the face of
present day social problems, man must learn or perish.
(2) Knowledge is a weapon.   Adult education has a heavy
responsibility for providing knowledge which is the basis
for understanding necessary to bring about cooperative
world and local relationships.   (3) The continuing character of adult education marks it as the phase and type of
education capable of training for civic efficiency.   (4) The
citizen needs to realize that the basis of a peaceful social
order is law.   Attitudes adult education must hope to
promote are: (1) We should value the good citizen or good
country by excellence, not size or power.   (2) We should
believe in and practice "liberty and justice for all."   (3)
We should appreciate that Americans are the luckiest, not
necessarily the wisest, of all people.   30

Cartwright, Morse A.   A Preview of Postwar Adult Educa-
    tion, In Educational Forum, 10 (March, 1946) 273-280.
    The necessity of making international adjustments with-
out war is paralleled by the necessity of achieving internal adjustments in critical areas of conflict without force.
Some of the areas of tension and conflict in the postwar
period are economic maladjustment, racial and intercultural antagonisms, problems of veterans and out-of-school
youth, social security, housing, recreational facilities, and
education.   Existence of these and other issues demonstrate the need for expansion of adult education activities.
The postwar period will see an ambitious forum and discussion group program developed under a variety of auspices; a widespread use of audio-visual tools; local information and counseling centers for veterans; expansion of
adult education activities of several types by institutions
of higher education; expansion of public school programs
for adults and of independent adult schools.   Other areas
of postwar expansion are workers' education, vocational education, education for Negro adults, and intercultural education.   Development of the adult education movement has
resulted in efforts at coordination of agencies through community councils, and state, regional and national associations.   Problems needing solution for successful expansion
of the movement are production of suitable materials for a-

dult classes, shortage of trained leaders, and need for
training programs.   Adult education is faced with the
greatest challenge in its history in the years ahead.   31

Cavanaugh, John J.   Adult Education and Catholics, In National Catholic Educational Association Bulletin, 49 (August,
1952) 151-157.
  Catholic influence on thought and action of leaders of
this country can be realized more quickly and surely
through the Great Books movement than in any other way.
Moral education is even more important than education of
the mind.   Moral virtue is not altogether a matter of
knowledge, but any consideration of moral education must
begin with knowledge.   Reading the Great Books should
help to discover the nature of the good life, but the revelation of religion is also needed.   Moral virtue requires
action in addition to knowledge.   Moral development, like
intellectual development, is interminable and requires systematic exercise.   If more Catholics were active throughout adult years in the education of themselves and non-
Catholics, the Catholic influence might be more evident,
and answers to questions posed by the necessity of improving moral education might emerge.   There is no richer
apostolic opportunity than that provided by adult education
in this chaotic age.   The interpretation of education for a-
dults as liberal education means altering our ideas of liberal education in the college.   The college student cannot
master all the materials of liberal education.   Rather he
should develop a pattern for exercising his powers to
think and choose, and the lasting desire to continue his
education throughout life.   Catholic educators can work
through alumni groups and directly in their own communities to foster true adult education.   The only requisite
is zeal for intellectual and moral growth in the members
of society.   32

Cox, Joseph G.   Organizing a Commission on Adult Education, In National Catholic Educational Association Bulletin,
51 (February, 1955) 7-15.
  The Executive Board of the National Catholic Education
Association has authorized formation of an Adult Education Commission to explore the field of adult education so
that the Association may be in a position to offer adequate
guidance and help in the formation of programs to meet
present needs.   Ends and means must be based upon the
philosophy of Catholic education which postulates development of the entire man, mind and body, intellect and will,

physical and intellectual, moral and social. A majority
of organized Catholic adult education programs are for
college credit with a traditional and formal approach. Another approach is the informal process, voluntary, more
individualistic, and less integrated. General objectives of
this type of program are: religious growth, social growth,
vocational advancement, recreation, development of a
Christian attitude toward things cultural, and development
of latent talents in areas constituting the cultural heritage
of our day. Topics requiring further study are the Catholic philosophy of education with specific reference to adult
education, objectives, optimum curriculum, techniques of
teaching, teaching personnel, advertising, and financing.
                                                            33

Crabtree, Arthur P.   The Philosophy of Public School Adult
    Education, In The Public School Adult Educator, 1 (No-
    vember, 1957) 19-20.   Same condensed: Education Di-
    gest, 23 (February, 1958) 50-52.
        Suggest elements that are minimum essentials of a phi-
    losophy of adult education: (1) Adult education must be
    conceived as genuine education.   (2) Those engaged in a-
    dult education must have a deep-seated conviction concern-
    ing its role in a dynamic society.   (3) Adult education
    must protect and preserve the interests of democracy by
    providing opportunities for learning that stimulate and en-
    rich the awareness of the individual for societal problems.
    (4) No individual adult should be compared with another
    for the purpose of determining rate of progress.   (5) A-
    dult teaching must be sympathetic, with the realization
    that the average adult is infinitely complex and that sub-
    ject matter is secondary in importance to the learner. 34

Dobinson, Charles H.   Adult Education in England and Wales,
    In Educational Outlook, 29 (May, 1955) 101-110.
        The fact that England's movement in the direction of
    democracy in the past fifty years has been smooth and
    peaceful is largely due to developments in adult education
    in the first decade of this century.   In the United King-
    dom the term "adult education" means liberal education.
    The term "further education" is applied to education hav-
    ing a vocational content or bias.   Pure economic theory
    and pure philosophy have been important ingredients of a-
    dult education in the United Kingdom throughout this centu-
    ry, as a result of the Workers Educational Association,
    extra-mural departments of universities, and of govern-
    mental policy which has given financial help to both. Early

adult education had so profound an effect upon social
thinking that many new developments have taken place in
the last few decades.   Local Education Authorities have
been providing or assisting voluntary organizations to provide a wide range of classes for adult interests.   Highest
development of cultural interests by a Local Education Authority has taken place in London through Literary Institutes which were built up between the wars.   There is a
wide range of liberal studies available now in all large
cities of the United Kingdom comparable with those in London as a result of the 1944 Education Act.   Despite a
lack of money since 1945, steady growth has been brought
about in almost all fields.   The highest standard of work
is that of university extra-mural classes and their joint
enterprises with the W. E. A.   In addition there is the work
of voluntary educational associations, of residential adult
education centres, and of voluntary bodies which are not
educative organizations.   Radio and television have had important cultural effects since the war.   The National Institute of Adult Education, founded soon after the war to coordinate the many aspects and act as a clearinghouse, now
plays a leading part in fostering international linkages with
adult education groups abroad which is probably the most
important aspect of all.   35

Dumazedier, J.   The Content of Adult Education, In UNESCO,
    Adult Education, Current Trends and Practices.   Prob-
    lems in Education, 2.   Paris: UNESCO, 1949.   Pp. 41-
    53.
        Although the aims of adult education vary in different
    cultures, there is a common ground in its increasing ad-
    aptation to the common aspirations of the masses.   Mod-
    ern adult education aims at the creation of a living cul-
    ture, firmly grounded in everyday life, in which all may
    participate.   Such a culture links knowledge with action in
    an essential unity by means of its principles and values.
    It "...aims at helping each worker to live the life of his
    times, at the same time giving him the means of render-
    ing it more humane."   The writer anticipates future de-
    velopments of general intellectual, social, scientific, and
    artistic education of adults.   36

Durrie, Paul H.   Introduction--Emerging Patterns of Growth,
    In Adult Education, 2 (September, 1952) 186-187.
        The adult education movement has been described as a
    jungle because of the luxuriant growth and tangle of inter-
    twined and interrelated activities.   Some of the patterns

of growth are: a continuing concern for meeting immediate and personal needs of the individual as he functions as
a worker, homemaker, creative individual, and citizen; an
increased recognition of the fact that the individual works
in a social setting which should influence the nature of his
instruction; a growing belief that we should do something
about neglected areas such as public affairs, human relationships, economics, government, social, and world affairs, with significant experimentation and activity in this
field; a movement from dealing with things to dealing with
people and ideas; a growing belief that methods of instruction and administration must recognize the individual's relationships and interests, and involve the individual on an
emotional as well as intellectual basis; involvement of
many agencies and institutions and the use of many media
with communication and joint projects.   37

Dyer, John P.   What Do We Fear? In Adult Leadership, 4
   (March, 1956) 5-7, 32. Same: Association of University
   Evening Colleges Proceedings. Seventeenth Annual Meeting, New Orleans, 1955. Pp. 31-37.
      Discusses present climate of conviction by innuendo,
   guilt by association, abridgment of civil rights, conformity
   and anti-intellectualism.   Points to four areas of fear:
   our new role in world leadership, the cold war and the at-
   om bomb, economic uncertainty and total social change.
   Liberal education programs growing out of adult experience
   are needed to help individuals gain insight into their own
   tensions and anxieties and translate this knowledge into
   terms of the world in which they live. Asks twelve questions which must be answered by liberally educated men
   and women.   38

Elsdon, Konrad T. "Reality and Purpose, a Visitor's Reflections on Some Aspects of American Adult Education."
   Notes and Essays on Education for Adults, No. 16.
   Chicago: Center for the Study of Liberal Education for
   Adults, 1957. 23pp.
      Discusses some of the major differences between adult
   education work in the United States and in England including scope of institutions of higher learning; attitudes toward degrees and diplomas; separation of vocational and
   non-vocational, credit and non-credit, high and low standards in the English system and their intermingling within
   one institution in the United States; status of adult educators; standards as judged by service to the community and
   to the individual; length of courses, etc. Criticizes A-

merican adult education for its concentration on credits,
degrees, and diplomas; for spreading adult education too
thin; for adult educators who are technician-administrators
rather than scholars with an interest in subject and in individuals.   Concludes that although some of the problems
and failures of British and American adult education are
very diverse, many of them are shared by both systems.
The major problem is the number and complexity of duties
and requirements for adult educators.   39

Essert, Paul L.   Adult Education in the United States, In
    American Academy of Political and Social Science Annals,
    265 (September, 1949) 122-129.
    Discusses trends in adult education in the United States
in relation to extent, means, motives, cultural influence,
studies of adult educability, the community, and financing.
Adult education as continued learning is becoming a necessity rather than a purely recreational or remedial activity.
The ways and means of study are numerous.   Motives for continued learning can be broadly summarized as education to
help adults adjust to cultural change.   Creative experiments
in control of environment through education suggest the possibility that one of the major emphases of adult education in
the next decade may be to focus the development of personality on community problems.   This trend is not a substi-
tute for education for meeting personal needs but an extension of it.   Since adult education is increasingly regarded
as essential to the welfare of the state, it should receive
more state and federal support.   40

Essert, Paul L.   "Creative Leadership of Adult Education."
    New York: Prentice-Hall, 1951.   333pp.
    Written to give adult educators "a better picture of the
scope, problems and potentialities of adult education.   It
is also intended as a presentation of some principles that
will give more unified and cohesive direction to the many
aspects of adult education, and some practical skills and
techniques of leadership in the field."   The book deals
with two major problems of adult education in relation to
maturity: (1) bringing into focus a core of experiences
which are natural laboratories of continued learning; and
(2) discovering processes and techniques by which the
leader can help adults educate themselves, thus bringing
into focus the vast array of agencies and institutions of
adult education.   Part One discusses "The Challenge of
Our Times to Creative Leadership," suggests a core of
adult experiences essential for maturing as criteria for

planning and evaluating a community program of adult education, and shows the relationship of creative leadership
to these experiences. In Part Two and Part Three these
criteria are applied to prominent and emerging forms of
adult education, and processes are suggested by which
each form may be improved in the development of human
beings and communities. Part Four is a "Discussion
Guide for Practical Education of Creative Leadership,"
based on practices in the field or in the literature as case
studies.   41

Essert, Paul L. The Future of Adult Education, In Teachers
    College Record, 49 (November, 1947) 89-97.
        Development of adult education in the United States has
    been somewhat meandering, with no system for which any
    individual or organization can take credit, with numerous
    individual elements making up a vast array of colorful and
    functional activities. The extent, scope, character, and
    costs of our vast "jumble" of adult education furnish an
    impressive pattern of growth and improvement, but it is a
    question whether people are making optional use of these
    resources. Structural and operational limitations are i-
    dentified, such as failure to convey to the people knowl-
    edge of resources and their availability; highly specialized
    teachers and leaders lacking training in general adult edu-
    cation, the psychology of adult learning, and the counsel-
    ing of adults; administrative confusion and fringe opera-
    tion of activities; lack of provision for needs of young a-
    dults; and lack of daytime facilities. Leadership for co-
    operation and development of public understanding of adult
    education resources should be a responsibility of public
    schools, with the school administrator serving as a "so-
    cial engineer." Public schools should also develop in-
    structional materials for adult education. Institutional a-
    dult education agency leadership needs an extensive in-
    service education program of training. General adult cen-
    ters are needed to act as information and counseling agen-
    cies and as coordinating links between all adult education
    resources. It is the function of colleges and universities
    to produce the type of leaders who will guide the people to
    resources in adult education which will lead to a more
    satisfying way of life.   42

Essert, Paul L. "Report to Teachers College on Adult Edu-
    cation in the United States and Its Implications to Educa-
    tion." New York: Teachers College, Columbia Univer-
    sity, 1948. 22pp. Condensed in Adult Education Bulletin,

14 (October, 1949) 15-16 under the title "Adult Education
in the United States."

Report of a survey of status and trends of adult education in more than seventy-five cities. The number of
persons studying in adult education will soon be greater
than the number of children and youth in regular schools
and colleges. This increase results from new patterns
of culture: (1) the shift from a predominantly juvenile
population to one largely adult; (2) demand and supply of
part-time learning continue during all economic periods;
(3) the citizen of today cannot become fully informed or
skilled in his occupation in his first twenty years. A program of workers education similar to agricultural extension is probable in the near future. The trend of adult
education seems to be toward education for world citizenship for improved community living. Colleges and universities are doing the best job in training adults in fields of
labor, agriculture, urban and rural planning, and industrial personnel research. These agencies are outstanding
in providing leadership for discussion groups in local communities, for home and family education, and in civic
planning. Universities and colleges show signs of strain
in trying to meet demands for all types of adult education
at local levels. There is a trend toward full-time day
and evening programs in adult education in public schools,
mainly where there is special state aid. State departments of education will speed up adult education activities
of public schools and to some extent of colleges and universities in response to two types of pressure groups,
state associations for adult education, and public school
and college pressure for junior colleges for adults.
Public libraries and museums will function increasingly as
centers to train adults through group discussion. Recommendations made to Teachers College are: (1) a seven-
year program of research and expansion in adult education; (2) five or six demonstration centers in community
planning to develop lay and professional leadership; (3) a
demonstration project in education for adult citizenship;
(4) a scholarship program to permit twenty full-time day
students on the graduate level to participate in the proposed university demonstration area.   43

Essert, Paul L. Significant Experiences for Maturing Adulthood, In Teachers College Record, 52 (October, 1950) 1-
10.

Learning tasks in adult education to have purpose and
meaning must be based upon experiences adults have with-

in their culture.   As people seek adult education there is
an interplay of five experiences which they are trying to
bring into equilibrium: (1) experience of occupational a-
chievement; (2) experience of search for truths and
beauty; (3) experience of self-government; (4) experience
of close fellowship; and (5) experience of intermittent
solitude.   Each is discussed in relation to adult education.
Beginning with any one of them the adult educator can expand learning tasks into broad plans for continuous learning.   Another implication of this balanced planning is that
some such series of criteria can furnish the basis for a-
dult educators from many agencies in a community to appraise, evaluate, and redevelop their community adult education programs.   Balanced experiences in adult education also suggest that the best laboratories are not necessarily found in artificial groupings of people, but in groups
which adults have already invented for themselves.   44

Frank, Laurence K.   "Education for Aging," In Wilma T.
Donahue, comp., Education for Later Maturity.   New
York: Whiteside and Morrow, 1955. Pp. 1-18.
To understand the philosophy and objectives of education
for the aging, it is necessary to recognize some significant aspects of contemporary life.   The number of older
people is increasing rapidly, with problems of social and
financial insecurity.   Limited capacity for change in cus-
tomary beliefs and for acceptance of new ideas for participation in the new global orientation is not entirely due
to aging; it also results from undesirable social conditions.
A democratic social order relies upon education to bring
about change.   Recognition of the dynamic relationship of
the individual to society and of society to the individual
gives increased significance to the need for adult education, especially for later maturity.   With older people education must be concerned primarily with "relearning" or
"unlearning."   For this process, group reading and discussion encouraging the individual to examine critically
his beliefs and consider new ways of thinking are essential.
Esthetic experiences are also important for older people
to keep alive their capacity for feeling and responding to
others.   Central to this education is the necessity of helping the older adult build up and maintain a feeling of his
own worth and the validity of his interests through understanding and guidance.   Older persons especially need to
participate in group programs of their own selection as
contrasted to a fixed curriculum of formal content.   It is
imperative that all agencies and professions in any way

concerned with older groups work together for the benefit
of the individual.   45

Friedenberg, Edgar. Liberal Education and the Fear of
    Failure, In Adult Leadership, 3 (January, 1955) 13-16.
    The most important and difficult purposes of adult edu-
cation in contemporary America are explored. The writer
summarizes the major services which liberal adult education should perform for adults: It should increase their
devotion to human freedom and their skill in making use
of it--their willingness to maintain and defend it. It
should increase their sensitivity to the meaning of their
feelings and those of others. It should increase the range
of their experience, enabling them to continue to learn
from the living and the dead, to accept the experience of
other persons whatever their mutual relationship. Liberal
education can promote better citizenship and more meaningful leisure by helping individuals to an improved self-
concept, to holding a better opinion of themselves, to
learning that they are valuable and why. Liberal education can be effective only by enhancing human dignity which
is blocked by an increasing acceptance of the virtues of
the group over those of individuals. Liberal education
must strike at the individual's fear of failure.   46

Friesen, John K. , Tannis Prendergast, and Guy Henson.
    Recent Trends in Adult Education, In Food for Thought,
    13 (October, 1952) 24-33.
    Addresses at the National Conference on Adult Education
in Montreal, June 2-6, 1952. John K. Friesen discusses
trends in Western Canada: in the occupational and technical fields, growth of agricultural extension, vocational
education, business education, workers' education, and in
university extension and correspondence credit courses;
in education for family, citizenship and leadership, increase in popularity of the residential short course, parent education courses, informal activities on current issues of political and general community interest, and education for immigrants through voluntary and civic agencies; increase of interest in arts and recreation, development in use of the small discussion group, in film use,
and expansion of libraries. Areas of needed research and
development are pointed out. Tannis Prendergast discusses trends in Central Canada: (1) increasing interest and
involvement of industry in adult education; (2) concern of
provincial governments for continuing education at the community level; (3) emphasis on parent education in Home

and School Associations; (4) expansion in labor union education; (5) concern about education and problems of the
immigrant. Guy Henson reports trends and developments
in the Atlantic provinces, including (1) greater coordination of efforts through the first Maritime-Newfoundland
Conference on Adult Education, other local meetings, and
establishment of a joint planning committee of educational
extension in Newfoundland; (2) in the field of labor, outstanding work by St. Francis Xavier Extension Department
and the Maritime Labor Institute, more willingness on the
part of labor to take advantage of services offered, and a
need for adult educators to be conscious of responsibilities
and needs of labor leaders for education for union membership and for good citizenship; (3) extension of the folk
school movement in rural areas; (4) increasing interest in
and provision for the arts in local communities; (5) development of libraries.   47

Fund for Adult Education. "Liberal Education for Adults."
   White Plains, N.Y.:   F.A.E., 1956. 78pp.
   Five speeches given at the Community Leadership Insti-
tute conducted by the Fund for Adult Education at Estes
Park, Colorado, July 15-20, 1956. See Nos. 14, 67, 89,
105 and 523.   48

Gold, Milton S. A Concept of Continuing Education, In Educational Leadership, 15 (November, 1957) 100-103, 106.
   The real issue is not provision of higher levels of education, but the content of this continued education and its
contribution to continuing self-education. The goals of
continuing education should be: (1) building interest in
and skills to pursue a program of continuing self-improvement; (2) preparation for vocational placement; (3) understanding human relationships; (4) development of satisfy-
ing and constructive leisure time interests; (5) building
values with respect to ethical considerations; (6) personal
development "per se." Effective utilization of opportunities for continuing education depends on the quality of the
job done by formal educational institutions in developing
competence necessary for effective continuation of education. If the school has done a good job in giving individuals the tools of learning, the adult can continue his education through many formal programs and informal associations.   49

Gordon, K.W. What Kind of Adult Education? In Food for
   Thought, 5 (April, 1945) 4-6, 48.

A reply to Watson Thomson's article, "Adult Education--New Model." (See No. 143). The writer believes the "new model" education threatens traditional values. Adult education need not "be social, leading people into action." People can study voluntarily by themselves, or in groups, or through classes in educational institutions. Action is all right in its proper place, but exciting people from outside, creating restlessness, is not true adult education. The true teacher in the field of adult education in a democracy tries to show students all sides of a question and trusts to their fundamental common sense to choose wisely. It seems under the "new model" the masses are to be given a special set of facts interpreted for them as the person in charge sees fit. Adult education should explore all theories and viewpoints, and explain the good and bad in any doctrine or theory to all who are interested.

50

Gould, Samuel B.   Adult Education, In Association of American Colleges Bulletin, 41 (December, 1955) 555-561.

Adult education is only beginning to capture the true spirit and conceptual basis for its importance. The spirit is identified by a creative urge which has its impact upon people seeking a finer life and individual maturity. The concept is that of education as a continuing process throughout life. In the last decade there has been widespread recognition that adult education must use the humanities as a resource and turn itself to the task of educating whole men. Democracy, better than any form of government yet devised, furnishes the climate in which whole men may develop. Mental maturity is the great hope for survival and progress of a democracy. Present methods of education should be examined in terms of their ability to plant in the human mind the concept of education as a continuing process. The idea that cultural and vocational pursuits go hand in hand all through life must be instilled from elementary school level upward. In order to emphasize continuity of education, we should break away from the highly compartmentalized approach to subject matter and rigidly separated levels of education. Efforts of individual organizations in the community should be coordinated to prevent overlapping in purposes and functions. There are possibilities of developing a full community college concept, a college sponsored by the community and available to all age and intellectual levels and to all types of interests. The local community must understand the needs, take the initiative in fulfilling the

needs, and build its program to adapt to the local environment and citizenry.   The college or university, as the cultural center of the community, must assume direct responsibility for stimulating intellectual growth.   51

Graney, Maurice.   General Extension Courses, Their Place
   in Publicly Supported Institutions of Higher Education.
      See No. 527   52

Grant, George.   Philosophy and Adult Education, In Food for
   Thought, 14 (September-October, 1953) 3-8.   Same: A-
   dult Education (London), 26 (Spring, 1954) 247-253.
      Philosophy makes demands on democracy, not vice ver-
   sa.   The idea that democracy makes demands on philosophy has done much harm to adult education in Canada.
   Causes for this confusion are that a pioneering and expanding society was taken up with pursuit of immediate
   goals, and that adult educators thought of education as a
   species of social engineering.   Neither can democracy demand anything of education; democracy is education's serv-
   ant, not its master.   Adult education stands for no limited social ends, but for the self-liberation of the human
   soul.   Programs with more immediate goals are but pre-
   liminaries to that end.   The curse of adult education in
   Canada is willingness to surrender to pressure of those
   who want to use it for some limited end.   Canadian universities and Protestant churches are falling down in the
   performance of their job regarding the higher reaches of
   education.   The adult education movement must supply its
   own spiritual power.   Amid signs of chaos hopeful
   signs of special significance for adult education are leisure time, which may be used profitably for education if
   peace and prosperity continue, and the move away from
   the old Protestanism and agnostic humanism which leaves
   an opportunity for a profound adult education to become
   unlimited.   53

Great Britain.   Ministry of Reconstruction.   Adult Education
   Committee. "A Design for Democracy." London: M. Parrish [1956] 222 pp.
      A republication in abridged form of the Report of the
   Adult Education Committee of the British Ministry of Reconstruction, commonly called the 1919 Report.   The Report is a history of adult education in England, and a detailed account of the movement at that time, with scholarly analysis and recommendations for development of the
   field.   Sponsored jointly by the Canadian Association for

Adult Education, The National Institute of Adult Education
of Great Britain, and the Adult Education of the U.S.A.,
this abridgment retains the basic theory and omits the now
irrelevant facts.   Contains a preface by Sir Ronald F.
Adams, and an introduction, "The Years Between," by R.
D. Waller, who calls the Report "the most important single
contribution ever made to the literature of adult education
... a work on the grand scale, a history, survey and
philosophy of adult education."   See also No. 151.   54

Green, Ernest.   "Adult Education, Why This Apathy?" See
No. 215.   55

Grierson, John.   Education in a Technological Age, In Food
for Thought, 5 (June–July, 1945) 4-8.
The basic problem of education today lies not so much
in acquisition of literacy or knowledge of skills as in the
pattern of civic appreciation, faith, and duty.   Knowledge
means nothing if it does not make for order in the world.
The crisis in education lies in the realm of imaginative
training for modern citizenship.   Educators have been too
isolated.   Education lies wherever the images and patterns
of thought necessary to a technological world are commu-
nicated to the people.   It is one of education's first duties
to recognize that it has many allies and to find out where
they are and what may be expected of them.   The forces
of government, whose responsibilities reach into the realm
of education, enjoy the highest license to secure understanding by the citizenry.   It is possible that we can
bring about an understanding between peoples and nations
based on an appreciation of our common possession in the
powers of science and mass production, and also based on
common needs and interests of men everywhere.   Canada,
especially, is in a position to further this progress because of its youth, vitality, and understanding of the social and politico--economic relationships of education. 56

Groombridge, Brian.   New Objectives for Adult Education,
In Adult Education (London), 30 (Winter, 1957) 197-215.
Considers problems of society and the part adult education can play in solving them.   Technical progress, together with economic need, will endow adult education with
a new and more important status.   It will begin to realize its limitless potentialities by abandoning concern about
which classes it is for, whether it is a movement or a
service, and by ridding itself of traditional and inappropriate concern for standards.   The British can learn from

the American philosophy that adult education must identify itself with the tasks of society and then translate those
tasks in terms of the people concerned. Realization of
the possibility of a new type of civilized life resulting
from increased leisure depends upon education throughout
life. Since the use of mass media is a principal feature
of this new culture, adult educationists need to decide
where they stand in relation to them. The writer examines the problem of leisure of the retired and aged, the
subject of an inquiry financed by a grant from the Nuffield
Foundation, on the following points: (1) extent of use of
existing provision for adult education; (2) extent to which
educational organizations not exclusively concerned with
elderly people provide for them specifically; (3) extent to
which those already in contact with elderly people develop
educational activities; (4) and (5) general and special provision for leisure; (6) adult education and adjustment to
retirement and old age; (7) interpreting the generations to
each other; (8) implications of this survey for philosophy
and method of adult education.   57

Gruen, William. A Pragmatic Criticism of Community-
   Centered Adult Education, In Adult Education, 6 (Winter,
   1956) 81-90.
   The extension of the university's activities beyond the
confines of the traditional areas of teaching and research
has been influenced by two tendencies: (1) social reform,
with increased social mobility gaining acceptance of the
idea of popular education; (2) the growth of naturalism
and scientific empiricism with consequent softening of traditional contrasts between pure and applied sicence. Some
educators have given the pragmatic philosophy of education a narrow interpretation, tending to orient education a-
round vocational and professional interests. Some adult
educators prefer "real-life" practical situations arising
in community projects to the abstractions of the classroom as vehicles of instruction. This "community approach" tends to exaggerate differences between theoretical knowledge and its applications and overlooks the distinction between two kinds of practical education, --applied
knowledge and empirical skill. The content and intellectual level of adult education courses must be adapted in
some respects to interests and capcities of the community,
but beyond this should be guided by the logic of the subject matter and social aims of education. One of the
greatest advantages of education, especially of adult education, is that it liberates thought and value from the lim-

its of local traditions and widens the scope of experience
and human association beyond the confines of local community.   58

Gruen, William. Preface to a Philosophy of Adult Education,
In Progressive Education, 34 (March, 1957) 49-51.
Discusses the need of adult education today for a philosophy whose tasks are the clarification of the aims of
continuing adult education, and the examination of the moral and social directives implicit in these aims. Consideration is given to two aspects of Kilpatrick's philosophy
which are applicable to adult education: (1) his theory of
individuality or selfhood, and (2) his dissociation of learning or education from preparation. The theory of adult
education developed from the ideas in Kilpatrick's philosophy converges on one central theme, the distinctive intellectual and social role of adult education.   59

Guehenno, Jean. Adult Education and the Crisis of Civilization, In UNESCO, Adult Education, Current Trends and
Practices. Problems in Education, 2. Paris: UNESCO,
1949. Pp. 27-37.
Culture is for all men; its purpose must be to give a
new meaning to life and strengthen hope. Decision in human affairs depends not upon illiterates or scholars but
upon the body between these extremes. Perhaps man's
deepest change is in becoming a mass-man manipulated by
systems based upon lies. Widespread literacy has failed
to make reason popular but has produced half-education
which makes it easier to fool and enslave mankind. "Reading means nothing unless it is the ability to distinguish
truth from lies on the printed page and recognize the subtle
and insidious combination in which they may sometimes be
found." Our most urgent problem is to reconcile erudite
thought and popular instinct. Popular education, popular
culture must be rooted in life itself and must furnish the
weapons needed to deliver man in his defense of truth. 60

Hallenbeck, Wilbur C. Building Working Philosophies in A-
dult Education, In Adult Education, 3 (May, 1953) 148-
152.
The work of A.E.A.'s Committee on Social Philosophy
in developing common objectives and a common philosophy
for those engaged in adult education has involved the for-
mulation of a tentative statement, distributing the statement to groups for discussion, study of the reports of
these groups, preparation for publication of the statement

32   Hallenbeck, Wilbur C.

with analysis and some of the group reports to stimulate
community groups to develop a working philosophy and put
it into operation.   Included are an outline of points to include in a working philosophy; a resumé of the assumptions, and suggestions for further cooperative thinking and
activity.   61

Hallenbeck, Wilber C.   A Sociologist Looks at Adult Educa-
    tion, In Adult Education, 7 (Spring, 1957) 131-143.
    Differences have arisen among adult educators regard-
ing objectives and methods.   Several assumptions important to rationalization on these issues are discussed.   In
the process of considering many different opinions, a more
balanced and adequate opinion will result.   The problem is
not to rid ourselves and others of bias, but to understand
what it is, how to use it, and how to be selective with
reference to the biases we hold.   Specialization, with resulting lack of sensitivity to inter-dependence and inter-
relationships, has often produced competition where cooperation is required.   The role of adult education in relation to the problem of integration is: (1) to develop a
united adult education movement in the U.S.; (2) to help
people understand the problem and their responsibility for
its solution; (3) to stimulate and participate in many endeavors to work on different aspects of the problem.   The
community must provide the framework within which integration takes place.   The role of adult education has several dimensions: propagating a sense of meaning of citizenship, helping people understand responsibilities of citizenship, interpreting meaning and importance of community development, helping to organize people in activities
for improvement and development of their community.
Ideas in adult education about which there is argument
seem to the sociologist more complementary than anti-
thetical.   Means and ends are of equal importance, but
a clear definition of goals is the keystone of the whole
structure.   There must be common ground on the concept
of the "mature personality," which is the ultimate objective of adult education.   Ideas and action are interdependent and inseparable and cannot be in competition or
thought of as providing alternatives.   Education must be
keyed to the action pattern of adult life if it is to fit real-
istically into living experiences of adults.   But action can
carry on only with ideas and information.   Content and
methods are both important, interdependent and inseparable in the education process.   A balanced fare of knowledge is required for the development of a well rounded

Hansen, Kenneth H.   33

person.   62

Hansen, Kenneth H.   "The Educational Philosophy of the
Great Books Program." Ph. D. Dissertation.   University
of Missouri, 1949.   232pp.   63

Hayakawa, S. I.   "Adult Education as a Time-Binding Process." Notes and Essays on Education for Adults, No. 8.
Chicago: Center for the Study of Liberal Education for
Adults, 1954.   16pp.
     Three stages of communication in the history of human
cooperation are: (1) organization around a physical sym-
bol; (2) organization around verbal symbols; (3) organization around shared perceptions.   Today we are in a transition from stage two to stage three.   A new system of
moral values is struggling to emerge out of the now inadequate morality of stage two.   In the light of necessi-
ties of communication in a diverse and heterogeneous society, it is possible to take an ambitious view of tasks of
adult education.   The mature citizen is a constantly growing person who has learned and continues to learn how to
share perceptions and therefore interact fruitfully with an
ever-widening community of people of common aims or
interests.   The purpose of adult education is to create
sub-communities in the open society for continuous solution of unpredictable problems.   Adult education thus conceived is a recent and highly refined aspect of the "time
binding" process.   A study of science, humanities, and
communication arts increases resources for interaction
with individuals and community.   Adult education, because
of immediate application of ideas to life, can contribute
directly and efficiently to the enrichment of our culture.
                                                           64

Herring, John W.   Adult Education: Senior Partner to
Democracy, In Adult Education, 3 (January, 1953) 53-59.
     Adult education has failed to make an important contri-
bution to education for democratic and world citizenship.
Some reasons for the default are: (1) Adult educators
reflect the hyper-individualism of our cultural pattern.
Trained to measure achievements of individuals, it is
hard to switch strategy to team attack on common problems.   (2) Teaching adults is usually a part time activity,
and adult education planners aim at quick and ready demand.   (3) The evening school manager lacks time to do
a quality job, and the result is mediocrity and almost
complete neglect of the "hard" subjects of the social sci-

ences.   (4) Adult educators have neither the skill nor desire to handle controversial subjects of social education.
(5) Adult education's role as senior partner to effective
functioning of society is not taken seriously.   Informal
programs of independent agencies have accomplished more
in the social field than more formally organized adult education programs.   The social vitality of informal programs should teach two lessons: (1) Present concepts of
professionalism both in make-up of program planning
boards and in picking teachers and administrators should
be largely outlawed.   (2) Immediate beginnings should be
made on new training programs with a radically changed
approach, starting with a description of the job to be done
and an analysis of people capable of doing it.   Suggestions
as to the type of community program of adult education
that should be set up include: the program should be
functional, with activities geared into the social living of
the community; the planning group should be people actively engaged in community activities; the right executives should be sought in several professions; the case for
action-education should be put to every live interest in the
community to obtain financing.   A functional program has
three elements which should not be separated: (1) con-
structing solid piers of thought and values to build upon;
(2) working out proposals and laying plans; (3) executing
them.   To develop a strategy of community-wide penetra-
tion there must be cooperative planning of all agencies including lay leaders, decentralization through neighborhood
units, program service to existing groups, and extensive
and imaginative use of mass media.   65

Hodgkin, T. L.   Adult Education and Social Change, In Adult
     Education (London), 23 (June, 1950) 7-15.
     Considers the relations between adult education and the
     needs of society.   Traces these relations in the historical
     development of adult education from 1900 to 1950.   Out-
     lines changes in the British society of 1950 that are of
     importance to adult education, and the implications of
     these changes for adult education in regard to changes in
     its forms and content required to fit the needs of the
     time.   66

Houle, Cyril O.   The Development of Leadership, In Fund
     for Adult Education, "Liberal Adult Education." White
     Plains, N.Y.: F.A.E., 1956.   Pp. 53-67.
     For the spread of liberal adult education through group
     discussion, a special kind of leadership is needed.   We

must conceive of leaders as wholly different from those
who teach children. Leaders of adult discussions have the
task of focusing and guiding the operation of the groups
and are themselves learners. In order to fulfill the ideal
of lifelong learning for everybody, we must accept the
fact that adults are different from children and cannot use
the same educational patterns. We must hold the ideal of
the individual as a responsible person who knows what he
wants to learn and who can be helped to learn it. To
serve needs of people adequately and to provide the enrichment of society that adult education can facilitate, we
must build an infinite diversity of programs and activities.
In any situation in which we teach or counsel others, we
should try to build within them a vigorous independence
and greater ability to direct their own further education.
The concept of self-directed learning is applied to development of leadership. There are three overlapping layers
in any pattern of adult leadership: the professionals,
those who combine adult education functions with other duties, and lay leaders. The three groups are intimately
related. Suggestions are made for developing programs
for lay leadership with respect to the qualifications and
selection of potential leaders, training of leaders, continuing development of leaders after they have been trained,
and the need for leadership in American life.   67

Houle, Cyril O. Emerging Programs of Adult Education, In
    School Executive, 64 (January, 1945) 61-62.
    Adult education in the United States has developed as a
result of significant social and economic trends, such as
increased proportion of adults in the population, technological change, improved methods of communication, and mobility of the population. Agencies of adult education which
have developed as separate pioneer efforts are: (1) institutions originally developed for another educational purpose, such as public schools, colleges, and universities;
(2) agencies originally developed for non-educational purposes, such as unions, prisons, hospitals, government
bureaus, industrial concerns; (3) agencies originally established to serve both young people and adults, such as
libraries, museums, settlement houses; (4) agencies in-
itially established entirely for adult education, such as
agricultural extension, correspondence schools, and small
local independent ventures. Predicts rapid growth of a-
dult education in the next fifty years.   68

Houle, Cyril O. Future for Adult Education, In Wisconsin

Journal of Education, 79 (September, 1946) 8-10; same:
Sierra Educational News, 42 (October, 1946) 25-27; Vir-
ginia Journal of Education, 40 (October, 1946) 69-70+;
Kentucky School Journal, 25 (December, 1946) 34-37;
Ohio Schools, 24 (December, 1946) 404-405; same con-
densed: Education Digest, 12 (December, 1946) 38-39.

Public schools must assume greater responsibility for
education of adults or yield the field to new institutions designed for that purpose.   Adult education is a greatly increasing activity and the future will bring about enormous
growth in opportunities for mature people to learn.   Four
major reasons why adults undertake further education are:
to remove deficiencies in childhood education, to maintain
and improve acquired skills and interests, to develop new
interests, to meet problems which are not encountered until maturity.   Several kinds of agencies are active in the
field of adult education.   Public schools will be affected
by the new development of adult education.   The school is
one of the most pervasive agencies in our society and can
serve more adults than other agencies.   Its program will
be more stable because of professional competence of
teachers and administrators.   The public school will become a different kind of agency than at present, better
able to serve the needs of society.   69

Houle, Cyril O.   How Useful Is a Liberal Education?   In
Adult Leadership, 3 (January, 1955) 17-20.
A liberal education is crucially important in building a
whole man, and as such is one of the most practical kinds
of education offering the best hopes for achieving rewards.
Houle examines the nature of liberal education, the kinds
of competence which have the greatest breadth and utility,
and the major fields of knowledge through which these competences may be developed.   The values of liberal studies
for the solutions of the problems of life include: basic
conceptions and categories necessary to problem solving;
a common core on which to base specialization and a necessary unity and integration; a context for new theories
of human behavior; and the means for equipping industrial
managers and leaders of other groups and organizations
with ability to see basic relationships, to integrate work of
specialists, and to fit various parts of an operation into
coherent patterns.   The ultimate value of liberal education
is that it gives man an opportunity to develop his whole
nature, not merely some part of it.   70

Hunter, Guy.   Challenge and Response in Adult Education--

New Offerings, In Adult Education (London), 27 (Winter, 1954) 182-188.

Address to the 1954 annual conference of the National Institute of Adult Education, in response to addresses of W. P. Alexander and R. D. Waller (See Nos. 5 and 152).

Adult education's main purpose is to enrich the spiritual quality of human lives in present day society. Too much attention is paid to the product of work in present times and too little to its quality, process and motive. Adult education has a contempt for studies directly connected with work. But at work can be discovered all qualities of mind and character to which liberal education can address itself, -- in human relationships and aesthetic feelings. A man cannot be taught to do his work properly with conscience and in the right social relationship unless he is educated as a man as well as a citizen, a citizen as well as a technician. Some new offerings being made through work are in residential college courses and university courses for men in industry and in other professions, which are humane, liberal courses. In citizenship there is needed a radical challenge to attitudes of mind nearer to men's daily lives. Study of citizenship should start with basic moral and religious questions of family life. There is much room for new offerings in liberal education in citizenship. There should be cooperation between those engaged in academic adult education and those in activities other than instructional, for when adult education is conceived of as addressed to the whole man, all these institutions are a part of the same purpose and must be inspired by the same spirit.   71

Hunter, Guy. 1950--a New Dedication, In Adult Education (London), 22 (March, 1950) 169-177.

The author summarizes his article in seven points: (1) The beginnings of adult education lie in local social activity, aided by the evening class. (2) Extent and quality of that activity depend on local leadership. (3) The residential college is peculiarly well adapted to train this type of leader, and by developing to the full this latent energy and idealism, we can best develop national resources. (4) Adult teaching must be designed to recreate culture. This culture must be seen as a series of links between an outlook on social and economic theory, science, the arts, and religion. (5) Much adult education effort is wasted in mere description of the social process or ornamentation in cultural subjects without relating them to contemporary human problems. (6) It is worth while

to re-establish the serious content of adult education at the
expense of popularity. (7) Adult education should set about
the gradual establishment and strengthening of civilizing influences throughout national life.   72

Hunter, Guy. Vocation and Culture--A Suggestion, In Adult
    Education (London), 25 (Summer, 1952) 7-19.
       Expansion of adult education in the last five or six
    years seems to be taking two main directions, --hobby or
    leisure interests, and vocational work. A vital question
    is whether it is legitimate to call this work humane edu-
    cation. Technical and humane education in the adult field
    had become almost completely segregated by the inter-war
    period, with the technical degraded in prestige. The er-
    ror in the vocational--humane distinction lies first in fail-
    ure to see the full range of human values within the life
    of the working man, and secondly in failure to analyze the
    relationship between intellectual culture of the élite and
    this working life. In solving the problem of transmission
    of culture, approach must be made through people's pri-
    mary interests, --their job, social position, their real con-
    dition of life, and relation to others. Success depends up-
    on the tutor's approach to the group and their vocation.
    In vocational courses, purely technical interest has to be
    transcended into humane teaching. A wider and more re-
    sponsible view of the world must be the ultimate object of
    vocational education. Emphasis on quality of teaching is
    the only safeguard against the danger implicit in the sug-
    gestion of rehabilitating vocational education. Rehabilita-
    tion of work and the working life as the principal medium
    of approach in adult education implies a sequence in which
    technical, vocational, and "pure" education will come
    naturally, and also a sequence in approach to a group
    movement from living interests and feelings toward phi-
    losophy and the arts.   73

Hunter, H. L. Motives in Adult Education, In Journal of Ed-
    ucation (London), 79 (February, 1947) 67-68, 70.
       There is a great challenge in the search for means of
    developing spontaneous interest in current affairs stimu-
    lated by international and national strife, and relating it to
    the need for responsible, active citizenship. To establish
    an imaginative and practicable plan it will be necessary to
    bring together a wide range of interests and personalities,
    investigate their respective motivating forces and provide
    the machinery for adult educators to function. A credit-
    able aim for adult education organizers is to develop

group activities in order to foster community spirit. All
concerned with the educational challenge of the age are
faced with the necessity to reexamine first principles in
the light of recent experience and to determine the motives
activating people to seek from adult education inspiration
and understanding to help in common problems and revive
community spirit in community service. 74

Hutchins, Robert M.   What Kind of Education?   In Food for
Thought, 13 (November, 1952) 5-7.
Hutchins offers evidence in support of his assertion that
the basic education in a modern, industrial, scientific
democracy should be liberal education, open to all citizens all their lives. It aims to help the individual think
for himself and develop his highest human powers.   Democracy and industry, rather than making liberal education irrelevant, have made it indispensable and possible
for all the people.   Subjects that cannot be understood
without experience should not be taught to the inexperi-
enced.   Men cannot solve their problems unless they learn
to think for themselves about fundamental issues of human
life and organized society.   The alternatives are democracy, with liberal education for all, or aristocracy, with
liberal education for the few.   Politically the world is
headed for unification either by conquest or consent.   If
it is to be achieved by consent it can be done only by effort toward world community and world organization.
The great productions of the human mind supply the framework for understanding one another.   We need an education designed to bring out our common humanity.   The
modern democracy requires wisdom.   The aim of liberal
education is wisdom. 75

Hutchinson, E. M.   Highlights of Adult Education: The British Scene, In Food for Thought, 16 (February, 1956) 207-
210.   Same under title Deeds and Words in Adult Education: The British Scene, Adult Education, 6 (Spring,
1956) 167-172.
A selection of recent happenings likely to effect future
developments of thought and action in adult education.   The
Ashby Report, published in 1954, by a Committee appointed by the Ministry of Education, made the following
points: (1) The continuing importance of voluntary action
in adult education is acknowledged.   (2) Universities,
through extra-mural departments, have assumed the main
burden of liberal adult education and have become heavily
involved financially and morally.   (3) The three-cornered

relationship of voluntary bodies, universities and the Ministry of Education is valuable.   (4) Tutors, especially
part-time tutors, are underpaid.   (5) In making grants
the Ministry of Education should scrutinize quality as well
as quantity of work being undertaken.   (6) Work should
not be excluded from grant support because it is related
to a vocational interest.   Since the war new interest has
developed in an overlapping area of liberal and technical
education and the humane aspects of employment.   In
broadcast education, educationally designed features have
been incorporated in BBC services, supplementing general
features of cultural value, with large-scale publicity in
conjunction with libraries and other educational bodies.
There has been an upsurge in demand for public school
evening classes or Evening Institute classes, and interest
in implications of this movement and the ways it can contribute to richer community life.   Residential colleges,
which have come into prominence since the war, are evidence that British adult education is not bogged down in a
tradition-ridden set up.   Examples are given of growing
contact in adult education abroad including a better set up
in the Adult Education Committee of U. K. National Commission for UNESCO, and study tours and conferences.

                                                                    76

Ingraham, Mary.   Development of Evening Programs, In
   "Association of Governing Boards of State Universities
   and Allied Institutions Proceedings. "   Thirty-Second Annual Meeting, New York, November 15-19, 1954.   Pp.
   57-61.
      In 1939 all evening students of the College of the City
   of New York were required to take the same courses and
   do the same type of work despite great variation in previous training and ability and in use that they would make
   of their educational opportunity.   Student turnover was
   high and only about six per cent were graduated.   Many
   teachers in the evening session were also teaching in day
   sessions or had outside employment.   Many had no teaching experience.   In order to improve the situation, potentialities of evening students enrolled and likely to enroll
   if more and different courses were available were explored.
   More adequate administration and instruction were provided.   Course offerings were increased.   Guidance and
   counseling and other supplementary services equal to those
   available to day students are gradually being established.
   In 1950 four Schools of General Studies replaced Evening
   Sessions or Extension Divisions at the several colleges.

A sound core of liberal educational courses and also specialized career training are provided.   Several examples
of unusual programs are given.   It is recommended that
the four-year degree program in Liberal Arts and Applied
Sciences be given on a basis of complete equality with day
sessions offerings.   The pattern of community colleges as
projected by New York State University is endorsed for
shorter degree and diploma terminal work.   77

Issues Confronting A. E. A., In Adult Education, 7 (Winter,
   1957) 99-103.
      A synthesis of replies to a letter sent out by the Social
   Philosophy Committee to persons who had attended the
   Committee's meetings at annual conferences asking for o-
   pinions on issues that lie ahead for A. E. A.   Some respondents reacted to the question of adult education as oriented to the community or to the development of the individual.   Some were concerned with the area of membership of the A. E. A. and the relationship of the organization
   to the local scene.   There were also suggestions as to
   the goals of A. E. A. and for activities such as experimental programs, education on international issues, summer workshops, publications, and developing adult education leaders.   78

Jessup, Frank W.   Synthesis of Group Reports, In UNESCO,
   Institute for Education, "Adult Education Toward Social
   and Political Responsibility."   Hamburg: UNESCO.   Institute for Education, 1953.   Pp. 58-75.
      Discusses the nature of social and political responsi-
   bility; the means of adult education, verbal and practical;
   types of adult education institutions; the state's responsibility toward adult education; need for a critical attitude
   combined with mutual trust among groups; subjects which
   give opportunity for strengthening the sense of social and
   political responsibility; the development of approaches and
   techniques in the categories of social sciences and humanities as a means of strengthening responsibility for political and social life.   79

Jessup, Frank W.   Trends and Resources, In Adult Education (London), 30 (Winter, 1957) 167-180.
      The writer's purpose is to assess the position which a-
   dult education has reached and suggest directions in which
   it ought to move in the future.   Methods and systematol-
   ogy in education are important, but our great concern with
   means rather than ends reflects the prevalent utilitarian

attitude toward education. This attitude is an incomplete
one and has the danger of mistaking only a part of education for the whole. All education has a social purpose.
It reflects and seeks to strengthen currently held ideals a-
bout man and society. The most acute revelation of the
ideal pattern of society a government lays up for itself is
its attitude toward and view of adult education. In the last
generation society has become egalitarian, economically,
politically, and educationally. More even distribution of
educational opportunity has led some to conclude that the
need for adult education is past. This attitude is based
upon two assumptions: (1) that the only social purpose of
adult education is to promote egalitarianism, and (2) that
the only quality the ideal society need possess is equality
among its members. We need the dynamic of a clear,
new social purpose in adult education. Adult education is
important in inculcating the self-discipline required in an
industrial society and can play an important role in the
area of the moral problems. Adult education should constantly be giving people opportunity to know and value the
best in art, literature, thought, industry, politics, professional ideals, and human character. If it were realized that by our attitude toward adult education we declare
more forcibly than in any other way our view of the ideal
society, and that through adult education we can do more
than in any other way to translate ideals into practice, a-
dult education would be accorded a central not a peripheral place. Clear ideas about the kind of society we want,
a social philosophy, would make the task of adult education easier.   80

Johnson, Earl S. Need for a Philosophy of Adult Education,
    In Journal of Negro Education, 14 (Summer, 1945) 272-
    282.
        Discusses "humanistic" versus "vocational" aims of a-
    dult education. Adult education in America is excessively
    preoccupied with vocationalism and is committed to a nar-
    row utilitarian needs philosophy.   Proposes starting with
    individual or group needs and interests and broadening a-
    dult education into a humanistic study of culture and val-
    ues.   81

Kallen, Horace. The Adult and His Education, In Harvard
    Education Review, 22 (Summer, 1952) 153-167.
        Summarizes political, social, economic and educational
    concepts which have influenced the development of adult
    education. The goal for the adult learner is defined as

"the consequential development, by acts of well-ordered
inquiry, by impartial yet sympathetic scrutiny of alternatives, by such trials as he can make and errors as he can
survive, of a vision of existence and destiny which shall
with its perspectives ennoble and transvalue the meanest,
the most routine and inconsequential events of his day,
and then to bet his life on his vision. For the teacher, it
is to lead the learner to achieve this development by free
exercise of his own powers, at his own risk and on his
own responsibility." World events have made adult education a national as well as a personal necessity. The present trend shows a growing awareness not only that knowledge brings power and advantage, but that education is
survival. Survival is the liberation and exercise of mu-
tually suffusing powers of seeing, understanding, and doing in every frontier which men and nature present. This
would end the divorce of vocation from culture, the segregation of the past from present relevancy and future consequences. It would seek to equip men for any emergency.
                                                                         82

Kallen, Horace. "The Liberation of the Adult." Notes and
    Essays on Education for Adults, No. 7. Chicago: Center
    for the Study of Liberal Education for Adults, 1954. 16pp.
    Adults are creatures of routine whose daily life autom-
atizes into a series of rigid and repetitive adjustments
to conditions of earning a living. Their ways of thought,
beliefs, and judgment also become habit bound into "principles" or "prejudices." Adult teaching proposes the
liberation of the learner by changing his status quo into
something altering and expanding, by transmuting "sames"
into a process of differentiation, of development in diversity, into a moving out into new directions. The American Idea postulates the notion of pursuit, mobility, and
change, with equal liberty an antecedent condition. In
neither the humanities nor the social sciences can the
how be kept alive except in and through its what. Any
subject matter which abandons isolation for union can become liberating. Methods depend upon the character of
each class. Best teaching starts where the learner is,
not where the teacher is.   83

Keenleyside, Hugh L. Education or Catastrophe, In Adult
    Leadership, 2 (December, 1953) 4-7.
    Danger to the future of humanity lies in the fact that
scientific progress and growth of population of the world
have outdistanced our capacity for social adaptation. While

we are preparing military defenses, we must work at the
process of universal education. The objective is a life of
peace and decency and kindness for all men. The educational campaign would have two aspects: (1) an effort to
convince people generally that war must not be allowed to
happen, which involves relinquishment of concepts of national sovereignty and the right to pursue individual interests by the use of war; (2) the task of convincing underprivileged peoples of the world that the more fortunate are
interested in their needs and are determined to do what is
possible to eliminate ignorance, poverty, disease, and in-
justice. To overcome these conditions it is necessary to
rid ourselves of national, racial, and social prejudice; to
support international, national, organizational, and private
programs for elimination of unnecessary evils; to participate actively in efforts to bring comfort and hope to the
underdeveloped areas of the world. Only to the extent
that we meet these demands can we pass on the opportunity to work out a permanent solution to the problem of
human existence.   84

Kempfer, Homer H. The President's Committee and Adult
     Education, In School and Society, 85 (January 19, 1957)
     22-23.
     The early work of the President's Committee on Educa-
tion Beyond the High School shows an emphasis on higher
education for adults with less consideration of non-college
forms of adult education. This is due to the fact that
higher education is well established and that adult education is not so well known. Sampling studies and area reports indicate that adult education is the most dynamic and
rapidly growing segment of American education. The
President's Committee, in studying this upsurge of interest, can perform its best service only if it gives the fullest consideration to non-college forms of post high school
education.   85

Kempfer, Homer H. We Move in New Directions, In School
     Executive, 67 (May, 1948) 35-37.
     After indicating the rapid growth of adult education in
New York State since 1945, especially in public schools,
the writer lists and discusses briefly the five essential
characteristics of a good community program of adult education, citing various programs throughout the state as
examples. A good community program (1) is comprehensive, serving all the learning needs of adults in the
community; (2) integrates all educational forces in the

community toward common ends; (3) involves adults in
both intensive and extensive educational activities; (4) has
a broad community base, with representation from all community agencies having educational objectives, and with
leaders of many types and grades; (5) seeks continuously
to develop feelings of community in the entire adult population.   New social inventions and techniques will have to
be found before the great majority of adults can be
reached, but in a democracy, public education must not
accept less.   86

Kidd, James Roby, ed.   "Adult Education in Canada. "
Toronto: Canadian Association for Adult Education [1950].
249pp.
     An introduction to adult education in Canada, written by
more than forty contributors, providing a background of
ideas and working principles, an historical outline of developments, and a description of significant programmes
and organizations. Section One, "Aims, Origin, and Development," contains "A Brief History of Adult Education
in Canada," "Present Developments and Trends," and
"A Working Philosophy for Canadian Adult Education."
Section Two, "Organization," is made up of chapters on
"The Canadian Association for Adult Education;" "Organization of Adult Education in the Provinces of Canada;"
"Adult Education in Some Major Institutions," (The University, The Library, The School, Specialized Organizations); "Adult Education in Rural Areas;" and "Adult
Education in Urban Centers, Including Business and La-
bour." Section Three, "Some Selected Programmes"
describes: I--The "Uncommon Schools" (Frontier College,
Banff School of Fine Arts, The School of Community Pro-
grammes--Camp Laquemac); II--Radio and Film (National
Farm Radio Forum, National Citizens' Forum, The Docu-
mentary Film); III--Rural Programmes (The Antigonish
Movement, Community Life Training Institute, Women's
Institutes); IV--Programmes Developed During World War
II (Adult Education in the Armed Services, Consumer Education and the Consumer Branch). Section Four contains
a bibliography of Canadian writing on adult education, and
a list of organizations concerned with adult education. 87

Kidd, James Roby, ed.   "Adult Education in Canada."
Toronto: Canadian Association for Adult Education [c1950].
A Working Philosophy for Canadian Adult Education,
pp. 24-39.
     A collection of statements from several sources each

dealing with an important concept that is central to adult
education, such as training for citizenship, adult education
for everyone, importance of both group and individual
goals, and importance of participation. The selections include a statement of goals prepared by a policy committee
of the Canadian Association for Adult Education; "Unlock-
ing Life to Free People," by M. M. Coady;   " 'Leaders
Who Can See Things Whole'--the Cultivated Individual,"
by Sir Robert Falconer; "Implications for Adult Education," by Gregory Vlastos; "Adult Education Demands
Participation," by E. A. Corbett; "Some Conditions of
Participation--The Role of 'Communications'," by John
Grierson; "Participation Develops in the Study Group,"
by David Smith; and summary statements of goals of adult
education by E. A. Corbett and M. M. Coady.   88

Kinney, Laurence F.   Liberal Education in a Free Society,
   In Fund for Adult Education, "Liberal Adult Education."
   White Plains, N. Y.:   F. A. E., 1956.   Pp. 5-12.
      Reflective thinking coupled with consequent action is re-
   quired for a society to be free. There is need to keep
   active a process of reflective thinking because of man's
   tendency to fall out of harmony with his environment.
   This disharmony robs him of freedom.   Man's relation to
   those around him tends to be exclusively utilitarian or
   superficial, leaving a sense of dissatisfaction.   In his isolation he seeks to establish relationships on false bases
   such as domination or submission.   Man tries to bend nature to his will rather than identifying himself with and
   participating in the common life and reality.   Educational
   and moral values which spring from assumption of public
   responsibilities suffer from neglect in contemporary society.   Because knowledge is so complex and precise
   thinking so technically demanding, it is assumed that experts must do our thinking for us.   Thus the minds of
   men are submitted to the authority of other men.   In seeking general understanding, although the limiting techniques
   of scientific method will not suffice, the same spirit of
   regard for facts, disciplined reflection, and willingness to
   learn from those with whom we differ, need to guide our
   inquiries.   Two ways in which elemental thought supplements scientific analysis are in the apprehension of persons as such and in the grasp of wholes.   The perspective given in comprehensive understanding is not the end
   of the matter.   Neither discovery nor contemplation is
   man's ultimate purpose.   His knowlege is achieved for the
   sake of intelligent and appreciative attitudes and action.

Adult education activities in communities provide the most
promising and practical means for achieving such perspectives through three avenues: (1) by group study--discus-
sion programs; (2) by stimulation of individuals to further
study and reflection; (3) by participation in serious community activities.   89

Knowles, Malcolm S.   Adult Education in the United States,
    In Adult Education, 5 (Winter, 1955) 67-76.
    Discusses meanings of the term "adult education," and
the forces that have made adult education a significant factor in modern social progress.   Describes the development of adult education in the United States from early beginnings to World War I, and new forces in the modern
era, which have pushed the adult education movement in
new directions: Federal aid, national and local organization, foundation aid, state aid, and new knowledge and
methods developed through research.   The scope and quantity of adult education are indicated by estimates of the
number of adults participating, and the number of persons
providing educational opportunities for adults (administrators, supervisors, leaders, and teachers).   A chart gives
figures for estimated number of participants by agency in
1924, 1934, 1950 and 1955, and for number of full time
and part time adult education workers by agency in 1955.
                                                            90

Knowles, Malcolm S.   Charting the Course of Adult Educa-
    tion in America's Future, In Adult Leadership, 6 (October,
    1957) 99-102, 118.
    Article written to provide a "thought starter" for dis-
cussions at the 1957 Annual A. E. A. Conference.   Discusses major challenges to adult education during its development in the United States; current status and trends;
major trends in American society today and their implications for the future course of adult education.   91

Knowles, Malcolm S.   The Coming of Age of Adult Educa-
    tion in America, In National Catholic Educational Associa-
    tion Bulletin, 54 (August, 1957) 376-378.
    Traces early beginnings of adult education in the United
States, which were lacking in direction and design, with
many agencies and a diversity of programs; and the drive
toward unity beginning by the end of World War I with formation of several organizations bringing together people
doing adult education work in different institutional settings,
such as the National University Extension Association,

the American Library Association, and the National Education Association, and in 1926, the American Association
for Adult Education, and in 1951 the Adult Education Association of the U.S.A. Trends that stand out as pointing the
direction of the development of adult education in its mature years are: (1) It will continue to expand. Within
our lifetime the education of adults will become accepted
as being as normal as the education of children and youth
is now. (2) It will become increasingly expert with growth
of knowledge through research about the adult, his needs,
and his learning process, which will make possible development of better methods and programs. There will also be more opportunities for advanced professional training for adult educators. (3) It will become better organized and integrated through more local and state councils
and associations. (4) It will become increasingly attuned
to the broad social needs of a changing civilization.
There will be less concern with literacy, remedial and vocational education, and more concentration on advanced and
liberal education. Adult education will become one of the
most significant social movements of all time.   92

Knowles, Malcolm S. Direction-Finding Processes in the
   A.E.A., In Adult Education, 8 (Autumn, 1957) 37-54.
      The second part of a working paper prepared by the A.
   E.A. Consultative Committee on Direction-Finding. (See
   also No. 95.) Past attempts of the Association at direction-finding are reviewed and described according to the
   type of process used: (1) assessment of needs, (2) discussion of aims, (3) survey of information and attitudes,
   (4) identification of social trends and gearing A.E.A.'s
   program to them, (5) empirical testing of direction decisions by translation into operational policy and imple-
   mentation in the areas of membership, program priorities,
   centralization versus decentralization, relationship with local and state organizations, relationship with foundations,
   relationship with other national organizations and the sub-
   groupings within the A.E.A.   93

Knowles, Malcolm S. Highlights of Adult Education in the
   United States in 1955, In Adult Education (London), 28
   (Spring, 1956) 313-315. Same: Food for Thought, 16
   (February, 1956) 212-214. Same under title "Deeds and
   Words in Adult Education: The U.S. Scene," Adult Edu-
   cation, 6 (Spring, 1956) 179-180.
      Lists major trends of adult education in the United
   States in 1955 as: (1) general expansion; (2) progress in

professionalization of the field; (3) emphasis on relationship between adult education and community development;
(4) liberal adult education the most rapidly expanding
area in the field; (5) improvement in financing; (6) expansion in the number of people in non-educational organizations who began to perceive themselves as performing
adult education roles. Other events of 1955 listed include
operation of educational television stations, conferences,
establishment of new departments of adult education in the
U.S. Office of Education and in some state departments of
education. Also listed are areas of research studies
made in 1955.   94

Knowles, Malcolm S.   An Overview and History of the Field,
   In Adult Education, 7 (Summer, 1957) 219-230.
      Sub-titled "A Working Paper Prepared by the A.E.A.
Consultative Committee on Direction Finding," written by
Malcolm Knowles in consultation with C. O. Houle.   Includes a brief history of national organization of adult education and a description of the groups and activities in
the field at community, state and national levels.   The
question "Is there a field of adult education?" is considered.   The characteristics of professionals and volun-
teers and their depth of commitment to adult education are
analyzed.   Estimates of the scope of participation in the
field are reviewed for 1929, 1934, 1950 and 1955.   Results are reported of surveys of A.E.A. membership in
1956 to determine occupational composition and major
areas of interest and concern in adult education.   Four
areas of most interest are: human relations training, community development, adult counseling and guidance, and
parent and family life education.   95

Knowles, Malcolm S.   Philosophical Issues That Confront A-
   dult Educators, In Adult Education, 7 (Summer, 1957)
   234-240.
      Three   outstanding points of disagreement in the field
of adult education are: (1) what ought to be taught, or
sources of objectives for adult learning; (2) how adults
should be taught; (3) the proper aims of adult education
in a democratic society.   Discusses various views as to
sources of objectives, such as the self-perceived needs
and interests of the learners, requirements of society,
requirements of the local community, institutional goals of
sponsoring organizations, and the more or less absolute
body of knowledge and wisdom.   The tension that these
differences arouse are inhibiting to cooperative planning

and action among adult educators.   Differences over how
adults should be taught are not great and arise more from
lack of adequate data about adult learning than from ideo-
logical differences.   The two opposing views as to aims of
adult education, namely freedom of choice for the learner
and the common aims of the adult education program, are
reconcilable.   For the field to deal adequately with these
three basic issues, adult educators must train themselves
out of the habit of defining positions in absolute and exclusive terms; develop an attitude that differences are acceptable and desirable; develop tolerance for the tensions
that differences produce; and obtain more knowledge
through research.   96

Lengrand, Paul.   Culture, Society, and Adult Education, In
    Adult Education (London), 21 (December, 1948) 53-58.
        The three elements of culture, life, and democracy are
    inseparably interwoven and when united can give meaning
    to the individual and collective life of man.   The task of
    adult education is to make each individual aware of his
    own potentialities, to equip him with means of self-ex-
    pression, and to assist the birth of a communal civiliza-
    tion where personality can flourish.   Proper significance
    of adult education can be seen only if it is put in its cul-
    tural perspective.   The communal civilization of today can
    grow only if education of the masses is full and complete.
    To rebuild the community of man is one of the most ur-
    gent cultural tasks.   True culture can only be a popular
    culture common to the whole people with unity of aims,
    values, ideals, and sentiment.   Two methods of rebuild-
    ing this unity of civilization are an authoritarian solution
    and a democratic solution.   For a democratic solution, a-
    dult education should aim at shaping the individual's
    habits, guiding his responses, and equipping him with
    tools for his work.   97

Lindeman, Eduard C.   Adult Education and the Democratic
    Discipline, In Adult Education Journal, 6 (July, 1947) 112-
    115.
        In order to furnish citizens with material which will
    help dispel confusions and keep them in a participant mood
    in regard to public issues, adult education should: (1) ac-
    quaint people with the nature of international, national and
    regional trends; (2) aid people in understanding nature of
    social movements of their time; (3) assist in discovering
    the moral factors involved in public issues; (4) reveal to
    people the nature of democratic disciplines which describe

thought and conduct of persons living within a democratic
culture. Democratic disciplines which should form the
code of behavior for a citizen in a democracy are: (1)
discipline of diversity, (2) discipline of the partial functioning of ideals, (3) discipline of avoiding false antith-
eses, (4) discipline of compatibility between ends and
means, (5) discipline of institutional correlation, (6) discipline of social and economic planning, (7) discipline of
"living with" contrary decisions, (8) discipline of humor.

                                                        98

Locke, Alain L. Areas of Extension and Improvement of A-
dult Education Among Negroes, In Journal of Negro Education, 14 (Summer, 1945) 453-459.

Adult educative effort must be systematic, standardized
and expertly administered to be entitled to be called "education." Two disadvantages of present Negro adult education are inadequate and inequitably segregated participation in public programs, and compensatory programs
which are amateurish and propagandist. These negative
factors provide criteria by which all adult education programs must be judged from the Negro's group position
and point of view. All special and separate programs
need to be absorbed into general programs of mass education, not only in the interest of integration of the Negro
clientele, but for all members of a truly democratic society. Adoption of interracial or common interest group
work in various adult education fields as a basic goal and
working principle is the most constructive prospect of improvement in respect to adult education for Negroes and
other minorities. There is prospect of progress in projects under private auspices because they are unimpeded
by restrictive legislation. In public adult education, prospects for improvement are: (1) standardization of racially
inequitable public school facilities through legal decisions
which will include pro-rata expenditures of public school
tax monies in which adult education programs will share;
(2) extensive Federal aid to all forms and levels of public
education in economically disadvantaged states, which is
likely to bring legal pressures for equitable distribution
and more progressive and standardized programs; (3) the
impending program of compulsory citizenship training,
which, if properly used, can be a crucial turning point in
basic educational policy and practice. Many programs of
Negro voluntary organizations are interracial, but often
their approach and motivating values are too narrow and
racially provincial to be democratic. The cause of mi-

nority rights is tending to be absorbed in mixed group
organizations with common interest objectives, such as
the Civil Liberties Union and the Committee to Abolish the
Poll Tax.   Such organizations have public education programs, and they educate by actual experience in democratic relations.   The tide of educational segregation is
ebbing.   99

Locke, Alain L.   Education for Adulthood, In Adult Education Journal, 6 (July, 1947) 104-111.
     The essential, commonly accepted aim of adult educa-
tion is the democratic widening of all sorts of educative
opportunities and experiences for more and more people
over greater areas not only of knowledge and skills but
for effective self knowledge and understanding.   Some
challenging implications of this basic idea are examined.
There is a need to revitalize and integrate the several a-
dult education programs by focusing them on a common
objective of the adult education effort, education for social
and cultural adulthood.   To achieve this, adult educators
must work out a mature and more explicit philosophy.
While it is hoped that indirect and internal pressures will
be the main sources of a more integrated program, it is
realistic to take note of external pressures such as support from public funds, further professionalization of the
adult educator, and international collaboration both within
and without channels of UNESCO.   Group education for social, intercultural and international understanding looms
as the paramount problem and concern of the educator.
The adult educator's responsibility is the task of making
people adult in their reactions and attitudes.   Consideration of adult education in terms of the community as a
whole, wider and more educative use of mass media, and
new emphases on education for democratic and world citizenship have close relevance to these new assumptions of
social responsibility.   Social and cultural illiteracy in the
complex, modern world is dangerous.   Adult educators
must accept responsibility for an adult society.   100

Loosley, Elizabeth.   Current Trends in Canadian Adult Education, In Adult Education (London), 28 (Spring, 1956)
321-327.   Same under title "Highlights of Adult Education: Canada," Food for Thought, 16 (February, 1956)
222-226.   Same under title "Deeds and Words in Adult
Education: The Canadian Scene," Adult Education, 6
(Spring, 1956) 172-178.
     Adult education in Canada reflects social changes.

Population growth has laid strong emphasis on education
for citizenship.   Current interest in "human relations"
and the "group process" results from urbanization.   Increased leisure and high standards of living undergird the
increasing concern of informal education with the arts and
humanities.   Business feels the need to educate its employees and the public as to its procedures and products.
Trade unionism educates its members for responsibility
within the movement.   Business is concerned with humanistic and rounded education for executives as well as with
human relations in industry.   Within trade unions there is
also a groping toward more comprehensive and liberal education.   Rural programs are adopting principles of the
group process, with growing interest in folk and rural
night schools.   Community development is a new concept
employing methods of fundamental education in problems
of contemporary culture.   The Canadian Association for
Adult Education has the task of coordinating changing patterns of adult education throughout Canada.   Adult education in Canada is based upon the fundamental concept of
adult education as individual development which liberates
the human spirit.   101

Lotze, Heiner.   Adult Education as a Public Duty, In Adult
    Education (London), 20 (September, 1947) 10-16.
    Adult educationists share the opinion that their work is
especially important for a particular age group (20-30) because of their susceptibility to learning, and for a particular social group, the manual workers, because of their
important role in economic, political, and social life.
There is need to educate adults for active cooperation in
public life, for understanding, and a sense of responsibility.   Adult education must free itself of its academic
past and select and present material suited to its task.
Rather than split up life into compartments of subject
matter, it should take cross sections of several compartments and make human problems the objects of study.   In-
terdisciplinary subjects should be selected from social,
cultural, and natural sciences which will serve as a central core for adult education schools.   If manual workers
and young people are not among the participants, it is a
result of mistaken selection and presentation of subject
matter.   102

Maaske, Roben J.   Needs in Adult Education Today, In
    School and Society, 69 (January 1, 1949) 9-11.
    Areas of interest upon which the educational program

for adults needs to focus attention are listed and discussed briefly: (1) education for world citizenship; (2)
preparation for social change; (3) education for technological change; (4) education for creative diversions; (5)
better education for special groups; (6) education for
family living.   Needs in organizing for effective adult education programs are summarized as: (1) more directors
of adult education in state education departments; (2)
more funds to enable extension divisions of universities
and colleges to offer broader programs; (3) training and
awareness of how to proceed in organizing community
programs in adult education on the part of superintendents
of schools; (4) better preparation of supervisors, leaders
and teachers of adult classes, discussion groups and other
types of adult learning opportunities.   103

McGhee, Paul A.   Adult Education and Community Action,
In Adult Education, 6 (Winter, 1956) 67-81.
     Attempts to answer recent attacks on university-spon-
sored, non-credit adult courses by both Robert Hutchins
and proponents of community development.   Reviewing
Hutchins' contention that colleges restrict themselves to
intellectual training of those qualified for such education
through study of the Great Ideas, the writer suggests that
the adult student must, on the contrary, be accepted where
he is, and the college should respond to whatever special
interest he has "if it falls within subject matter areas appropriate to a college or university."   The community development approach to adult education is insufficient because "the meaning of life is not to be found in a desper-
ate concentration on the outward forms of living with other
people."   Discusses the difficulty of an urban university
to define its community and to determine how best to serve
it.   He concludes: "We shall become less effective and
less trusted if instead of analyzing and clarifying issues
as dispassionately as we can, we become a party to them."
                                                              104

McGhee, Paul A.   Liberal Education for Adults: Some Problems in Marketing, In Fund for Adult Education, "Liberal
Adult Education."   White Plains, N.Y.: F.A.E., 1956.
Pp. 29-51.
     Liberal education for adults is referred to as a product
which is to be merchandised and marketed.   Statistics on
numbers of adults attending school are impressive, but the
percentage who have a genuine, serious-minded, and sustained experience of liberal education of an organized char-

acter is discouragingly small. There are several adult
education "publics": the mass to whom the ultimate appeal must be made in a democratic society and who are
essentially non-involved; the mildly concerned and mildly
involved; those who appear heavily involved but are motivated by self-interest or corporate direction; a large
group of people who actively seek intellectual experience;
and finally the searchers or leaders. We should think in
terms of our different publics and what our message
should be to each. To reach the mass of the non-involved
we should operate on the "begin-with-them-where-they-
are" theory and provide good teachers so that students
will learn the excitement of learning. The most effective
influencing of public opinion must take place through
teachers and leaders in adult education. An examination
of the leadership of the field and of attitudes and motives
of all who work in the field is of greatest importance.
The writer discusses the status, roles and attitudes of the
college president, the dean of the evening college or director of the program of liberal education for adults,
members of the advisory board, the professional teacher
and the lay leader. Close contact with and sensitivity to
the community are needed. Provision of other types of a-
dult courses can be first steps toward liberal education as
well as a financial necessity. Our merchandising efforts
often fail because we are not professionals in marketing,
and lack funds to employ them. Some unsolved problems
related to cultivation of public response to programs of
liberal education are: (1) to find the time and means by
which teachers of "bread and butter" and semi-professional courses can be brought to see that their purpose is a
step in the education of whole men; (2) to provide proper
counseling of adults; (3) to give adult students a sense of
belonging and proprietorship in a community of adult students.   105

McGhee, Paul A. Merchandising Adult Education, In Adult
  Education, 5 (Spring, 1955) 146-152.
     Examines the reasons why adult educators resist the
thought of "selling" adult education as a product. To
sell the concept of continuing education and its content
they should adopt merchandising techniques of getting the
attention of potential consumers while guarding against the
'merchandising orientation.' Consumers should especially
include teachers, professors, librarians and community
leaders who in turn can help to sell the concept and un-
affiliated individuals who rarely participate in group ac-

tivity. Adult education competes with other merchandisers for people's time, not essentially their dollars, so that adult educators' merchandising aims can be achieved by working through and in collaboration with other merchandisers, as in the area of mass media.   106

McGlothlin, William J. A Basic Confusion, In Adult Education, 3 (February, 1953) 98.

Adult education still has a basic confusion between a belief that people can determine what is good for them and a belief that educators know what is good for them. This latter position developed because adult education activities often grew out of institutions which are primarily responsible for the education of youth in which this is the prevailing assumption. Adult educators who believe that people are the best judges of their own problems and can best determine how to deal with them must be ready to organize, aid and uphold, but not direct, the educational activities of those with whom they work. These skills in dealing with people who are their own masters are not considered academically respectable but are indicative of a willingness to live democracy even in education. Adult educators must hold fast to this belief in people rather than to a belief in what is good for people.   107

McHugh, Vincent.   Toward a Theory of Approach in Adult Education, In Adult Education, 1 (June, 1951) 171-176.

There is a diversity and fecundity of techniques in use in adult education which may be valuable not only for immediate adaptability but also for possibilities in experimental discovery. A common factor in all teaching situations encountered in adult education is that all derive their conventions in some measure from larger social patterns outside the classroom and look toward goals beyond the classroom. Thus, adult education is a phase in the continuous current of adult life, and should be approached in terms of major social attitudes rather than the specialized attitudes of the pedagogic tradition. The question of technique goes straight to the question of what the teacher is trying to do and what the student wants. Like other fruitful group experiences, adult education is developed and controlled by participants; it should produce certain objective results; it proceeds by the interaction of personalities; and it brings about changes in each personality involved. This governing concept can be applied as an orientation and a positive technique. The most workable techniques in adult education will tend to be derived from

(1) the socially analogous or related situation with which
the student is familiar, and (2) the professional situations
implicit in the subject matter itself. The professional
person would move from working to teaching with little
change in professional attitudes. Because of his sense of
this continuity he would create the psychological atmosphere of his profession in the classroom. Thus learning
may escape the disadvantage of a separate process and
become an apprenticeship in the profession itself.   108

MacLean, Malcolm S. Challenges in Adult Education, In
   Adult Education Bulletin, 11 (February, 1947) 69-76.
   Traces the early development of adult education and
the great stimulus and developments of the World War II
period and early post-war years, and discusses the challenges ahead. These challenges are: (1) international
organization for peace; (2) intercultural relationships; (3)
character education; (4) adjustment in home and family
affairs; (5) adult education for leisure for enjoyment and
growth. The great pressures and changes of society
challenge adult education to expand its thinking, step up
its planning, and widen and intensify its activities to meet
the challenges of the present and future.   109

Maud, Sir John. The Significance of Adult Education, In
   UNESCO, "Adult Education, Current Trends and Practices." Problems in Education, 2 Paris: UNESCO,
   1949. Pp. 17-26. Same condensed: Food for Thought,
   11 (March, 1951) 21-25.
   The significance of adult education is that it can free
people from insignificance, from the sense of being power-
less, and from the sense of being lonely. The need
which adult education must meet today is the need to find
significance in work, to find significant and creative possibilities in leisure time, and to know how political responsibilities as citizens of one's country and of the world
can be discharged. Some principles necessary to accomplish this are: (1) Adult educators must have an adequate philosophy of life. (2) The student in adult education must be sovereign. (3) Adult education is an end in
itself. (4) The instrument through which adult education
can best be pursued is the small group. (5) The various
groups must cooperate with each other. (6) Cooperative
relationship must exist between groups of different nations so that adult education will become a world movement. Adult education can become a world wide movement through national adult education organizations, inter-

national conferences, use of mass media, and the work of
UNESCO.   110

Melby, Ernest O.   World Understanding--the Community's
     Job, In Adult Education Journal, 7 (July, 1948) 121-126.
     Education has not been a panacea for the problems of
the world.   Democracy cannot be made to work without
a different kind of education than that provided in the past.
One reason for past failure lies in too narrow a conception of democratic values.   We have not given enough attention to democracy's economic, social, and human relations aspects.   A thorough program in the meaning of
democracy is needed from kindergarten through college
and adult life.   We have also failed to give the average
citizen abiding faith in freedom because of overemphasis
on organizational forms and machinery.   The foundation of
successful democracy is a successful working local community.   Education must have a larger content in the area
of community organization, leadership and participation.
Past failures in education have been due in considerable
degree to excessive verbal efforts with a lack of vitality of
real life situations.   The Montana Study is cited as an illustration of community examination of its educational
problems and working out their solution.   In placing attention on the realities of community life we overcome the
verbal character of education and also emphasis on method, machinery, and form.   Through a total program of
community development a vital education can be developed
for the recapture of faith in the common man and democratic processes.   111

Miller, Harry L.   What's Your Line? In Adult Leadership,
     6 (September, 1957) 69-72, 85, 89.
     The diversity of the field of adult education makes it
difficult to define the work of adult educator.   The significant kinds of specializations in the field and the tasks
of the adult educator are discussed.   The field can be divided by type of institution, subject matter, or more
meaningfully, in terms of Houle's pyramid with lay leaders
at the base, professionals who combine adult education
functions with other duties in the middle, and professionals whose primary concern is in adult education at the
top.   Describes changing social forces which have shaped
education in the United States and concludes that "adult
education has tended to respond, much more than traditional forms of education, to the major thrusts of the
society."   Adult education is characterized as "a sort of

trade school for the skills needed to adjust to social
roles." To guard against pressuring people to adjust to
basically unstable roles or to encourage conformity, all
adult educators have an additional common task--liberal
education. More liberal studies should be offered. Vocational or role education should be liberalized. Teaching methods should lead learners beyond the specific
skills involved in learning roles by showing connections to
underlying principles in the field or other fields, examining personal and social consequences of a role, and expanding the meaning of the role to include aesthetic, moral and social implications.   112

Mills, C. Wright. "Mass Society and Liberal Education."
    Notes and Essays on Education for Adults, No. 9. Chi-
    cago: Center for the Study of Liberal Education for A-
    dults, 1954. 17 pp.
    Discusses the transformation of a community of publics
into a mass society and its concomitant psychological and
political problems. Sets forth four dimensions necessary
for distinguishing between public and mass: (1) the ratio
of givers of opinion to its receivers, (2) the organization
of communication which determines the possibility of an-
swering back an opinion without reprisal, (3) the ease
with which opinion is effective in shaping important decisions, (4) the degree to which instituted authority infil-
trates the public with sanctions and controls. In a community of publics, discussion is the ascendant mode of
communication, and mass media link one primary public
with the discussions of another. In a mass society, communication is dominated by the formal media, and the
publics become media markets. Major trends transform-
ing the public into mass are delineated. The task of the
liberal college for adults is "to help produce the disciplined and informed mind that cannot be overwhelmed,"
"to turn personal troubles and concerns into social issues and rationally open problems" and to fight the
forces which are destroying genuine publics.   113

Morris, C. R. The Aims and Content of Adult Education,
    In Adult Education (London), 18 (December, 1945) 85-92.
    The writer recognizes the values of technical education
for general educational purposes, but in discussing aims
and content of adult education, he speaks of adult education in the academic sense. British universities have a
tradition of scholarly learning, much of which has carried
over to adult education. Adult education has managed to

bring academic learning to a much greater number of
people and in some ways in a much better way. Many
subjects can be studied profitably only by adult minds.
Adult students have reached the stage where what they
want is not to be instructed, but to see the subject studied and to join in the study themselves, and adult educational techniques have developed accordingly. Four points
are made concerning adult education: (1) General discussion is fundamental, but an immense amount can be
done by a professional student to set the atmosphere and
tone. (2) Adult education does not consist exclusively of
very advanced classes in liberal studies. (3) Steadiness
and solidarity of public opinion is due to the large number of people accustomed to thinking. The widest opportunities possible should be given for study of subjects that
can be studied only by mature people. (4) Adult education is valuable because it can bring everybody at some
stage of his life to the common study of eternal verities.
This kind of education can be enjoyed by many mature
people who cannot live the life of the full-time student and
scholar.   114

Morris, C.R. Is Adult Education a Luxury? In Adult Education (London), 24 (Spring, 1952) 247-251.
     The greatest value of earlier education is that it
builds up for the education that can come only in maturity.   While learning may be acquired by self study, per-
ceptiveness is enhanced and good judgment is formed and
nourished by discussion with others. The question may be
asked whether the understanding and enjoyment resulting
from liberal adult education are not too costly to the community. Training in technical skills can be more easily
defended in terms of utility. Maintenance of the life of
the community demands judgment in human affairs, and
it is with human subjects that liberal adult education is
concerned. The British have a reputation for good judgment politically. They also have a high reputation for a-
dult education. There can well be a connection between
the two.   115

Mumma, Richard A. Trends in Adult Education Offerings in
Region II. See No. 384.   116

Nietz, John A. Expand Adult Education, In American School
Board Journal, 114 (March, 1947) 23-25.
     It has been estimated that approximately half the adult
population in the United States has a general reading abil-

ity insufficient to provide a sound basis for independent
thinking on important matters.   Psychological studies
have determined that adults can and do learn.   What a-
dults should learn should be determined in terms of the
learner, although he may not know what he ought to learn.
This problem may best be resolved by determining his
purposes for learning: (1) to learn certain basic things
which he failed or neglected to learn when he was a child;
(2) to learn things for which a particular need has arisen,
not foreseen during formal schooling, usually of a vocational or professional nature; (3) to learn those things
which deepen and enrich his understanding and appreciation of what he has learned; (4) to learn those things
which will help him meet the diverse problems of life
other than vocational or cultural.   These types of adult
education should be offered both formally and informally
and by many diverse agencies.   Consideration should also
be given to methods and techniques most suitable to adult
learning.   Surveys have determined that a large number
of adults want to learn.   The problem is to provide proper opportunities for learning.   As long as educational
programs are to be based on meeting needs, programs of
adult education cannot be neglected.   117

Peers, Robert.   The Future of Adult Education, In   Adult
   Education (London), 25 (Autumn, 1952) 87-95.
   Discusses purposes which adult education served in the
past, the complexity of social organization of present day
society, and implications for education in general and a-
dult education in particular.   Among these implications
are the needs for adult education of specialists, of the
aging, and for increased leisure.   In the analysis of present day needs and possibilities, adult education cannot be
conceived of in terms of limited objectives, either in relation to sections of society or subjects.   Methods must
be as diverse as material and objectives.   118

Peers, Robert.   The Meaning of Adult Education, In Adult
   Leadership, 2 (April, 1954) 2-3, 32-33.
   In examining the question of whether academic studies
can be effective for social purposes, the writer considers
social conditions in the light of which the place and purpose of adult education should be defined.   Implications of
these conditions for society and adult education are discussed.   Adult education's character, purpose, standards,
and ability to perform tasks proper for it must depend upon education of the individual at earlier stages which must

be strengthened. Circumstances demanding more specialized training also make more urgent the need for general, liberal education which aims at development of
qualities upon which democracy depends. Principles which
should govern and inspire adult education are: (1) It
should be the kind of education appropriate to the stage of
life in which the individual is released from preparation
for earning a living and is ready to assume responsibilities and privileges of a fuller citizenship. (2) It should
be concerned primarily with studies relevant to interests
of men and women as human beings and with responsibilities as democratic citizens and with skills for making creative use of leisure. (3) Organization and method of a-
dult education must be suited to needs and characteristics
of mature persons. (4) The relation between teacher and
student should be one of active sharing in the whole educational process. (5) Adult education must be completely
free from propaganda or censorship. (6) Adult education
must be of the highest quality if it is to achieve its ends.
Emphasis should be on quality rather than arbitrary standards. Critics of this conception of adult education argue
that adult education should aim at influencing behavior
rather than at accumulating knowledge. But action not
based on knowledge can be dangerous. The argument
that liberal studies do not change behavior is a generalization from the wrong kind of academic studies for adults.
Assuming that liberal education produces better persons,
it also produces better communities. The shift in emphasis from knowledge to action brings the danger that a-
dult education may take the form of propaganda in the interest of particular doctrines or kinds of social action.
Mere propaganda without freedom of critical discussion
must induce a passive and indiscriminating habit of acceptance destructive to the ideal of democracy.   119

Pell, Orlie A. H. Social Philosophy at the Grass Roots, In
    Adult Education, 2 (April, 1952) 123-134.
        A report of the work of the Adult Education Associa-
    tion's Committee on Social Philosophy "to re-define the
    function of the new organization with regard to continuing
    interpretation of the social scene in the light of its effects
    on the educational needs of adults." The Committee pre-
    pared a statement of seven "Principles Which Should
    Guide the American Adult Education Movement" and seven
    opposing social philosophical value judgments which was
    circulated among one hundred fifty adult educators. These
    representatives were asked to present the statement to

small groups for discussion. Eduard Lindeman, summarizes and discusses the principal general areas of criticism by the groups. Principles formulated by the Committee include: (1) The focus of adult education is the
local community. (2) Citizenship requires realization
that one lives in an expanding environment and local problems must be viewed in regional, national and world perspective. (3) Adult education must conform with the ide-
ological traditions and aspirations and traditions of the society of which it is a function, i. e., democratic goals and
methods. (4) Adult education should be guided by the
truth-seeking disciplines of scientific method. (5) "Social action on behalf of reasoned social change is the
functional raison d'etre of a modern adult education movement." (6) Each step in directed social change should be
accompanied by a rigorous examination of its ethical meaning. (7) Adult education, although "based upon social
goals and utilizing social methods, is founded upon the belief in the individual as the ultimate seat of responsibility,
integrity and worth." An appendix to this report was
prepared by the Committee of Social Philosophy of the
Springfield (Mass.) Adult Education Council. Included is
a statement of the persistent needs of self, family and
community, nation and world; of values--enhancement of
self, developing good human relations, increasing sensi-
tiveness to larger realities; and of principles of the organization of adult education, the role and orientation of
adult teachers, use of mass media and evaluation in the
field.   120

Powell, John W. Adult Education: American Plan, In Adult
    Education Journal, 8 (July, 1949) 169-175.
    The picture of adult education in the United States is
one of diversity, having many programs and agencies, with
no established institutional pattern, no accepted curriculum,
and no professional body of leaders. Yet its very diversity is an expression of affirmative principles underlying
American institutions. The writer offers five clues to
these principles as they concern the character of education in this country and explains each: (1) The method of
liberty is to offer the widest available variety of options
and let the people choose. (2) Dynamic differences--of
background, experience, opinion, valuation, aim--furnish
both the occasion and the content of educational activity.
(3) The individual adult is an active complex of functions,
interests, aims, memberships and relationships, and is
uniquely defined by his own combination and patterning of

these elements which he shares with others.   (4) The
master function of education shall be to increase people's
power to make intelligent choices; but education itself is
non-partisan.   (5) Education consists of experiences in
activity-situations shared with others, leading to increase
in individual skills and resources and to growth in awareness of one's relatedness with other people.   121

Powell, John W.   "Education for Maturity; an Empirical
    Essay on Adult Group Study."   New York: Hermitage
    House [c1949].   242 pp.
        The writer's thesis is: "...education now has a meth-
    od and a vehicle for providing experiences, on an adult
    level, which can be implemented and controlled for the
    promotion of maturity, and which can sustain itself by the
    enjoyment and rewards which men and women find implic-
    it in it.   This vehicle is group study based on a book
    curriculum under leadership oriented to major questions
    of common concern."   Part One discusses "The Meaning
    of Maturity," in ten chapters.   Part Two discusses the
    nature of the group process.   Part Three describes two
    enterprises of which the writer served as director, The
    School of Social Studies, established in San Francisco in
    1933, and The Group Reading Program of the Public Li-
    brary, Washington, D.C., begun in 1945, with chapters
    on methods; use of books; role of the leader; use of ma-
    terials other than books such as films, forums, field
    studies, and radio;   "Questions--and Some Answers;"
    "Group Reading as a Library Service."   Part Four con-
    sists of four appendices: "Some Tested Sequences;"
    "Books for Group Reading;"   "Index of Books Used in
    Groups, 1933-48;" "A Tool for UNESCO."   122

Powell, John W.   "Learning Comes of Age."   New York:
    Association Press [c1956].   235 pp.
        A "general survey of the present state and future pros-
    pects of adult education."   Part I, "Aims of Adult Learn-
    ing,"   "Introduces the Reader, the Author and the
    Theme,"   "Looks at the Growth in Adult Learning Activi-
    ties,"   "Suggest Some Major Areas of Adult Concern."
    Part II, "Agencies of Adult Learning,"   "Discusses the
    Principal Agencies of Adult Learning,"   "Discusses Asso-
    ciations and Councils," and "Denies that the Present Pat-
    terns are Adequate."   Part III, "Areas of Adult Learn-
    ing," discusses education for citizenship, education for
    family life, the relation of education and the job, educa-
    tion for the enrichment of living, and education for self-

Powell, John W.   65

understanding. Part IV, "Toward a Structure for Adult
Education," "Suggests Some Institutional Patterns,"
"Proposes a Profession," and "Discusses Financing of
Adult Education." Part V, "Toward a Philosophy of A-
dult Education," "Derives the Values of the Educator."
                                                              123

Powell, John W.   Toward a Philosophy of Adult Education,
     In Adult Leadership, 5 (November, 1956) 133-134.
     This essay is the final chapter of the book "Learning
Comes of Age." New York: Association Press, 1956.
Because individuals come to maturity of function only in
a social context, an absolute requirement for society is
communication. The range of inclusion of concern which
the individual makes his own is one measure of the maturity that education seeks. The "ultimate fulcrum on
which all the leverage of education rests is the communication within the individual." Education must oppose
everything which impairs communication--irrational com-
pensation, lying, prejudice, ignorance, anger, fear, par-
tiality, behavior which contradicts precept, barriers to
community integration--and seek to assist learners constructively to change their behavior in the opposite direction. Thus the values of adult education are not just as-
serted but are implicit in the task of serving society
through communication. A more reasonable community
for adult learners must be made by them by widening the
common circle of shared communication; the adult educator is committed to democracy as a social method. Because it is valuable for adults to learn within a context of
intimate response and to become sensitive to the quality of
their own intimate responses to each other, the adult educator emphasizes group processes as the matrix within
which adult learning can take place most effectively.   124

Reller, Theodore L.   Adult Education in a Democratic So-
     ciety, In Educational Outlook, 29 (January, 1955) 49-54.
     Despite the social need for an advance in adult educa-
tion, progress seems to be slow, possibly as a result of
lack of understanding and vision. In considering this
problem, the writer gives attention to democratic society
and adult education; goals of education and their attainment; peculiar relevance of adult education to the goals;
and brief consideration of a selected group of problems
or issues. Adult education has a large role in helping to
clarify the meaning of democracy and in determining results of various applications of its basic principles.   A

high level of adult education should insure an increasing
achievement of democracy.   The goals of education are to
produce free men, able to judge and plan so that they can
truly govern themselves, and men universal in their motives and sympathies.   Among adult education's special
attributes or opportunities to contribute to or enhance
these aims are the following: (1) further attainments begun in formal schooling; (2) open up new areas which
have gone largely undeveloped; (3) consider matters which
have developed since elementary or secondary school attendance; (4) stimulate higher achievement because of
greater maturity of students; (5) contribute to attainment
of essential critical powers because of greater willingness
of society to permit adults to pursue truth more objective-
ly; (6) more readily see action as a fundamental aspect of
the educational process; (7) have to respond less to immediate economic demands and therefore give more attention to experiences which contribute most to the freeing
of men.   Public understanding of the significance of adult
education, the concern and involvement of professional
educators, clarification of aims, program coordination,
commitment of more resources, and development and use
of more effective forms of adult education are some of
the keys to needed progress in the field.   125

Rowley, C. D.   Ends and Means--an Australian View, In
Adult Education (London), 24 (Spring, 1952) 277-283.
      There is a difference between educational policy and
practice, and even non-technical courses planned to promote general culture may result chiefly in more highly
trained recruits for processes of production.   Educational
experience is a process through which individuals grow
into harmony with the community and environment.   It is
a task of adult education to attempt to arrest the social
disintegration of industrial society.   It can promote cooperative and constructive activities with direct appeal to
all levels of ability and attainment.   In addition to equality of competitive opportunities, there is need in the field
of adult education for extension, proliferation, and integration of cultural opportunities.   There is lack of demand
for what adult education organizations have to offer, little
research, and no training facilities for adult education
workers.   There have been proposals for organization of
general and cultural activities, new publications for adult
education purposes and new adult education organizations.
But the scale of present activities is too insignificant.
Subsidies to cultural education activities are needed.   Cer-

tain difficulties arise if this principle is accepted. First,
there cannot be provision for activities until there is demand for them. If need for cultural education exists, the
problem is to get people to demand what they need. The
second difficulty is in the limitation of central government
action. Local authorities should be given responsibility
for promotion of general educational and cultural activities,
with subsidies from governments for approved activities.
Collateral expenditures would have to provide for research
and training of personnel. In these two functions universities could make their greatest contribution to adult education work.   126

Royall, Norman N., Jr. Adult Education's Major Premise,
In Adult Education, 4 (February, 1954) 94-100.
      Defines adult education as "a type of communication
within the open society whose proximate objective is the
creation of sub-communities within that society, these
sub-communities being created for the continuous solution
of essentially unpredictable problems which arise in the
open society. The ultimate objective of adult education is
the transformation of the entire open society itself into the
pattern of a great university." Differentiates between o-
pen and closed societies, discusses the relationship of communication and community, the time binding process, and
"Building Cooperative Intelligence for the Open Society."
                                                           127

Ruthven, Alexander G. The Role of the College in Adult
Education. See No. 593.   128

Schwertman, John B. Adult Education: Means or End, In
Adult Education, (Autumn, 1954) 37-41.
      Agencies of adult education are usually parts of a het-
erogeneous group of social institutions which have other
major activities and purposes. The agencies having the
most successful adult education programs are those most
committed to partisan, specialized or utilitarian ends however socially desirable those ends may be. There is an
inverse relationship between program success and education, "culture" and arts for their own sake. Adult education programs may be placed on a three point continuum:
(1) the highly partisan or utilitarian programs, limited in
the organizational clientele appealed to, with evaluation in
terms of contribution to the institution's own group and its
specific goals; (2) programs committed to broad social
goals, appealing to broader clientele and with evaluation

in terms of the public interest; (3) the "art for art's
sake" programs with aims generally synonymous with
those of liberal education.   Adult education should direct
its efforts at helping make the ideal of an open society a
reality.   To create such a movement adult education agencies must permit and encourage study and discussion sub-
jecting organizational goals and institutionalized norms to
constant rational inquiry, and the public must support liberal education programs.   The Adult Education Association should act as a practical service agency for adult educators, social agencies and voluntary organizations;
should provide the means of posing crucial questions, research findings and ideas; and should provide a national
forum for conflicting aims and philosophies.   129

Schwertman, John B.   The Need for Theory in Adult Educa-
    tion, In School and Society, 77 (June 27, 1953) 405-408.
      Adult education in the minds of most college and uni-
versity people is divided into three parts: (1) The aspect providing academic programs leading to college degrees.   These programs are held to be the proper concern of universities, and it is believed they should have
the same objectives, content, methods and standards as
day programs for full-time students.   (2) The aspect
which provides non-credit short courses, lecture series,
institutes, etc., which most academic people feel concern
the university only to some extent.   University extension
and certificate programs also fall into this category.
(3) The aspect which is generally held not to be the concern of the university, including what is done by public
schools, adult education councils, Y.M.C.A.'s and other
non-collegiate agencies.   Since at least some adult education programs connected with institutions of higher learning should be something more than day school at night, a-
dult education needs to develop some theory of its own.
The main obstacle to better adult education is the lack of
an appropriate way of looking at it.   The aspect of adult
education connected with higher education is in a frame
of reference which is, at least in part, inappropriate for
adult education.   Learning principles and practices more
appropriate for adults will emerge only when adult education develops a reason for its existence, a theory of its
own to discover what it really is.   130

Sharer, Robert E.   Community's Program of Continuing Edu-
    cation, In Adult Education, (January, 1953) 59-62.
      Lists and discusses ten essential characteristics which

Sheats, Paul H.   69

constitute the minimum structure for a community program of adult education: (1) a foundational philosophy;
(2) educationally sound approaches; (3) provision for the
discovery and training of effective leadership; (4) clarification of legal authority to provide for assumption of
roles in adult education by public agencies; (5) adequate
financial support; (6) recognition of the fact that continuing education is characterized by a constantly expanding
scope of program and by a continually changing content;
(7) concern with the continuous improvement of the quality of the program; (8) a sound administrative structure;
(9) provision for continuous evaluation; (10) provision for
research.   131

Sheats, Paul H.   Luncheon Address at Founding Assembly,
    In Adult Education, 1 (August, 1951) 212-215.
    Guidelines evolved in discussions of the Assembly, to
which the A.E.A. should hold in the years ahead are:
(1) The community approach in adult education.   Vitality
of the American system depends on the quantity and quality of citizen participation in the cooperative effort of
community life.   (2) Willingness to stand for things that
preserve and extend the free society in which adult education alone may continue to serve as an instrument for
social advance.   (3) Engaging in and applying findings of
research and evaluative studies to basic problems of communication as they affect both content and methodological
aspects of adult education.   (4) Establishing priorities a-
mong the many tasks of adult education.   One which
should be near or at the top of the list is equipping people
with knowledge and skills   needed for effective citizen participation in world affairs.   132

Sheats, Paul H.   A Middle Way in Adult Education, In Adult
    Education, 7 (Summer, 1957) 231-233.
    Suggests a continuum upon which to analyze "the focal
issue of adult education today."   At opposing ends of the
continuum are those who perceive adult education's primary role as that of facilitating individual learning, growth
and development, and those primarily concerned with the
responsibility of adult education for strengthening society
and the solution of group problems and who see the individual's cultural development as a by-product of his participation in the group life of the community.   A middle
way philosophy may be based upon the following questions: "(1) Are we working collaboratively with those
whom we hope to influence as staff members, as learners,

as academic colleagues? (2) Are the experiences which
we are providing to our staff and in our classes and
conferences genuinely educational for the participants?
(3) Are we maintaining an experimental attitude toward
our work? (4) In the discharge of our daily tasks are we
'self-centered' in our approach or do we use work settings to satisfy personal needs for power and prestige?
(5) Are we conducting ourselves in all that we do, so as
to recognize continually the sacredness of human personality and the right of the individual to areas of privacy
which even the educator shall not invade?''   133

Sillars, Robertson.   An Approach to Adult Education, In
    Adult Education, 7 (Summer, 1957) 240-244.
    States briefly the opposing positions of the Traditional-
ist and the Modernist on five issues: content versus
method, action versus ideas, social science versus humanities, teacher-directed versus collaboratively directed
education, individual improvement versus social improvement.   On the basis of the position that the central responsibility of the educator is to enable individuals to formulate and pursue their own goals for personal development and social policy, the writer outlines three tasks of
adult education: (1) to examine programs of communication in various sectors of adult population as to purposes,
contents, methods, and effects; (2) to examine social
structures and processes, group and class relationships,
and challenges confronting individuals at various points in
the life cycle; (3) to experiment with methods of program
planning, promotion, operation and evaluation.   In con-
clusion the author states a position on each of the five issues dividing the Traditionalist and Modernist which is
consistent with the approach taken in this paper.   134

Sillars, Robertson.   Are the 'Great Books' the Answer?   In
    Food for Thought, 8 (December, 1947) 14-18.
    Although the Great Books Program has value and is a
worthwhile undertaking, it is not the best or only way to
educate adults.   The writer suggests that a more promising alternative for acquiring principles for evaluation and
action is a problem-centered rather than a book-centered
orientation, dealing with present day challenges of real
life.   The kind of books needed and motives for reading
them will be determined by the nature of the problems
faced and the level on which we are in a position to deal
with them.   135

Smith, David. The End of Adult Education, To Learn 'To
Live in Fellowship,' In Food for Thought, 11 (April,
1951) 10-13.

Attributes of educated men or men of character all describe the way these men relate themselves to others. It
is easier to gather and impart information, make and carry out decisions in the study group approach because relations between members are good, communication is effective, decisions include everyone and are therefore carried out. Whatever an adult's interest or concern, the
pursuit of it is carried out in association with other people.
The role of the adult educator is to help citizens relate to
one another with optimum effectiveness as they carry out
their purposes. The specific responsibility of the adult
educator is for the learning of attitudes of responsibility,
reliability, tolerance, understanding and cooperation. 136

Smith, Russell F. W. Education for a Lifetime, In Journal
of Educational Sociology, 30 (January, 1957) 216-220.

Two kinds of specialized training for retirement can be
distinguished, each of which leaves the main job undone:
(1) Post-retirement training. Activity programs and adult
schooling will always have a useful place in work with
people after retirement, despite the fact that they come
too late to be thoroughly effective. The closer post-retirement training can come to being unsegregated adult education, whether vocationally or culturally oriented, the
more satisfactory it will be. (2) Pre-retirement training.
Specialized training in preparation for retirement will always continue to have real value. An increasing number
of agencies are undertaking such training. There is much
room for improvement in these programs. The important
factor is necessity for preparation for retirement to begin
early. The only preventive measure for unhappiness after
retirement is not specialized training, but education aimed
at life-long activity of a kind that is rewarding in itself
and which, if necessary, can become self-supporting.
General education has an enormously important role in
preparing people for retirement. It provides adults an opportunity to consider whether and how they can prolong
their careers and life interests, and provides chances to
experiment with and develop secondary interests and careers. Most important, it can provide "a continuing ac-
quaintance with the world of ideas, with literature, art,
music and... philosophy that are in the last analysis the
only real preparation for life, for retirement, and for
death."   137

Some Trends in Adult Education; a Symposium, In Adult Education, 2 (September, 1952) 185-216.
   Title of the entire issue. Contents: "Introduction--
Emerging Patterns of Growth," by Paul Durrie (See No.
37 for annotation); "Agricultural and Home Economics
Work," by M. L. Wilson; "Agricultural Education in Pub-
lic Schools," by Herbert Hamlin; "Vocational Education
for Adults," by H. C. Thayer and William Wilkins; "Par-
ent Education for Home and Family Life," by Mary S.
Lyle and Freda S. Kehm; "Public Health Education," by
H. N. Calver; "Education for Mental Health," by D. H.
Ruja; "Education for Creative and Recreative Leisure,"
by Joseph Prendergast and J. B. Kessel; "Education for
Industrial Relations," by Abbott Kaplan.   138

Some Trends in Adult Education; a Symposium, In Adult Ed-
ucation, 3 (November, 1952) 19-33.
   Continuation from the September, 1952 issue. "Work-
ers' Education," by E. G. Coit, O. A. H. Pell, I. L. H.
Kerrison, and L. Rogin; "Fundamental Education," by
Ambrose Caliver; "Education for the Foreign Born," by
Benjamin Shangold; "Civil Defense Training," by Leon
Weaver.   139

Spence, Ralph B.   Education's Stake in Adult Education, In
Teachers College Record, 54 (February, 1953) 275-284.
   All educators have a large stake in adult education.
An expanded adult education program can make possible
important development in other phases of education.   The
present trend of the adult education movement is to
broaden the concept to include the complete range of activities in which an effort is made to help adults learn
more effectively.   Four identifiable emphases of adult education, accepted as characteristic of good education, are:
(1) Adult education emphasizes the functional approach,
starting from things adults accept as important for themselves, but at the same time, recognizes a responsibility
for broadening horizons.   (2) It sees education as a continuous activity throughout a person's entire life.   (3) It
emphasizes the place of groups in modern life.   (4) It
uses an expanding concept of the community.   The following results of a strong adult education program are suggested: (1) more freedom to other parts of education to
develop on a functional basis; (2) new possibilities for
family education; (3) new possibilities for lay understanding of educational programs; (4) new opportunities to give
work its appropriate place in the educational picture; (5)

a more creative approach to a period of national service;
(6) new vistas in the creative use of leisure; (7) improved standards of health and safety; (8) new significance for guidance. In developing a total program of
democratic education, we need to achieve more unity of
purpose. We also need to achieve more unity within education. Adult education can contribute toward a more unified program by helping to make clear the interplay between adults and children, and by building a well informed
citizen group who will make decisions on what they want
the schools to be.   140

Stoddard, Alexander J.   Adult Education in Relation to Our
    Country's Purposes, In Adult Education, 4 (November,
    1953) 41-48.
        There have been four dominant points of view towards
    the function of education established in the United States
    during the last fifty years: (1) Education is the right of
    all people. (2) Schools are an avenue for the pursuit of
    happiness or the abundant life by transmitting our cultural
    heritage. (3) People should be trained to search for and
    find truth, i.e., to develop their ability to create, ex-
    press and implement ideas. (4) We should teach an un-
    derstanding freedom and its implications for living: "...
    discipline is the price of freedom; freedom is positive,
    not negative; freedom is something that we can have indi-
    vidually, only as we help others find it."   141

Styler, W. E.   Adult Education and Social Planning, In Brit-
    ish Journal of Educational Studies, 5 (November, 1956)
    37-46.
        Because of the dominance of the academic tradition in
    British adult education, little attention has been given to
    the type of adult education which is deliberately organized
    to assist plans for social development. The writer gives
    several examples of this type of adult education and con-
    siders the question of whether such education, which so
    far has been conceived and organized to meet needs of
    agricultural regions, has significance for a developed, in-
    dustrial society such as the United Kingdom. This use of
    adult education violates the traditional practice of British
    adult education. There is a strong case for the view that
    adult educationists in Britain should closely examine forms
    of adult education in other countries designed to assist ful-
    fillment of short term social objectives. Statistics re-
    veal that a small proportion of students in adult education
    are interested in subjects relating to political, economic,

and community development. If satisfactory projects having some realizable aim or close relationship to social action could be devised, it is probable that the number of
people studying social subjects could be increased and
new vitality given to study of social sciences in Britain.
Active adult education, as compared with academic or
theoretic, is necessary where men need to plan for improvement of their environment and conditions of social
life. It is complementary to rather than opposed to academic adult education and is desirable as an aid to good
citizenship. Needed experiments should be made to develop more of this type of adult education in Britain. 142

Thomson, Watson. Adult Education--New Model, In Food
    for Thought, 5 (January, 1945) 4-8.
      To meet the new social situation, adult education has
had to acquire new methods, new programmes and a new
philosophy. The philosophy can be described as social
and activistic, that is, education for action. The main
drive of adult education is now toward a coming together
of citizens, not just to be instructed, but to discuss common social problems, to clarify and define common social goals. Adult education is a part of the social process, challenged by the crisis of our time. The new
programmes are as varied and complex as the society they
reflect and seek to change. The new methods, social and
cooperative on the one hand, are streamlined and mecha-
nized on the other. Lectures have been replaced by participation of the study group and community forum, and
the use of radio and films has come to the forefront. A-
dult education is as much concerned with communities as
with individuals. Adult educationists cannot be neutral a-
bout fundamental issues of our times. Adult education
must be on the side of social change and democracy. 143

Tomlinson, Laurence E. "Adult Education, Its Vital Sig-
    nificance for Your Town." Portland, Oregon: Education-
    al Studies [c1951] 46 pp.
      Part I, "Development of Adult Education," includes
sections on (1) Definition; (2) History and Development--
Beginnings, Formal Development of the Movement, Examples of Organized Programs, Forms of Adult Education,
Relation to Objectives of General Education; (3) Bases of
Adult Education in Psychology, in Sociology, in the Responsibility of a State. Part II, "Parent Education," defined broadly as any form of adult education which has influence and bearing on the family environment and parental

attitudes and behavior, includes sections on Social Significance; Objectives: Physical and Mental Health, Fundamental Knowledge of Practical Value, Stabilization of
Family Relationships, Vocational Adjustment and Social
Security, Responsible Citizenship, Fuller Enjoyment of
Life, Ethical Character in Human Relationships; State Responsibility for Parent Education.   144

Torres Bodet, Jaime. Adult Education and the Future of
our Civilization, In UNESCO, Adult Education, Current
Trends and Practices. Problems in Education, 2. Paris:
UNESCO, 1949. Pp.9-16. Same: Adult Education Journal, 8 (October, 1949) 219-224; same: School and Society,
70 (October 1, 1949) 209-212; same condensed: Education Digest, 15 (December, 1949) 11-14.
    Adult education should be based on the idea of the
brotherhood of human destiny. Man is a social being and
a member of the community, which in the present day is
world-wide. World-wide aims, together with freedom in
the means of pursuing them, constitute the two cardinal
tenets to guide action to foster, through universal education, a culture whose principle is personal responsibility.
Civilization can progress only if the masses are trained
systematically and coherently for the task before them.
That is the ultimate aim of adult education.   145

Townsend, Willard S. Toward Full Equality; Labor Works
for Democratic Adult Education, In Adult Education Journal, 5 (October, 1946) 162-165.
    The great challenge to adult education today is to serve
as a means of making the democratic process effective.
In a world of rapid change, adult education must take the
offensive in teaching adults to think and act for themselves. The primary purpose of the adult education
movement is to serve as a channel whereby adults learn
to understand, live with, and tolerate each other. In the
struggle to become a vital instrument in the democratic
process, adult education has a strong ally in the trade
union movement. The narrow confines and methods of
approaching labor problems have disappeared and the labor movement has become an integral part of the community, with a fusion of labor and community problems. It
is at the point where labor meets community that adult education can render a great service with strong support
from the labor movement. One of the basic jobs of labor
and adult education cooperation is establishing in the public school system a liberal system of community adult ed-

ucation services to serve the needs of democratic citizenship.   146

Trends and New Ideas in European Adult Education, In Adult
  Education, 5 (Autumn, 1954) 5-10.
      The first of four articles in this issue reporting the
impressions gained by ten adult educators from the United
States and Canada from their participation in four international seminars on adult education conducted in Europe
during the summer of 1954.   The following general trends
are noted: (1) There is an emphasis on intellectual en-
lightening through an examination of the roots and values
of civilization through philosophy, economics, psychology
and history.   (2) Programs call for earnest purpose and
serious application by the participant.   (3) The traditional
lecture method is being supplemented by a discussion period, and public forums and informal week-end institutes
are common.   (4) The social value of the residential
school has gained increasing recognition.   (5) More provision is being made for occupational studies.   (6) There
is a recognition among European adult educators of the
need for a world-wide exchange in their field, and progress is being made through the European Adult Education
Association.   Impressions gained of significant developments in Europe are presented: the fight against illiteracy in Italy, university extension in Sweden, the Salsburg
folk high school, residential colleges in Scandinavia and
Britain, community centers in Britain, leisure time programs in Austria and Italy, and the Swiss Klubschulen.
                                                            147

UNESCO.   "Adult Education, Current Trends and Practices."
  Problems in Education, 2.   Paris: UNESCO, 1949. 148
  pp.
      One of three UNESCO publications designed to depict
the state of adult education at the mid-twentieth century.
This volume supplements the Summary Report of the Elsi-
nore Conference on Adult Education (1949) and the International Directory of Adult Education (1951).   Contributions to this symposium were prepared independently of
each other but fall logically into three groups which cor-
respond closely to the method of work adopted at the Elsi-
nore Conference: Part I: Role and Functions, includes
articles by Jaine Torres Bodet, Sir John Maud, and Jean
Guéhenno; Part II: Content and Development, articles by
J. Dumazedier, E. M. Hutchinson, and Ernest Green;
Part III: Methods and Institutions, articles by W. C.

Hallenbeck, Paul Lengrand, R. A. Sims and Eugene
Bussière, J. Farenc, Marion E. Hawes, and G. H. Ri-
vière. A selected reading list from UNESCO documents
and publications is appended. For selected articles see
Nos. 36, 60, 110, 145, 806, 952.   148

United States. President's Committee on Education Beyond
the High School. "Second Report to the President." Washington, D. C.:   Government Printing Office, July, 1957.
Adult Education, pp. 66-69.

The Committee recommends wider understanding and
acceptance of the potentials of adult education, more
careful planning of its future, clearer definition of its
aims, better organization of its programs, and new approaches for doing its work better in order to realize
fully its potential. There is need for research data national in scope so that problems and prospects of adult
education can be assessed. Established institutions such
as colleges and public schools should continue to extend
their cooperation and leadership. More teachers are
needed, new methods, improvements in information and
counseling services, encouragement of programs for rural
areas, better coordination of federal programs, reexam-
ination of the role of public and non-public institutions
and agencies. Developments in leadership, participation
of more organizations, and projects to measure effectiveness of adult education programs show promise of new directions and increased rewards from this dynamic educational field. Such activity should be encouraged and
means found for exchange of information on plans, organization and accomplishment.   149

Verner, Coolie. Adult Education for Tomorrow's World, In
Adult Education (London), 26 (Summer, 1953) 32-41.

Both the force of criticism of adult education and its
changing relationships with society indicate the need for
a new evaluation. The ultimate aim of adult education is
the development of constructive social responsibility. To
achieve this, it is essential to devise a methodology that
will provide continuity in learning while people are involved in experiences of everyday living, thus providing
both education of value in a changing society and strengthening democracy through intelligent participation. Existing institutions must be modified to accomplish this or be
replaced by a new dynamic process for the education of
individuals related to improvement of their environment.
Patterns of the past must be replaced by more creative

innovations. Academic disciplines and the specialist are a-
mong many resources for education, and one principal function of the adult educator is to help people identify and use
these resources. Many problems of adult education today
will be replaced by new ones as a dynamic methodology
replaces classical concepts. Community development has
been recognized as offering the most powerful medium
thus far developed for educating adults to responsibilities
of democracy. Research in community development has
uncovered many useful ideas for working with informal
groups which can be applied directly to adult education
programs as a means of developing a more dynamic methodology. Adult education must exercise creative leadership in directing the course of change, and design the
democratic methodology and train leaders for the future.

150

Verner, Coolie. The British Charter for Adult Education,
In Adult Education, 4 (February, 1954) 119-121.
   The Adult Education Committee of the Ministry of Reconstruction of Great Britain issued in 1919 its final report on the role of adult education in post-war reconstruction. (Great Britain. Ministry of Reconstruction, Adult
Education Committee. Final Report: Presented to Parlia-
ment by Command of His Majesty. London: H.M. Stationery Office, 1919. 407 pp.)
   As a prelude to study, the Committee formulated nine
propositions upon which to base its analysis and conclusions. These propositions epitomize the principles of a-
dult education in a democracy and are a Charter for A-
dult Education. They are, in brief: (1) That the main
purpose of education is to fit a man for life, and therefore
in a civilized community, to fit him for his place as a
member of that community. (2) That the goal of all education must be citizenship, that is, the rights and duties
of each individual as a member of the community; and
the whole process must be development of the individual
in relation to the community. (3) That education in a
democratic country must aim at fitting each individual
progressively not only for personal, domestic, and vocational duties, but above all, for duties of citizenship.
(4) That there is latent in the mass of our people a capacity far beyond what has been recognized for rising to
the conception of great issues and facing difficulties of
fundamental problems when these can be visualized in
familiar form. (5) That adult education must not be regarded as a luxury for a few nor as a thing which concerns

only a short span of early manhood, but as a permanent
national necessity, an inseparable aspect of citizenship,
and therefore should be universal and lifelong. (6) That
the opportunity for adult education should be spread uni-
formly and systematically over the whole community, and
that every encouragement and assistance should be given
to voluntary organizations. (7) That economic recovery
of the nation and the sound exercise of their responsibilities by millions of new voters depend on a far wider body
of intelligent public opinion which can be created only
through a universal process of education throughout the life
of the adult. (8) That such a process needs to be planned
and set in operation immediately as part of the general
work of reconstruction. (9) That this plan should build
upon existing lines or develop from popular institutions,
and should utilize existing facilities while providing for
their extension and removing obstacles which at present
hamper them.   151

Waller, Ross D.   Challenge and Response in Adult Education,
the Established Tradition, In Adult Education (London), 27
(Winter, 1954) 173-181.
An address to the 1954 annual conference of the National Institute of Adult Education, in response to the address
of W. P. Alexander (See No. 5). Waller defends the value of the traditional academic type of adult education.
Alternatives to this type of adult education are a vast
range of non-vocational activities in evening institutes, education centers and community centers, residential colleges, and activities of independent organizations, all of
which are socially valuable and provide knowledge of limited applicability. Universities, as repositories of knowledge, must be involved in the traditionalist type of adult
education, but they need allies who share the conviction
that knowledge is worth acquiring, and can help universities give relevance to common life today. The W. E. A. is
such an ally. An essential feature of traditional modes
is that they are based on the teaching situation with tutors
and students. The modern way is based on the learning
situation with study groups, workshops, and projects, with
advice and information at points where participants want
them. Knowledge can be acquired only through study,
with guidance. Seeking understanding of society is an intellectual pursuit, sustained by a sense of social and moral responsibility. All forms of education express the
spirit and values of their world and are shaped by forces
deeper and stronger than the efforts of educators. Con-

tinuing education for all after the secondary stage is a
matter of highest priority. It is a field for which a large
number of teachers will have to be trained, and to maintain their own general education teachers should be able
to turn to the traditional field of adult education which is
the responsibility of the university.   152

Waller, Ross D. "Learning to Live; a Short and Long
   View of Adult Education." London: Art and Educational
   Publishers, Ltd., 1946. 63 pp.
      A discussion of what adult education is; influence of
   education in H. M. Forces; adult education before World
   War II, origins, the Workers' Educational Association,
   the universities, Local Authorities, other bodies, such as
   Y. M. C. A., Y. W. C. A., residential colleges, etc., coordination through organizations; institutions in adult education since the war: community centres, urban and civic
   institutes,   residential colleges; importance of discussion
   groups; adult education as a career; the purpose of adult
   education.   153

What Is Adult Education? Nine 'Working Definitions', In
   Adult Education, 5 (Spring, 1955) 131-145.
      The "working definitions" are brief essays embodying
   several contributors' conceptions of the field as it is and
   their various visions of what it ought to be, by Wilbur C.
   Hallenbeck, Paul H. Sheats, Stanley Sworder, Per G.
   Stensland, David L. MacKaye, Carl E. Minich, John B.
   Schwertman, R. J. Blakely and Lawrence K. Frank.
   Some of the writers stress growth in awareness, sensitivity, and intelligence as the major aim of adult education;   others stress ability to fill the social roles of
   group member: parent, worker, and citizen.   One emphasizes the need to learn how to achieve the traditional values of dignity and worth of the individual personality under today's radically changing conditions of technology,
   social organization, and knowledge.   Insofar as the definitions reflect differences in focus, emphasis, and purpose, they indicate the variety of human problems with
   which adult educators must cope, the interrelatedness of
   these problems, and hence the real basis for unity of the
   adult education movement.   154

Wirtenberger, Henry J.   Goals for Evening Education and
   the Education of the Whole Man, In Association of University Evening Colleges Proceedings.   Fifteenth Annual
   Meeting, St. Louis, 1953. Pp. 47-52.

Although evening education is part time and limited, it should make the education of the whole man its primary objective. Educating the whole man means helping him develop his mind, acquire a mature attitude toward the problems of living, train the will so that choices will be made on the basis of reasoned convictions. This is a difficult goal to attain, especially in technical education. Three devices which reinforce each other in the process of liberal education are: (1) Technical and factual information can be imparted with some awareness of its philosophical implications. (2) There must be ample opportunity to study a number of well taught cultural courses. (3) Integrating courses can be devised to aid the student to pull together and focus what he learns.   155

Young, Kenneth. The End of Adult Education, the Self-Education of the Whole Man, In Food for Thought, 11 (April, 1951) 14-18.

Regardless of demands of expediency and temporary shifts in priorities in adult education in times of tension, there should be certain fundamental aims and values which remain constant. Although adult education carries a heavy responsibility to society, its first responsibility is to the individual. The approach to education which can offer a maximum of opportunity to every individual to develop to his fullest potential is a conditioning of youth in school and college to a broader concept of the purpose of education so that he enters the adult world cognizant of the need for and sources of further education. Adult education should be prepared to meet educational needs of all men and women, extending laterally over a range as wide as that of human motivations and interests, and vertically from classes for illiterates to post graduate study. New approaches should be explored in the process of conditioning people to accept adult education as a normal function of living. Democratic society demands a high standard of education in its citizens.   156

II. Research and Bibliography

A. Research

1. Reviews of Research

American Educational Research Association. Adult Education, In Review of Educational Research, 20 (June, 1950) 161-246.

Reviews the literature in this area through September, 1949, concentrating on the last five years and including earlier studies of special significance. Each section reviews the literature in a specific area of adult education and includes a bibliography of works cited. Areas include an overview of the field, characteristics of adults and groups basic to adult education, content, methods, audio-visual aids, organization and administration, and the agencies of adult education.   157

American Educational Research Association. Adult Education, In Review of Educational Research, 23 (June, 1953) 191-283.

Reviews the literature for the period October, 1949, through October, 1952. Covers research on aging, fundamental education, group behavior in adult education, community development, adult education about education, and other developments.   158

Bradford, Leland P. Characteristics of Groups Basic to Adult Education, In Review of Educational Research, 20 (June, 1950) 185-197.

Examines briefly the need to educate and train people in more effective participation in group and community problem solving, and the need to make use of group and community forces acting on the individual to increase learning and problem solving; analyzes trends in the study of group discussion; reviews in detail recent study and research in group behavior and leadership training; and suggests areas of needed research in community structure and functioning.   159

Calvin, Allen D. and others. Studies in Adult Learning
  Since 1930, In Journal of Educational Research, 50 (December, 1956) 273-285.
     The studies reviewed are concerned primarily with
  three basic considerations: the effectiveness of older a-
  dults in a learning situation; the effect of "rustiness" on
  adult learning; and the effect of intelligence on intellectual decline.   160

Essert, Paul L.   Adult Education - An Overview, In Review
  of Educational Research, 23 (June, 1953) 195-201.
     A review of forty-four studies, published 1949-1952,
  covering qualitative trends, trends in organization for research, needed research.   161

Hand, Samuel E.   "A Review of Physiological and Psychological Changes in Aging and Their Implications for
  Teachers of Adults."   3d ed.   Bulletin 71 G-1.   Tallahassee: Florida State Department of Education, Division
  of Vocational and Adult Education, 1957.   31 pp.
     A review of forty-six studies published since 1923 on
  physiological and psychological changes in aging.   The
  section on physiological changes is divided into three
  parts: changes in vision, changes in hearing, and miscellaneous physical changes.   The section on psychological changes is divided into: changes in intelligence and
  learning, changes in interests and attitudes, and miscel-
  lanesous psychological changes.   Findings of the studies
  are summarized.   Implications for teachers of adults as
  indicated by these research findings are given after each
  section.   162

Hendrickson, Andrew.   "A Review of Post-War Literature
  on Public School Adult Education."   Columbus: Bureau
  of Special and Adult Education, Ohio State University,
  1951.   Pp. 1-18.
     A selective review of the literature in this field for the
  years 1944-1950, under the headings: Philosophy; Principles of Organization and Administration; Aims and Objectives; Programs; Methods; Teacher Training; Veterans' Education; What of the Future?   163

Hieronymus, Albert N.   Research in Adult Education, In
  Phi Delta Kappan, 32 (April, 1951) 373-374.
     A review of the June, 1950 issue of Review of Educa-
  tional Research, which is devoted to recent studies in
  this and related fields.   A summary of each section of

the Review is given.   164

Houle, Cyril O.   Other Developments, In Review of Educational Research, 23 (June, 1953) 268-276.
    A review of fifty-nine studies, published 1949-1952, on
  common interests of adult educators, other attempts at
  synthesis, collection of basic data, public-school adult education, the public library, other agencies, analyses of
  adult education leaders, leadership training, development
  of program, education by television, methodological studies.   165

Houle, Cyril O. and William Bowden.   The Content Of Adult
  Education, In Review of Educational Research, 20 (June,
  1950) 198-206.
    A review of fifty-eight studies, published 1945-1949, on
  general approaches to curriculum development, approaches
  to content selection, relation of content and method, the
  diverse agencies and fields of adult education, public
  school adult education, university extension activities, other agencies of adult education, important fields of adult
  education.   166

Lorge, Irving and Rose Kushner.   Characteristics of Adults
  Basic to Education, In Review of Educational Research,
  20 (June, 1950) 171-179.
    Reviews eighty-seven research studies since 1944 on
  characteristics of adults basic to education - psychological characteristics, intelligence, learning, memory, and
  adjustment.   167

McClusky, Howard Y.   Adult Education for Citizenship, In
  Review of Educational Research, 17 (October, 1947) 293-
  298.
    A critical and descriptive review of publications, 1942-
  1947, related to citizenship education for adults.   Includes
  studies on attitudes toward public affairs, political behavior, participation in civic activities, programs of self-
  study, programs of community self-help.   168

Palmer, Orville H.   Significant Research Studies in Adult
  Education, In Association of University Evening Colleges
  Proceedings.   Fourteenth Annual Meeting, Atlanta, 1952.
  Pp. 48-55.   Also published as: "Significant Research in A-
  dult Education," Notes and Essays on Education for Adults,
  No. 2.   Chicago: Center for the Study of Liberal Educa-
  tion for Adults, 1952.

Reviews significant research studies since 1927 in these
areas: (1) why adults attend school and needs of adult
students; (2) improvement of methods of teaching in adult
education; (3) administrative practices in adult education
programs. Palmer concludes that a substantial number
of studies have been made in certain areas of adult education but results are not widely publicized or easily accessible to others. He recommends that the Association
through the Center for the Study of Liberal Education for
Adults (1) serve as a clearing house for information on
existing research; (2) study areas in which there appears
to be need of research for continued growth of adult education through the evening colleges, and carry out carefully planned research producing suggested courses of action; (3) the Association, acting as a unit, would lend
significance and prestige to such research so that funds
could be secured to make research possible.   169

Palmer, Orville H. Studies and Research, In Association of
University Evening Colleges Proceedings. Fifteenth Annual Meeting, St. Louis, 1953. Pp. 69-81.
Report of research studies reported during the past
year as completed or in process by member institutions of
the Association. Thirty-four studies are listed in four
categories: (1) evaluation of teaching methods; (2) evaluation of needs of adults; (30 evaluation of various types of
programs offered through evening colleges; (4) evaluation
of problems in other areas.   170

Raybould, Sidney G. Research in Adult Education, In Adult
Education (London), 23 (June, 1950) 16-22.
Discusses lack of research in adult education and reasons for this gap. Extra-mural departments of universities, the natural agencies to promote research in adult
education, have made no contributions in book form. One
reason may be lack of staff competent or with sufficient
time to carry on research. A secondary cause is the
lack of suitable channels of publication. A recognized
journal specializing in publication of research studies is
needed. Tutors are interested in research in teaching
methods; administrators, in research in organizational
matters. Both are interested in research on the nature
and purposes of the adult education movement. The lack
of original work is most startling in the psychology of a-
dult study. Studies are needed on nature of maturity,
subjects suited to adult study, the most profitable ages for
study, the importance of experience, intelligence, and

prejudice. For such research to be done, there must be
persons with definite responsibility to initiate research,
and conditions designed to enable them to do so.   171

Research Review, In Adult Education, 5 (Winter, 1955) 114-
127.
   The first of the reviews of current research on adult
education in the United States, published in Adult Education. Includes studies in progress or completed since the
beginning of 1954. A classified and annotated list of
seventy-five research studies, mostly Ph. D. and Master's
theses. For each study there is included a summary of
the purpose and major findings, and where it is available.
Studies are categorized under the following headings: A-
dult Learning Process, Audio-Visual and Printed Materials, Clientele of Adult Education, History of Adult Education, College and University Adult Education, Community
Development, Leadership and Leadership Training, Determining Policy and Program, Public School Adult Education, Research Methods, Rural Adult Education.   172

Research Review, In Adult Education, 5 (Summer, 1955) 240-
246.
   A classified, annotated list of twenty-nine research studies to supplement the listing in Research Review, In A-
dult Education, 5 (Winter, 1955) 114-127. New categories of research include: Areas of Adult Study, Library and Adult Education, Religious Adult Education, and
Voluntary Associations.   173

Research Review, In Adult Education, 6 (Summer, 1956)
234-243.
   The annual review of research studies, a classified,
annotated list of fifty-four studies, giving summary of
purpose and major findings, and availability of each study.
                                                       174

Research Review, In Adult Education, 7 (Summer, 1957)
196-207.
   The fourth report of research in adult education by
Adult Education. The listing of sixty-nine studies is preceded by an introduction by Abbott Kaplan comparing the
number of studies by classification in the four reports,
1955-1957.   175

Sheats, Paul H. and Laurence K. McLaughlin. Methods in
Adult Education, In Review of Educational Research, 20

Spence, Ralph B.

(June, 1950) 207-215.
A review of sixty-nine studies published 1934-1949, on
interpersonal communication and communication in small
and large groups. 176

Spence, Ralph B. Adult Education-An Overview, In Review
of Educational Research, 20 (June, 1950) 165-170.
A review of fifty-one studies, published 1937-1949,
covering trends in adult education, climate for adult education, evaluation and further research. 177

Spence, Ralph B. and Louise H. Evans. Dropouts in Adult
Education, In Adult Education, 6 (Summer, 1956) 221-
225.
Brief descriptions and summaries of research studies
on dropouts in adult education, made in the last ten years.
In making a study of the subject in 1955, the AEA Research Committee found: (1) There has been almost no
comprehensive research on adult education dropouts. (2)
There have been some related studies in other areas.
(3) There have been suggestions from several adult educators regarding handling of dropouts, but few are based
on experimental evidence. The Committee recommended
that comprehensive research on the problem be carried
out in the near future. The Committee is contacting a-
dult educators to encourage them to gather data on the
subject and to report to the Committee. 178

Tibbitts, Clark and Wilma Donahue. Developments in Education for Later Maturity, In Review of Educational Research, 23 (June, 1953) 202-217.
A review of one hundred twenty-four studies covering
previous reviews, changing capacities, adjustment to aging, programs, professional personnel research. 179

Verner, Coolie. Research-Based Publications, 1955, In
Adult Education, 6 (Summer, 1956) 226-233. Condensed
under title: U.S. Research Review, In Adult Education
(London,) 28 (Spring, 1956) 315-321. Same: Food for
Thought, 16 (February, 1956) 214-221.
A critical review of thirty-six books, periodical arti-
cles, and reports published in 1955, categorized under the
headings: General, The Adult, Institutional Developments,
Methodology, and the Social Setting. 180

2. Adult Learning

Anderson, John E.   Teaching and Learning, In Wilma Donahue, Education for Later Maturity. New York: Whiteside, Inc. and William Morrow, 1955. Pp. 60-94.
Changing needs and problems of the aging, purposes of
education for older persons, learning in older persons,
adapting instruction to the group and individual, principles
of instruction, types of education, counseling older persons, rehabilitation.   181

Brown, Giles T.   Never Too Old to Learn: A Gerontological Experiment in General Education, In School and Society, 74 (November 3, 1951) 279-281.
A report on a college sponsored night class in world
affairs for adults aged sixty and beyond. Methods used
were discussion based on background material and current
events, outside speakers, visual aids and reading of current periodicals. Some suggestions developed from the
experience are: (1) Teacher-education institutions should
be more aware of this type of employment for future
teachers and the differences required in techniques. (2)
Colleges should encourage on-campus and off-campus
classes in general education for senior adults. (3) Visual aids should be used and a sense of what is useful
should be developed.   (4)Informality and "give and take"
attitudes between class and leader proved helpful. (5)
Since most adults are not interested in academic credit,
grading and covering a certain amount of material can be
ignored. A growing population in the aged sixty and beyond group offers a distinct challenge to organized education.   182

Buswell, Guy T.   Conditions for Effective Adult Learning, In
Institute for Administrative Officers of Higher Institutions
Proceedings, 1948. Vol. 20, The Community Responsibilities of Institutions of Higher Learning. Chicago: University of Chicago Press [1948]. Pp. 14-23.
Scientific studies indicate that the most important factors relating to effective adult learning are in psychological and social conditions rather than biological changes of
maturation. Five conditions that are examples of ways
to increase effectiveness of adult learning are: (1) opportunity for continuous practice and experience in learning, with activities appropriate for the various periods of
life; (2) motivation adjusted to varying levels of maturity;
(3) methods of teaching and learning appropriate for vari-

ous levels of adulthood; (4) a community "curriculum"
consisting of a coherent organization of activities appropriate for adults at various levels of maturity; (5) suitable facilities which will meet the peculiar needs of a-
dults.   183

Calvin, Allen D. and others.   Studies in Adult Learning
Since 1930.   See No. 160.   184

Charters, Alexander N.   "An Evaluation of the Development
of Certain Aspects of the Ability to Think by Participation
in an Adult Education Program."   Ph. D. Dissertation.
University of Chicago, 1949.   179 pp.   185

Davies, John L.   "A Study of Participant Interests and A-
bility in Adult General Education Programs of Iowa."
Ph. D. Dissertation.   Iowa State University, 1950.   186

Donahue, Wilma.   Experiments in the Education of Older A-
dults, In Adult Education, 2 (December, 1951) 49-59.
   Describes experimentation at the University of Michigan
to determine whether the use of any psychological function
will retard its aging; whether exercise of an ability which
has declined can restore its function; whether aging
people who realize the need to prepare for the later years
will become motivated to learn about aging and how to adjust to it.   Courses offered through Extension and on
television are described as to content, method, evaluation
and student characteristics.   Address before the International Gerontological Congress, St. Louis, September 13,
1951.   187

Eckert, Ralph.   The Psychology of Adult Learning: An In-
service Course for Adult Teachers, In Adult Education
Bulletin, 14 (December, 1949) 55-59.
   A description of week-end courses for teachers of a-
dults in California offered jointly by the University of
California Extension and the Bureau of Adult Education of
the State Department of Education.   At the first session,
led by Harry and Bonaro Overstreet, causes of dropout of
adult students, analysis of the adult learner, and psychology of adult leadership were discussed.   A dynamic concept of education applicable to adult learning, personality
needs, psychological steps in problem solving, and counseling were discussed in the second session led by the
writer.   The third session, led by Robert Haas, was
centered around the concept of interpersonal and group

maturity, the concept of roles, and problems of leadership.   188

Farnum, Hollis B.   "A Study Comparing the Academic Aptitude of University Extension and Campus Students." Ph. D.
Dissertation.   University of Rhode Island, 1956.   189

Goldin, Frank S.   "The Effect of Program Format in Educational Broadcasts On Adult Retention."   Ph. D. Dissertation.   Boston University, 1948. 298 pp.   190

Guerin, Quinon.   Some Observations on Adult Reading Skills,
In Adult Education, 4 (February, 1954) 115-118.
   Observations based upon studies conducted while helping over four hundred adults improve reading abilities.
Discusses the relation of interest in subject matter to
reading speed; relation of nature of subject matter to
reading speed, recall and inference; relation of vocabulary
to reading speed and comprehension; adult recognition
problems; remembering what is read.   191

Jenkins, David H.   On Educating Adults, In University of
Michigan School of Education Bulletin, 22 (April, 1951)
110-112.
   Characteristics of adults which make them differ educationally from other students are: (1) Adults are independent.   (2) Adults resist the "learner" role.   (3) They
have a background of life experience.   (4) They have a
wide variety of motivations, the least of which may be to
learn.   (5) Much adult learning is relearning rather than
new learning.   (6) They come to a learning situation with
definite expectations about goals and methods which they
do not readily change.   (7) Most adult learning involves
change in attitude if it is to be effective.   192

Kuhlen, Raymond.   Patterns of Adult Development.   See
Murphy, Gardner and Raymond Kuhlen.   Psychological
Needs of Adults.   No. 198.   193

Leestma, Robert.   Some Problems Reported by Teachers of
Adult Students and Some Suggestions for Their Allevia-
tion, In University of Michigan School of Education Bulletin, 22 (April, 1951) 107-109.
   A summary of problems in teaching as reported by two
hundred thirty-four leaders of adults in eight Michigan
cities.   Problems appearing most frequently are listed
under five categories: (1) characteristics of the adult

student; (2) size of and time for classes; (3) meeting individual needs and differences; (4) attendance and dropouts; (5) inadequacies of equipment and other facilities.
The writer suggests way of alleviating each of these problems, stating that the first step is acquiring data on the
way the problems appear to those responsible for their
management.   193

Lorge, Irving.   Adult Intelligence, In Walter S. Monroe,
"Encyclopedia of Educational Research." New York: Macmillan, 1950. Pp. 32-35.
A review of twenty-six research studies on the testing
of adult intelligence, made before 1950.   194

Lorge, Irving. Adult Learning, In Adult Education, 2 (June,
1952) 156-159.
Implications for teaching adults of the changes during
maturity in speed of performance and sensory activities,
and of the adult's past knowledge, skills and attitudes. 195

Lorge, Irving. Never Too Old To Learn, In Baltimore Bulletin of Education, 33 (June, 1956) 1-7.
Psychological tests and experiments have proved that
adults do not deteriorate in mental ability.   Older people
are slower in learning and in making adjustments, but
have the advantages of wisdom in dealing with people and
situations, more stable attitude judgments, a stable core
of intellectual interests, and a background of stored
knowledge and skills. Successful teachers of adults know
the sources of difficulty for adult learners, such as their
attitudes toward themselves, and are aware that such attitudes can be changed only by changing the learners' concepts of themselves, of the task, and of the role of the
teacher. Adult education must use facts about the adult
that are available now and must encourage further studies
for information on the general and special psychology of
the adult which can be used by adult educators to improve
instructional techniques.   196

Murphy, Gardner. Teaching the Individual, In Adult Leader-
ship, 3 (March, 1955) 19-21.
Also published as part of the next entry under the title,
Individuality in the Learning Process.   197

Murphy, Gardner and Raymond Kuhlen. "Psychological Needs
of Adults; A Symposium." Notes and Essays on Education
for Adults, No. 12. Chicago: Center for the Study of

Liberal Education for Adults, 1955. 25pp.

In Individuality in the Learning Process, Gardner
Murphy discusses individual differences in perception, recall, thinking, feeling, disposition to act, and self-image
governing student response to learning materials. Suggests methodological and programming implications for a-
dult education. In Patterns of Adult Development, Raymond Kuhlen reports findings on psychological differences
among adults at different age periods as further indication of what subject matter areas, materials, and experiences are desirable in adult education programs. Topics
include: Changes in Capacity and Physical Characteristics; The Urge for Expansion - A Positive Force; Defense Against Loss - A Negative Force; Time Perspectives in Need Changes; Specific Needs and Individual Differences.   198

Siegle, Peter E. The Adult Learner, In Adult Leadership,
    3 (March, 1955) 16-18.
    A discussion of ability of adults to learn and of other
characteristics of adults which affect their educability.
Psychological studies have proved that adults never lose
the ability to learn though there is a loss in speed of reaction and physical stamina. Learning ability consists of
social and psychological as well as physical factors. The
educability of adults is limited by a number of characteristics such as: fear of self, personal uncertainties in
economic or community status, fear of others, fear of i-
deas, lack of continuity in pursuit of education, confusion
about what the academic program has to offer. On the
positive side are the adult's eagerness for learning, relatively free scope of action and lack of distractions, self-
identification with a program he seeks of his own volition,
more integrated purposes, more coherent life program,
etc. Obstacles in teaching adults are often intensified by
the failure of teachers to adapt techniques to the adult
personality.   199

Siegle, Peter E. Mountains, Plateaus and Valleys in Adult
    Learning, In Adult Education, 4 (March, 1954) 146-150.
    Fundamental propositions in learning theory, levels of
complexity of learning, kinds of learning, plateaus in
learning, typical patterns of learning. The writer concludes that more important than age in adult learning is
the combination of basic capacity, energy, experience,
motivation and guidance.   200

Thompson, Warren C.   93

Thompson, Warren C. "A Comparative Study of a Book-
Centered Course Versus a Machine-Centered Course in
Adult Reading Improvement." Ph.D. Dissertation. Uni-
versity of Southern California, 1954.   201

3. Student Needs and Interests

Anderson, John E. Teaching and Learning. See No. 181.
                                                       202

Barron, Howard H. "A Study of Adult Educational Interests
and Programs in Salt Lake County." Ph.D. Dissertation.
University of Utah, 1954.   203

Brown, Robert S. "A Survey to Determine the Post-Second-
ary Needs of Youth and Adults in Summit County and Proposals for Meeting These Needs." Ph.D. Dissertation.
Ohio State University, 1955.   204

Carey, James T. "Why Students Drop Out; Study of Evening
College Student Motivations, Research Report." Chicago:
Center for the Study of Liberal Education for Adults,
1954. 54 pp.
    A study to determine reasons for dropout of adult stu-
dents in eight evening colleges in the Chicago area. Eight
hundred dropouts were contacted by telephone interview,
mail questionnaire and personal interview, with three
hundred-fifty responding. Students are categorized as vocationally or culturally oriented, with over two-thirds having vocational goals. Reasons given for dropouts are tab-
ulated and students' future educational plans are reported.
In their order of frequency, the following reasons for
dropouts are reported: course not available, reasons not
connected with the university, job cause, financial reasons, etc. Most respondents were satisfied with college
courses, policies and services but over half did not plan
to return to evening college.   205

Costin, Frank. "Relationship of Employees' Problems and
Various Other Factors to Interest in an Adult Education
Program." Ph.D. Dissertation. University of Chicago,
1949. 269 pp.   206

Davies, John L. "A Study of Participant Interest and Ability in Adult General Education Programs of Iowa." Ph.D.
Dissertation. State University of Iowa, 1950.   207

94 Deane, Stephen R.

Deane, Stephen R. "A Psychological Description of Adults
Who Have Participated in Selected Educational Activities."
Ph. D. Dissertation. University of Maryland, 1949.
165 pp.   208

Dirks, Henry B. "Dropout in the Evening Adult Schools."
Ph. D. Dissertation. University of Southern California,
1955.   209

Donahue, Wilma. Experiments in the Education of Older A-
dults. See No. 187.   210

Dressel, Paul L. Educational Demands Arising From Individual Needs and Purposes, In National Society for the
Study of Education, Yearbook 55, Part 1: Public Junior
College. Chicago: University of Chicago Press, 1956.
Pp. 41-63.
    The problems and educational needs of prospective
college students of varying ages and backgrounds, motivation factors in seeking further education, the demand for
more and varied education, and the implications for post-
high school education especially as applied to junior colleges.   211

Evans, Helen M. "A Survey of the Citizens and Civic
Leaders of Selected Michigan Communities to Determine
Need, Interests, and Motives Related to Adult Education."
Ph. D. Dissertation. Michigan State University, 1957.
227 pp.   212

Flood, W. E. and R. W. Crossland. Origins of Interest and
Motives for Study of Natural Sciences and Psychology A-
mong Adult Students in Voluntary Courses, In British
Journal of Educational Psychology, 18 (June, 1948) 105-
117.
    An account of an investigation made in 1947 to deter-
mine motives of adults attending courses in natural sciences and psychology, to determine relative importance
of these motives, to investigate significant variation of
motive with subject, sex, and age, and as a subsidiary
aim, to determine origin of interests. Questionnaires
were sent to the extra-mural departments of all universities and university colleges in England and Wales. Information was received from fifty-five classes in natural science and fifteen in psychology. In general the predominant origin of interest in natural sciences is the study of
science in school, with books and lectures important influ-

ences.   Motives in natural sciences were grouped as vocational, general desire for knowledge, and social and
recreational.   Conclusions were: (1) Motives are mixed
and show variations with subject and age.   (2) Males
have a greater vocational interest in science, but in general motives show little variation with sex.   (3) The predominant motive is the desire to understand the present
world with the implication that science is necessary for
this purpose.   (4) Social sciences are thought best to
provide this general scientific culture.   In the field of
psychology, interest originated mainly from reading and
the influence of friends.   For psychology the study found:
(1) The predominant motives are practical but non-vocational.   (2) The strongest single motive is understanding
other people.   (3) Vocational motives are strong.   (4)
There is little difference in the motives between males
and females, but motives of males are almost independent of age, while those of females vary with age.   213

Graves, Perdue B.   "An Investigation of Adult Education
Needs and Interests in Topeka."   Ph. D. Dissertation.
University of Kansas, 1949.   214

Green, Ernest.   "Adult Education, Why This Apathy?"
London: Allen and Unwin [1953].   145 pp.
An analysis of material based upon two questionnaires
and a syllabus for study groups.   The purpose of the first
questionnaire, "Present Day Apathy in Adult Education,"
was to ascertain the point of view of adults who had taken
part in adult education.   The object of the second questionnaire, "Educational Background and Interests," was to
secure reactions of those who had little experience of a-
dult education.   The "Group Syllabus" was for study
groups competent as students and workers in adult education to suggest the main reasons for apathy and to propose remedies.   The writer was concerned to discover to
what extent adults' experience of school had stimulated
continued educational interest in adult life and in what
form.   Findings are discussed in seventeen chapters.   The
last four chapters are a summary which attempts to draw
conclusions helpful in solving the problem of apathy.   The
major reason for apathy given is inadequacy of school education.   Recommendations are: that the school should
provide more liberal education, with more emphasis on
moral and spiritual values, and wider significance of the
full life; the curriculum of technical and professional institutes should be broadened, and more stress given to

liberal and humanistic aspects of subjects, and that consideration be given to possibilities of synthesis between
technical and professional studies and liberal adult education; that a different approach be used by organizing
bodies; that better physical facilities be provided; that a
vigorous effort be made to train discussion group leaders;
that more use be made of films; and that the W. E. A. and
universities should concentrate on the problem of the educationally underprivileged.   215

Havighurst, Robert J. and Betty Orr. "Adult Education and
    Adult Needs, a Report." Chicago: Center For the Study
    of Liberal Education for Adults, 1956. 66 pp.
        Explores the implications for adult education of a study
    of the activities and goals of adults in Kansas City.
    Chapters are: The Wisdom of Maturity; Adult Needs and
    Developmental Tasks; Personal Motivation for the Achieve-
    ment of Developmental Tasks; Implications for Adult Ed-
    ucation - Illustrative Cases; Qualities of an Effective A-
    dult Education Program.   216

Havighurst, Robert J. "Social Roles of the Middle-Aged
    Person, A Method of Identifying the Needs of Adults."
    Notes and Essays on Education for Adults, No. 4.   Chi-
    cago: Center For the Study of Liberal Education for A-
    dults, 1953.   14 pp.
        A methodology for the study of middle age through rat-
    ings of social roles or activity patterns, and the relation
    of role activities to adjustment, health, economic secur-
    ity and self-concept.   217

Haworth, Edward.   "The Expressed Educational Needs of
    Older-Age Adults in Two Senior Centers." Ed. D.   Dis-
    sertation.   Stanford University, 1956.   218

James, Bernard J. and Harold W. Montross.   Focusing
    Group Goals, In Adult Education, 6 (Winter, 1956) 95-
    101.
        Discussion of some problems of education based on ex-
    perience with adult groups in 1953 and 1954, and implica-
    tions of the research for a general theory of adult educa-
    tion.   Work with the first group, composed of farmers
    and laborers, concerned primarily the design of a film
    discussion series to enable estimating flexibility of goals
    and leadership requirements.   The study of an amateur
    theater group in a small city was primarily an attempt to
    build a sociometric case history of the group based on ob-

servation-participation. Two conclusions drawn were:
(1)' Professed motives for adult education participation
should not be interpreted necessarily as real motives.
(2) Because of the flexibility and lack of clarity of goals
in adult education groups, especially of the "cultural"
sort, the adult educator must assume responsibility for
focusing group goals.   219

Kempfer, Homer E. "Identifying Educational Needs of Adults."
U.S. Office of Education. Circular No. 330. Washington, D.C.: Government Printing Office, 1951. 64 pp.
Summary: Adult Education, 2 (October, 1951) 32-36.
This study evaluates and describes thirty-seven common
practices followed by administrators of adult education
programs in identifying educational needs and interests of
adults. The method consisted of comparing practices
used in superior and inferior programs.   220

Kuhlen, Raymond. Patterns of Adult Intelligence. See
Murphy, Gardner and Raymond Kuhlen. Psychological
Needs of Adults. No. 198.

Love, Grady E. "A Study of the Interests and Needs for A-
dult Education in Greensboro, North Carolina." Ph.D.
Dissertation. University of North Carolina, 1957.   221

Love, Robert A. A Call for Action, In School and Society,
70 (October 8, 1949) 227-231.
Results of studies of dropouts made at New York City
College School of Business, Evening and Extension Division, show that fewer than ten per cent of evening students complete the curriculum and receive degrees. In addition to transfers, twelve major reasons for dropouts
are: (1) wrong selection of school or course; (2) lack of
orientation; (3) work load; (4) illness; (5) scholastic difficulties; (6) home responsibilities; (7) business or military reasons; (8) financial difficulty; (9) student inactiv-
ity; (10) inattention to problem of dropouts; (11) ineffec-
tive teaching; (12) meaningless curriculum. Discusses
steps that may be taken to correct these conditions.   222

Love, Robert A. Use of Motivation Research to Determine
Interest in Adult College-Level Training, In Educational
Record, 34 (July, 1953) 210-218.
A study made by the Extension and Evening Division of
New York City College School of Business and Civic Ad-
ministration in 1952 to determine underlying attitudes of

students and non-students toward education which might
motivate persons to overcome obstacles in order to obtain adult education at the college level.   The study was
aimed at seeking a sounder basis for obtaining additional
enrollment.   Motivations of students and of non-students
were compared as to nature and intensity.   A preliminary
statistical analysis was followed by "depth interviews."
As a result two preconditions and a sequence of enrollment were discerned.   Preconditions are that education
is seen as desirable for solving problems and is equated
with success and happiness.   Awareness of a problem to
be solved and of the availability of a course of study, selection of a school and actual matriculation comprise the
sequence of enrollment.   At each step the prospective en-
rollee encounters barriers which tend to increase near the
end of the process.   Some other observations obtained
from the study are: (1) A higher proportion of women
than men take liberal arts courses and the youngest women take a larger proportion of liberal arts courses.
(2) The attitude of employers is a major deterrent to
their employees' seeking further education.   (3) The easi-
est group to enroll is the group which has had the most
previous education.   (4) New students, mostly men, usually start with business training courses and later switch to
liberal arts courses.   Calls for a promotional program
to generate a recognition of adult extension education in
colleges as a highly desirable activity for society and for
the individual.   223

Mack, John A.   "Determining Community Needs for Adult
    Education Based Upon an Analysis of Educational Interests
    of Eight Hundred Adults in the Ithaca High School Area."
    Ph.D. Dissertation.   Cornell University, 1951.   224

McMahan, Frederick J.   "The Educational Needs of 1946 and
    1949 Parochial High School Graduates in Iowa."   Ph.D.
    Dissertation.   State University of Iowa, 1952.   225

Maloney, Martin.   Six O'Clock Scholars, In Adult Leader-
    ship, 4 (May, 1955) 4-6, 28.
    An anecdotal "miscellaneous anthology of impressions
    and guesses" concerning motives of adult students for tak-
    ing courses, by an experienced teacher.   226

Minnis, Roy B.   "Educational Needs of 1946 and 1949 High
    School Graduates in Twelve Selected Iowa Counties."
    Ph.D. Dissertation.   State University of Iowa, 1955. 227

Murphy, Gardner.   Teaching the Individual.   See No. 197.
                                                          228

Murphy, Gardner and Raymond Kuhlen.   Psychological Needs
    of Adults: a Symposium.   See No. 198.   229

Myers, Eugene E. and Francis E. Drake.   Keeping Pace
    With the Needs of the Student, In Adult Education Bulle-
    tin, 14 (June, 1950) 144-146.
        A report on devices used to maintain a continuing
    check on the needs of students at the Academic Instruc-
    tors Division of the United States Air Force Special Staff
    School, Craig Air Force Base, Alabama.   Devices used
    are: (1) the advisory system, by which each staff mem-
    ber is assigned to five to ten students for weekly con-
    ferences; (2) the tutorial system, in which ten students
    meet with their critic teacher to discuss previous instruc-
    tion and select teaching topics; (3) a critique sheet by
    which students selected periodically at random comment
    on pertinency of instruction, methodology used, and in-
    structors; (4) course conferences in which students meet
    in small groups with the director to discuss strong and
    weak points of the course.   Several curriculum changes
    have been made on the basis of data received from these
    techniques.   230

Nicholson, David H.   "Why Adults Attend School: An An-
    alysis of Motivating Factors."   Ph.D. Dissertation. Uni-
    versity of Missouri, 1948.
        The same title was published as: University of Mis-
    souri Bulletin Vol. 56, No. 30, Educational Services No.
    57.   Columbia: University of Missouri, 1955. 23 pp.
    The same title was also published in Adult Education
    Bulletin, 13 (August, 1949) 172-177.
        Report on a survey conducted during the school year
    1946-47 to ascertain the major reasons for school at-
    tendance of adults.   Additional purposes were to analyze
    and classify motives of adults for attending school, and to
    discover how such variables as sex, age, marital status,
    veteran status, employment, years of schooling, and types
    of courses taken are related to purposes given for school
    attendance.   Eighty-nine hundred inquiry forms were dis-
    tributed to students in part-time or evening schools, trade
    and business schools, and day colleges.   The article in-
    cludes a table showing percentages for each of the thirty
    reasons for attendance included in the questionnaire.   The
    study revealed that adults were motivated by a considerable

number and variety of purposes. Students want a broad
program of adult education, additional technical or specialized knowledge relating to their occupations, cultural
subjects to broaden their mental horizons and develop
their personalities and to find friends and develop social
skills.   231

Reynolds, Mildred M. "The Identification of the Needs of
Senior Citizens and an Analysis and Critique of Selected
Programs Designed to Meet These Needs." Ed. D. Dis-
sertation. Temple University, 1957.   232

Ride, Dale B. "Public Education for the Aging - A Determination of the Educational Desires of the Aging and Recommendations for More Adequately Involving Them in the
Santa Monica Adult Education Program." Ed. D. Dissertation. University of California, Los Angeles, 1955. 233

Spence, Ralph B. and Louise H. Evans. Dropouts in Adult
Education. See No. 178.   234

Styler, W. E. The Motives of Adult Students, In Adult Education (London), 23 (September, 1950) 106-112.
    Summarizes the findings of inquiries on motives of a-
dult students as reported in Learn to Live, by W. E.
Williams and A. E. Heath, 1933; in "Origins of Interest
and Motives for Study of Natural Sciences and Psychology
among Adult Students in Voluntary Courses," by W. E.
Flood and R. W. Crossland, published in British Journal
of Educational Psychology, June, 1948; in Tutorial Class
Students, published by Leeds University Extra-Mural Department in 1949; in the Manchester 1947-48 inquiry.
The following conclusions are drawn, based upon the limited amount of research done in this field: (1) In social
and political subjects and in natural sciences, the chief
motive is interest in the world in which the students live.
(2) In psychology, the present interest in social psychology relates the motives of many psychology students with
those in the social and political group. (3) In appreciation of music, the chief motive is prior interest. (4) Desire for additional education is very important and may be
regarded as a result of the general advance in education.
(5) Vocational motives appear to be more powerful in natural sciences than in any other subject. (6) 'Personal'
motives are much more powerful than 'social' motives,
the desire to improve society. (7) A statement of motives does not measure their strength. Degree of inter-

est in a subject varies and may be strengthened or weakened by experience after joining the adult education activity.   235

Wilkins, Ralph W. "A Study to Determine the Adult Education Needs of Providence, Rhode Island." Ed. D. Dissertation. Boston University, 1955.   236

Wright, Grace S. "Persistence of Attendance in Adult Education Classes." U. S. Office of Education. Circular No. 353. Washington, D. C.: Government Printing Office, October, 1952. 8 pp.
     A study of attendance and dropout in three hundred thirty-one public school adult education programs in thirtynine states. Among the conclusions are: (1) Subjects vary as to the degree of their holding power. (2) Dropouts occur less frequently when students pay a high fee for the course than when the course is free or the fee nominal. (3) There are more dropouts in states which provide financial support for adult education than in those which do not provide such support.   237

Zander, Alvin. Student Motives and Teaching Methods in Four Informal Adult Classes, In University of Michigan School of Education Bulletin, 22 (April, 1951) 103-106. Same: Adult Education, 2 (October, 1951) 27-31.
     A summary of part of a study on the teaching of adults, the purpose of which was to explore the nature of problems in teaching adults, specifically in regard to the way in which teachers dealt with motives of students. Findings are presented in three areas: (1) motives of students and teachers; (2) procedures in the classes; and (3) evidence on fulfillment of these motives. A majority of students in four small night school classes had strong motivation to acquire something beyond information, such as social or recreational interests. Although the teachers were aware of student interests, and described their teaching methods as intended to help the students meet their needs, the methods actually used were not as flexible as described and were of limited value toward the goal of meeting student needs. The students were getting primarily information from the courses different from that which they had hoped to get.   238

4. Student Characteristics

Anikeeff, Alexis M.   Scholastic Achievement of Extension
and Regular College Students, In Journal of Applied Psychology, 38 (June, 1954) 171-173.
    Report of a study made to evaluate scholastic achieve-
ment of extension students in comparison to that of regu-
larly enrolled students in an attempt to determine whether
extension students should receive regular college credit.
Procedure, results, discussion, and summary. In view
of obtained results, the advisability of granting college
credit for work in evening off-campus courses is ques-
tioned.   239

Blum, Lawrence P. , Ben A. Sullivan, and J. David O'Dea.
Identifying Problems of Adults in Evening Schools, In
Personnel and Guidance Journal, 31 (March, 1953) 376-
379.
    The Mooney Problem Check List was administered to
eighty-five day school and eighty-five evening school students at the University of Wisconsin, Milwaukee Extension
Division to determine similarity of problems.   Results
are presented in three tables: (1) Distribution of Day
and Evening School Population; (2) Frequency of Problem
Category Indications; (3) Frequency Ranking of Problem
Items and Percentages of Total Responding.   Conclusions
and implications are: (1) Since evening students indicated
fewer problems than day students, it may be assumed that
increased maturity brings a reduction in problems, reluc-
tance to admit their existence, or improved facility in
problem solving.   (2) Problems indicated by evening students as being of serious concern seem to be related to
the relative maturity of the group.   The authors believe
differences in maturity level account for differences in
problem types and intensity.   (3) Implications of these
data seem to support research in that the same counseling
techniques are applicable to evening and day students. (4)
Even though basic counseling techniques should remain the
same, the implication seems justified that counseling
tools, instruments, and aides may differ when used with
day or evening students.   240

Deane, Stephen R.   Who Seeks Adult Education and Why; a
Description of Adult Education Participants, In Adult Education, 1 (October, 1950) 18-25.
    Reports a study made at the University of Maryland in
the Spring of 1949 wherein three adult education programs

were investigated to determine educational, vocational, and social values and characteristics of the student population of each. The three programs were: (1) Great Books Reading and Discussion Groups at Washington, D. C. Public Libraries; (2) non-credit evening school groups of Baltimore high schools; and (3) college credit students registered with the College of Special and Continuation Studies at the University of Maryland. Marked differences were found in student characteristics among different programs.   241

Dirks, Henry B. "Dropout in the Evening Adult Schools." Ph. D. Dissertation. University of Southern California, 1955.   242

Evraiff, William. "Characteristics of Continuation School Students in Selected Communities." Ph. D. Dissertation. Stanford University, 1955.   243

Farnum, Hollis B. "A Study Comparing the Academic Aptitude of University Extension and Campus Students." Ph. D. Dissertation. University of Rhode Island, 1956.   244

Guerin, Quinon. Some Observations on Adult Reading Skills. See No. 191.   245

Hand, Samuel E. A Review of Physiological and Psychological Changes in Aging and Their Implications for Teachers of Adults. See No. 162.   246

Jenkins, David H. On Educating Adults. See No. 192. 247

Knox, Alan. "An Analysis of Certain Characteristics Related to the Nature of Adult College Students." Ed. D. Dissertation. Syracuse University, 1957.   248

Kohn, Nathan. Analysis of Students Carrying Full-Time Loads in Night School, In Association of University Evening Colleges Proceedings. Fourteenth Annual Meeting, Atlanta, 1952. Pp. 112-116.
      Report of a study of two hundred students taking nine semester hours or more in night school at University College, Washington University. Analysis was made as to age, previous education, plans for working toward a degree, grades earned. Following a one-year period spent in University College, students were interviewed as to vocational adjustment, vocational attitude, avocational par-

ticipation, distribution and use of time, alternate goals
vocationally and professionally and their appraisal of the
value of adult education. The study indicates that many
adults can profit from carrying a larger academic load
than sometimes considered advisable. Adult students with
relatively stable vocational patterns and indications that
constructuve use of energy may result in advancement,
tend to be able to absorb a considerable amount of academic training in relatively concentrated doses even when
holding full-time positions. Students accepted for such
programs should be carefully investigated and selected.
The study recommends analysis of students' personal goals
and aspirations, social patterns of living, and vocational
adjustment.   249

Ladd, Ernest E. "The Characteristics of Adults Enrolled
    During 1951-52 in the Gary, Indiana Night School Classes
    for Credit Toward High School Graduation." Ph.D. Dis-
    sertation. Indiana University, 1953.   250

Lorge, Irving. Adult Intelligence. See No. 194.   251

Love, Robert A. A Call For Action. See No. 222.   252

McLaughlin, Lawrence K. "Student Population in University
    of California Extension Classes." Ph.D. Dissertation.
    University of California, Los Angeles, 1951.   253

Nicklin, John R. "Characteristics of Students in a Credit
    Telecourse Offered by University of California Extension,
    Southern Area." Ed.D. Dissertation. University of Cali-
    fornia, Los Angeles, 1956.   254

Olds, Edward B. Adult Students and Their Teachers; A
    Study Based on Six Communities, In Adult Education, 5
    (Summer, 1955) 210-219.
        A study based on six public school adult education pro-
    grams to obtain data on students' ages, incomes, occupa-
    tions, educational level, reasons for attending classes,
    etc., and on teachers' ages, incomes, education, prepa-
    ration for adult teaching, and interest in further profes-
    sional development.   255

Preston, James M. "Characteristics of Continuing and Non-
    Continuing Adult Students." Ed.D. Dissertation. Univer-
    sity of California, Berkeley, 1957.   256

Spence, Ralph B. and Louise H. Evans. Dropouts in Adult
   Education. See No. 178.   257

Stratton, Burton E. and Lawrence Lipsett. An Extension Division Evaluates Its Program, In Adult Education Bulletin,
   13 (December, 1948) 240-244.
      Report on a survey of student opinion by the Evening
   and Extension Division of Rochester Institute of Technology, giving results as to why students take courses; how
   they find out about courses; their opinions of staff and
   services, plant and facilities; how they rate forms and
   procedures; and their suggestions.   258

Styler, W. E. Two Manchester Inquiries, In Adult Education
   (London) 22 (March, 1950) 184-191.
      A summary of a detailed report, published by the Na-
   tional Institute of Adult Education under the title, "Who
   Were The Students," 1951. During the 1947-48 and 1948-
   49 sessions inquiries were undertaken by Manchester Extra-Mural Department to discover characteristics of their
   students such as average age, occupational distribution,
   educational background, and lengths of membership in a-
   dult classes. Findings indicated: (1) a decline in the
   number of manual workers and 'educationally underprivileged' in adult education; (2) a high turnover of students
   from one year to another; (3) adult education is accepted
   by a large section of the community as a public service
   available in accordance with interest and inclination. 259

Whipple, James B. "Especially for Adults." Notes and Essays on Education for Adults, No. 19. Chicago: Center
   for the Study of Liberal Education for Adults, 1957. 70 pp.
      A study to identify characteristics of adulthood which
   may be factors in planning courses or other educational
   experiences for adults. Six areas are identified in which
   there are distinctive characteristics of adults relevant to
   the educational experience: (1) adult experience, (2) e-
   motional meanings; (3) adult patterns of thought, (4)
   time perspective of adults, (5) variation in time available
   for organized educational experience, (6) adult motivations.   260

Wright, Grace S. Persistence of Attendance in Adult Education Classes. See No. 237.   261

106   Avril, Edwin F.

5.   Program Planning and Evaluation

    a. Program Planning

Avril, Edwin F.   "A Plan for the Development of an Arts
    Program at the Sonoma Community Center, Sonoma, Cali-
    fornia."   Ph. D. Dissertation.   Columbia University,
    Teachers College, 1954.   262

Bunge, Adolph F.   "An Experimental Study of a Process for
    Program Planning in Adult Education." Ph. D. Disserta-
    tion.   Columbia University, Teachers College, 1955. 263

Dalton, John E.   "The Organization and Administration of
    Adult Education Programs in Small Population Centers."
    Ph. D. Dissertation.   University of Nebraska, 1956. 264

Degroat, Fannie M.   "Elements That Seem to Contribute to
    Successful Adult Education Programs in Selected Public
    Schools of the State of New York."   Ph. D. Dissertation.
    Cornell University, 1954.   265

Garber, Leonard.   "A Plan for Meeting Most Completely the
    Post-High School Educational Needs of Hartford Youth."
    Ph. D. Dissertation.   Columbia University, 1950.   266

Gilligan, Thomas J. and William T. Van Orman.   "Planning
    a State Adult Education Program in Colorado."   Ed. D.
    Dissertation.   University of Denver, 1956.   267

Hand, Samuel E.   "Community Study As a Basis for Pro-
    gram Planning in Adult Education."   Ed. D. Dissertation.
    Florida State University, 1956.   268

Harris, Albert T.   "Analysis of Selected Socio-Economic
    Data for the Purpose of Determining the Content of and
    the Conditions Under Which a Program of Education May
    Be Carried on by and for the Negro Adults of Chesterfield
    County, Virginia."   Ph. D. Dissertation, University of
    Michigan, 1948.   269

Harrison, James W.   "Designing Education Programs   for
    Adults: A Comparison of Non-Credit and Credit Courses
    in University Evening Colleges."   Ph. D. Dissertation.   Uni-
    versity of Chicago, 1957.   270

Morrow, Evelyn.   "Long Range Integrated Programming for

Adult Education." Ph.D. Dissertation. University of Chicago, 1957.   271

Mumma, Richard A. Barriers to the Development of an Adult Education Program, In Adult Education, 1 (February, 1951) 106-113.

A report on the barriers to development of an adult education program in public schools. Information was obtained from a questionnaire sent to school superintendents in seven hundred sixty-five cities. Analysis showed a relationship between needs expressed and the size of the city; the smaller the school system, the greater the number of classes checked as needed. Also indicated was a relationship between the number of administrators checking a type of class as needed and the state where the school is located. An assumption is that other media of adult education also are needed. Chief barriers to development of a program of adult education were: (1) lack of financial support; (2) lack of interest by adults; (3) school board limitations; (4) adult education offered by other agencies. The administrator, himself, because of insufficient leadership, interest, or time, should not be overlooked as a possible obstacle to meeting educational needs of adults.   272

Rounds, Lester E. "A Plan for Meeting the Post High School Educational Needs of Older Youth in Rockland County." Ph.D. Dissertation. Columbia University, Teachers College, 1954.   273

Siegle, Peter E. and James B. Whipple. "New Directions in Programming for University Adult Education." Chicago: Center for the Study of Liberal Education for Adults, 1957. 96 pp.

New directions in program planning by extension divisions and evening colleges, using interesting or outstanding programs in operation as illustrations. Chapters are: Programming for Liberal Arts; Programming for Businessmen, Professionals, and Technicians; Programming for Community Groups and Interests; Programming for Adult Degrees and Certificates; New Challenges-Programming and Mass Media, Programming for Aging, Programming for Alumni, Residential Programming.   274

b. Program Evaluation

Adult Education Association of the U.S.A., Committee on

Evaluation. "Program Evaluation in Adult Education." Chicago: Adult Education Association, 1952.   32 pp.

Purpose of evaluation, the evaluative process, principles of program evaluation, the role of research in evaluation, evaluation in action as illustrated by three cases, the challenge of evaluation.   Selected references.   275

Banta, Clarence O.   Sources of Data for Program Evaluation, In Adult Education, 5 (Summer, 1955) 227-230.

Devices used by seven public junior colleges of Colorado to determine the effectiveness of their adult education program; and the importance of data secured toward improving programs.   Most frequent evaluative techniques used by the colleges were: growth in enrollment, personal conferences with students, observation and supervision of program, and record of student enrollment.   Also reported were testimonials of advisory committees, student evaluation forms, and follow-up of former students.   276

Blackwell, Gordon W.   Evaluation of Present Programs of Adult Education for Negroes, In Journal of Negro Education, 14 (Summer, 1945) 443-452.

In evaluating adult education for Negroes, three questions are considered as criteria: (1) Do programs reach all the people?   (2) Do programs meet the more important interests and real needs?   (3) Are programs effective?   Influencing factors in the application of these criteria are: (1) existing patterns of Negro-White relations; (2) differences between urban and rural populations; (3) educational level; (4) economic situation of the people.   In discussing the first question, the writer considers the work of various agencies and concludes that present coverage is far from adequate, with the smallest proportion of population being reached in rural areas, especially in the South.   In considering meeting of interests and needs, he evaluates programs of adult education in five categories: remedial, health and nutrition, cultural, vocational and social.   In considering effectiveness of programs, four points are stressed: (1) the need for research materials for general adult use, and close collaboration between research specialists and educators; (2) the trend toward group action as a method of adult learning; (3) the need for adequately trained staff; (4) the need for coordination and joint planning by adult education agencies.   277

Blakely, Thomas A., Jr.   "An Evaluation of the Administration of the Educational Program at San Quentin Prison."

Ph. D. Dissertation.   University of California, Berkeley,
1949.   278

Burns, Norman.   Self Evaluation in the Evening College, In
   Association of University Evening Colleges Proceedings.
   Seventeenth Annual Meeting, New Orleans, 1955. pp. 23-
   30.
   The fact that the evening college deviates from established traditions of institutions of higher learning should
not lower its prestige.   The important thing is that it offer evidence it is doing well what it has set out to do.
The accrediting agency has had an important place in providing evidence of institutional quality based on conformity
to standards, and has accomplished much in bringing order to American education.   However, the limitation of
concern only with attainment of minimum status, the fact
that standardization may retard educational improvement
by stifling individual initiative and creativity, and loss of
confidence in measures of excellence expressed in quantitative terms, have led to current interest in self-evaluation as a measure of quality and stimulus to further improvement.   To be maximally effective in self-evaluation,
an evening college should take account of accumulated experience of other evening colleges and of other educational institutions.   Guide lines for continued growth and self-
evaluation should be set up by agencies such as the AUEC.
These guide lines may be of two kinds: (1) suggested solutions to educational problems, and (2) techniques by which
answers to educational problems may be found.   A typical
breakdown for purposes of evaluation provides for discussions
of institutional purposes, curriculum, faculty and the instructional program, library, plant, business management, financial structure, student personnel services.   The writer
makes suggestions relative to those areas presenting peculiar
problems for the evening college.   He concludes that the evening college, which differs significantly from the day college,
needs to establish its own guide lines to mark its progress
toward its own goals.   279
Burch, Glen.   Evaluating Adult Education, In Adult Education
   Journal, 6 (April, 1947) 70-75.
   Places responsibility for providing adequate opportunities for adult education on the local community, discusses
the role of various local agencies and institutions and
lists principles for evaluation of a community-centered
program.   280

California.   State Department of Education. "A Survey of the

California Adult Education Program." Sacramento: State
Department of Education.   June, 1953.   231 pp.
    A survey of public adult education in California, made
in 1952 for the purpose of evaluation of the program.
Part I, "Foundations of Public Adult Education in California," is a review of the legal provisions, provisions in
the Administrative Code, and appropriations of state funds
for adult education.   Part II, "The California Adult Education Program in Action," sets forth criteria for judging the value of education activities and interprets data in
the light of these criteria.   Part III lists recommendations
for improving adult education offerings at local and state
levels.   281

Charters, Alexander N.   "An Evaluation of the Development
    of Certain Aspects of the Ability to Think by Participa-
    tion in an Adult Education Program."   Ph. D. Dissertation.
    University of Chicago, 1949.   179 pp.   282

Cheskie, Sophie V.   "An Appraisal of the Adult Education
    Program of the Highland Park Public Schools, Highland
    Park, Michigan."   Ed. D. Dissertation.   Wayne State Uni-
    versity, 1957.   283

Deming, Robert C.   Characteristics of an Adequate Adult
    Education Program, In Adult Education, 1 (October, 1950)
    25-26.
    Eight characteristics of adequate programs of adult ed-
    ucation for communities in New England as outlined at a
    workshop conference for New England adult educators,
    conducted by the U. S. Office of Education and the Office
    of Education of the State of Connecticut, June 26-30, 1950.
                                                          284

Evaluating Program and Performance, In Adult Leadership,
    1 (April, 1953) 32 pp.
    The title of the entire issue, composed of eight articles
    including a "Tool Kit," devoted to the evaluation of adult
    programs.   Articles are: "What Price Honesty?" by
    Charles E. Hendry; "Where and How to Look for What's
    Wrong;" "Hurdles for Evaluators;" "Evaluating Your
    Program" (Tool Kit); "Evidence of Things Hoped For;"
    "Evaluating Goals;" "Adult Education for a New World;"
    "Consultation, Please."   285

"Evaluating the Evening College as a Teaching Institution."
    Report of the Southern Regional Faculty Seminar, New Or-

leans, Louisiana, November 10-13, 1955. Chicago:
Center for the Study of Liberal Education for Adults,
1955. Pages unnumbered.

    This report summarizes three days of intensive work
by a group of faculty members from nine colleges and
universities in the Southern Region, joined by five faculty
consultants from other regions. The final reports were
used in the AUEC annual meeting which followed the seminar. The reports are: (1) Criteria for the Evaluation
of Programming; (2) Criteria for the Evaluation of Instruction; (3) Criteria for the Evaluation of Administration.

    286

Evaluation of Adult Education, In Baltimore Bulletin of Education, 25 (January-March, 1948) 153-248.

    Title of the entire issue on the Baltimore Cooperative
Survey and Work Survey Conference which contains: a
foreword on the significance of the Baltimore Survey by
W. H. Lemmel; a developmental chart of the Work-Study
Conference; "A Community Problem," by Angela Broen-
ing and Mrs. Simon Sobeloff, stating values of the survey
to participating agencies; "A Community Survey Through
Cooperative Action," by Thomas A. Van Sant, discussing local and regional values, development of plans, successful aspects and parts that could be improved;
"Launching the Work-Survey Conference," pre-conference
briefing sessions for chairmen and recorders; "Summa-
rizing the Work-Survey Conference," by Everett Preston,
Kenneth Benne, Glen Burch, William Wythes, and Homer
Kempfer, regional consultants. The remainder of the issue consists of reports from agencies and services surveyed, and a list of individual participants in the Work-
Survey Conference.   287

Fishback, Woodson W. "An Evaluation of Teacher-Training
Methods Used in an Adult Education Program." Ph.D.
Dissertation. University of Chicago, 1948. 242 pp. 288

Frasure, Kenneth J. "Did the 1946-1947 Offerings and
Practices of Selected Illinois High Schools Outside Cook
County Meet Standards for Judging Adult Education Pro-
grams as Suggested in the Literature of Adult Education?"
Ph.D. Dissertation. University of Illinois, 1948.   289

Freeman, Samuel D. Criteria for Adult Activities, In
Jewish Center Program Aids, 12, June, 1952.
    Presents factors affecting standards, statement of

twelve criteria, response to a survey of criteria used to
measure the success of adult programs in fifty-four Jewish Community Centers, joint responsibility of professional and lay leadership for planning. An evaluation form
for the adult program is included with questions designed
to direct evaluation of the adult activities committee, the
total adult program, individual group activities, professional leadership, and methods and materials.   290

Hendry, Charles E. What Price Honesty?, In Adult Leadership, 1 (April, 1953) 3-5.
   Cites cases in which administrative personnel in national organizations were resistant to and suspicious of
evaluation research. These attitudes are also found in
local groups. Evaluation is one of four indispensable
steps in any process of educational development: (1) determining objectives, (2) formulating a plan of action,
(3) carrying out the plan, and (4) evaluating results. If
evaluation is to be used in programs of adult education and
action, realistic strategy must be devised to identify areas and degrees of readiness and resistance to evaluation
in organization. Experimentation must be attempted to
discover ways of advancing evaluation against distrust.
Suggests ways of cultivating readiness for evaluation. 291

Hensarling, Paul R. "A Study of the Accreditation Standards
for Adult Academic Programs in Elementary and Secondary Education in the United States." Ed. D. Dissertation.
University of Houston, 1957.   292

Hershey, Edna-Jean. "The Development of Evaluative
Guides for Use in Adult and Vocational Educational Programs." Ph. D. Dissertation. University of Denver,
1954.   293

Kempfer, Homer H. "Checklists for Public School Adult Education Programs. U.S. Office of Education. Circular
356. Washington, D. C.: Government Printing Office,
1952. 17 pp.
   Checklists by which the local director of a public
school adult education program can assess his direction,
gauge progress, and analyze performance in size of program, population segments served, flexibility of schedule,
approaches used, methods of coordination, and cooperative practices.   294

Kempfer, Homer H. Formula for Measuring Adult Educa-

Kropp, Russell P.   113

tion Programs, In Adult Education Bulletin, 13 (October,
1948) 195-198.
    Explanation of the "clock-hour index" proposed as a
measure of the amount of public school adult education
provided in a community, with reports on application of
the formula from forty-four directors of adult education.
                                                    295

Kropp, Russell P. and Coolie Verner. An Attitude Scale
  Technique for Evaluating Meetings, In Adult Education, 7
  (Summer, 1957) 212-215.
    Description of a Thurstone-Chave type attitude scale,
developed and tested by the authors, that was designed to
evaluate short-term educational programs for adults by
measuring the reaction of a total group in attendance.
Items are categorized on an eleven point scale. The me-
dian for all responses is computed, thus giving a measure
of the success of an activity. In addition to measuring
overall reaction to a program, this scale is useful within meetings to measure and compare participant satisfaction with one process against another. It is valid as an
instrument for measuring attitudes in general; it is not
suitable for evaluating content or diagnosing particular aspects of program design or management.   296

Lindemann, Eduard C. and the Issue Committee. Evaluating
  Your Program, In Adult Leadership, 1 (April, 1953) 13-
  20.
    Steps in evaluation, evaluation of organizational and
small group functioning, and standards and methods of e-
valuation of their own learning by adult students in voluntary groups. A "Tool Kit" of procedures and materials
for evaluating adult programs.   297

London, Jack. Evaluation: Continuing Problem in Adult Education, In California Journal of Secondary Education, 28
  (December, 1953) 472-474.
    Discusses essential factors of evaluation of adult educa-
tion programs: determination of values, clear definition
of goals, and application relevant to the program under
study.   298

Miller, Harry L. "Evaluating Courses, Not Students, An
  Evening College Experiment With Objective Devices."
  Notes and Essays on Education for Adults, No. 3. Chicago: Center for the Study of Liberal Education for A-
  dults, 1953. 8 pp. Condensed in: School and Society,

77 (March 21, 1953) 180-183.

Evaluation usually means measurement by examination of students' assimilation of material of a course. Reasons why courses, not students, should be evaluated in evening colleges are: (1) Range of interests, backgrounds, and abilities among evening students is great. (2) Aims of adult liberal arts students differ greatly from undergraduate or professional school aims. (3) Many adults in evening colleges take a hand in formation of curriculum and methodological policy by dropping out of a class not relevant to their aims. Describes five experimental courses prepared in 1951 by the Center for the Study of Liberal Education for Adults for use in evening colleges. The writer, who planned the course and wrote the discussion guide, taught the course at Northwestern University, University College. To test whether the course met educational needs, he first defined the purposes of the course. Subjective and objective techniques used for obtaining evidence of success in relation to these goals are described. As a result of evaluation, several decisions were made concerning the next presentation of the course. The most important generalization to be drawn from this experience is assertion of the need to abandon the guess method of evaluation. Increased and widespread testing of evaluation devices that measure courses rather than students can lead to greater effectiveness of general education.
299

Moss, Ira M. "A Description and Appraisal of Programs and Services in Selected Homes for the Aged." Ph. D. Dissertation. Columbia University, Teachers College, 1956.   300

Powell, Oscar R. "A Study of Peer Evaluation in an Adult Group Learning Situation." Ph. D. Dissertation. University of Denver, 1954.   301

Rushing, Joe B. "A Critical Analysis of Adult Education in Junior Colleges in the United States." Ph. D. Dissertation. University of Texas, 1952.   302

"Score Card for Community Adult Education Programs. East Lansing, Michigan: Continuing Education Service, Michigan State College, June, 1951. 20 pp.

Lists forty items for evaluation divided into five sections: community, organization and staff, programs, publicity and promotion, evaluation. Appendixes list immedi-

ate, intermediate, and long-term objectives; and explain
the use of the clock-hour formula.   303

Stratton, Burton E. and Lawrence Lipsett.   An Extension
Division Evaluates Its Program.   See No. 258.   304

Timken, Joseph E.   "A Study to Determine the Adequacy of
Three Selected Oklahoma Public School Adult Education
Programs." Ph.D. Dissertation.   Oklahoma Agricultural
and Mechanical College, 1952.   305

U.S. Office of Education.   Evaluation of Adult Education, In
Adult Education Ideas.   Issue No. 12.   Washington, D.C.:
Government Printing Office, November, 1950. Pp. 1-2.
    Evaluation is defined as the process of comparing ac-
tual characteristics with desirable characteristics and
must be in terms of immediate, intermediate, and long-
term objectives.   Evaluation is most useful in revealing
opportunity for improvement and in stimulating growth.
Maximum growth occurs in self-evaluation which involves
all of those affected by a program.   Ideally evaluation
should be continuous although appraisal points occur at
specific times.   To compare one program directly with
another is unsound; results can best be compared with
previous results in the same situation or with an ideal.
Public school directors of adult education programs should
be concerned with evaluation of the quantitative aspect, or
scope of the program, and the qualitative aspect, concerned with changes in behavior made by the program from
the community viewpoint and from the individual viewpoint.
Checklists, rating scales, committee judgment, questionnaires to and interviews with participants, and judgment
of outsiders are among evaluative tools useful in measuring operational efficiency.   306

Van Sant, Thomas A.   The Baltimore Cooperative Survey and
Work-Survey Conference, In Adult Education Bulletin, 12
(February, 1948) 87-93.
    Describes techniques used in the Baltimore Survey Pro-
ject which included two main parts: a survey of the adult
education program of one city by the adult education leaders of that community; a three-day work conference at
which adult educators from other cities and states worked
with local leaders in evaluating, resurveying, and reform-
ing survey reports.   The article gives the over-all plan
of the project and the values and results of the venture.
                                                            307

Van Sant, Thomas A.   A Community Survey Through Cooperative Action, In Baltimore Bulletin of Education, 25
(January-March, 1948) 156-168.
    Values of the 1947 Baltimore Cooperative Survey and
Work Survey Conference locally and regionally; development of plans and organization of the Survey and Conference; a list of successful aspects, and a list of parts
that could be improved as a result of Baltimore experiences if undertaken by another group.   308

6.   Research Needs and Methods

Benne, Kenneth D.   The Future of Work-Survey Conferences,
In Adult Education Bulletin, 12 (February, 1948) 93-96.
    Comments on the value of the Baltimore Survey and
Work Conference of adult education.   Observations on the
importance of the convergence of two significant movements in adult education: (1) the work group conference
movement, and (2) the cooperative action research movement.   Discusses each movement as to purpose and function.   Ends with a statement of the possibility of applying
the principles and methods of this conference to future
development of adult education.   309

Deane, Stephen R.   Interview as a Tool of Adult Education
Research, In Adult Education Bulletin, 14 (June, 1950)
150-157.
    The second article on the study to produce information
of value to adult education administrators and to demonstrate a methodology for further research in education and
social science areas.   Discusses advantages of the interview over the mailed questionnaire, such as providing
greater opportunity for use of discussion type questions,
inclusion of more items, greater response, more detailed
answers, etc.   The article includes the schedule of questions used in the interview with a discussion of the questions.   310

Deane, Stephen R.   Sampling Control in Adult Education Re-
search--A Case Study, In Adult Education Bulletin, 14
(February, 1950) 84-88.
    The first of two articles on the use of scientifically
valid controls in adult education research.   Discusses
sampling methods, - randomization, stratified random
sampling, quota technics, and how these principles are
applied to research in adult education as illustrated by ref-

ence to the author's study of students in three major
types of adult education: (1) a Great Books discussion
group; (2) non-credit courses by various agencies; (3)
college credit courses by university extension.   311

Eckhoff, Harry C.   General Educational Development Tests
in Adult Education, In Adult Education Bulletin, 13 (June,
1949) 144-149.
Describes the United States Armed Forces Institute
Tests of General Educational Development, and implications for their use in adult education programs.   312

Flanagan, John C.   Contribution of Research in the Army
Air Forces to Educational Policy, In Educational Record,
28, Supplement 16 (January, 1947) 78-90.
Describes the research programs in the Army Air
Forces for evaluating individual differences, determining
critical requirements, and providing predictive tests and
scientifically developed courses and counseling services.
Recommends that techniques and procedures found success-
ful in the coordinated research program in the Army Air
Forces be utilized for research in education.   313

Harrison, J. F. C.   The Materials for the Early History of
Adult Education, In Adult Education (London), 23 (March,
1951) 273-278.
States the need for research on the histories of individual aspects of adult education in the 19th century, with
a view to their ultimate assimilation into a general history
of adult education in Great Britain. Discusses the questions of how the subject material can be broken down, and
where the material for the study can be found.   314

Havighurst, Robert J.   Social Roles of the Middle-Aged Person, A Method of Identifying the Needs of Adults. See
No. 217.   315

Lorge, Irving.   Research Needs, In Adult Education, 1 (December, 1950) 73-79. Same condensed: Education Digest, 16 (March, 1951) 34-37.
Areas of needed research are: the mental functioning
of the adult, with preparation of adequate tests of intelligence and abilities; the nature of the learning process,
including relation of learning to previously learned materials and established habits, relation to meaningfulness,
basic concepts of retention as a function of meaning and
influence of meaning on transfer of training; effectiveness

of various media of communication for adults; adjustment
problems of the aging, with studies on motivation, interests, attitudes, values, and other aspects of personality;
the influences of early learning on adulthood; educational
preparation for later maturity.   316

Love, Robert A.   Use of Motivation Research to Determine
Interest in Adult College-Level Training.   See No. 223.
                                                           317

Maaske, Roben J.   "Needed Research in Adult Education;
Report."   National Education Association.   1949.   32 pp.
Same condensed in: American Educational Research Association, "Growing Points in Educational Research; Official Report," 1949.   Pp. 101-111.   Excerpts: Adult Education Bulletin, 14 (April, 1950) 120-121; A. L. A. Bulletin, 44 (April, 1950) 121-122.
     The Chairman of the Joint Committee for the Explora-
tion of Needed Research in Adult Education explains methods used in preparing the report.   Five members of the
committee were appointed in 1946 jointly by NEA Department of Adult Education and American Educational Research Association.   Twenty-five main categories or areas
were identified and significant research problems within
each area were compiled.   Each committee member selected five areas and enlisted the cooperation of leaders
in these areas in stating the most significant needs for
research data and information.   The report lists the
categories with their suggested study and research problems and a brief introductory paragraph for each section.
                                                           318

Raybould, Sidney G.   Research in Adult Education.   See No.
171.   319

Spence, Ralph B.   Role of Research in Adult Education, In
Adult Education, 3 (February, 1953) 76-79.
     Ways in which social science research can help adult
educators.   Author urges cooperation between educators
and social scientists to systematize needed research on the
education of adults.   320

7.   Training of Teachers of Adults

Fishback, Woodson W.   "An Evaluation of Teacher-Training
Methods Used in An Adult Education Program."   Ph. D.

Dissertation. University of Chicago, 1948. 242 pp.   321

Hendrickson, Andrew and John A. Spence. Professional
   Training Programs for Adult Educators, In Adult Education, 3 (September, 1953) 191-192.
   Report of a survey of institutions offering professional
training in adult education for the 1952-53 academic year.
Responses from seventy-five per cent of the ninety-six
institutions included disclosed that forty-one were including professional adult education offerings, with fourteen
offering Master's and Doctor's degrees. In addition,
twenty-seven institutions provided special programs rang-
ing from non-degree institutes to a total of twelve semester hours of work. A wide variety in numbers of offerings and in the nature of the courses was evident. See
No. 327 for reference to the complete report.   322

Hockabout, Marvin C. "The In-Service Teacher Training
   Program for Teachers of Adults in California." Ph.D.
   Dissertation. Stanford University, 1952.   323

London, Jack. Are Adult Teachers Being Trained? In
   California Journal of Secondary Education, 32 (February,
   1957) 96-102.
   Report of a survey of a public school adult program in
an industrial community in the San Francisco Bay Area
examining characteristics of eighty-three professional and
lay teachers with respect to their professional training.
This paper is concerned only with phases of the problem
of providing professional training for practitioners in a-
dult education under auspices of the public schools. This
discussion focuses on examination of the extent of professional training secured by these teachers since obtaining
their initial positions in adult education and on their attitudes toward need for securing additional professional
training in adult education. It was found that a larger
percentage of lay than of professional teachers take professional training in adult education after initial appoint-
ments, feel the need for more training, and are willing to
take more training. Although California provides a statewide in-service professional training program in adult education, relatively few adult administrators and teachers
are utilizing this service. There are few direct pressures upon adult teachers to obtain professional training in
adult education, but findings reveal that a considerable percentage had secured such training and that those who had,
appreciated its value. Findings imply that adult adminis-

trators should undertake more systematic programs of educating their staffs on the value and importance of professional training.   324

Mumma, Richard A.   Effective Instruction in an Evening Program for Adults, In Adult Education, 1 (June, 1951) 183-189.
Research is needed to adumbrate effective instruction in adult classes which present special problems because of the heterogeneity of students' ages, interests, abilities, academic backgrounds and educational objectives.   Qualities essential to good adult teaching are presented and suggestions are made regarding selection and organization of content and teaching methods.   325

"Professional Preparation of Adult Educators; A Symposium." Notes and Essays on Education for Adults, No. 15.   Chicago: Center for the Study of Liberal Education for Adults, 1956.
Includes: Professional Education for Educators of Adults, by Cyril O. Houle, with discussion by Paul Bergevin, Robert J. Blakely, Watson Dickerman, Paul L. Essert, Andrew Hendrickson, Abbott Kaplan, Burton W. Kreitlow, Jack London;   Some Common Interests of Adult Education Leaders, by Thurman White;   A Review of Professional Preparation Programs, by Elwin V. Svenson. These articles are reprinted from Adult Education, Vol. 6, Spring, 1956. See Nos. 328 and 332 for annotations.
                                                      326

Spence, John A. "Opportunities for Professional Training In Adult Education Offered by Colleges and Universities in 1952-53, Exclusive of Summer Sessions." Ohio State University, Bureau of Special and Adult Education, 1953. 8 pp. See No. 322 for annotation.   327

Svenson, Elwin V.   A Review of Professional Preparation Programs, In Adult Education, 6 (Spring, 1956) 162-166. Reprinted in No. 326.
This article, adapted from a doctoral dissertation (see next item), attempts: (1) to identify institutions of higher learning whose departments or schools of education provide opportunities for professional study in adult education; and (2) to analyze those study programs leading to advanced degrees in adult education.   States four hypotheses, summary of findings in terms of the hypotheses, and some implications of the study for the role of universities

in this field, for other agencies providing professional
training in adult education, for professors of adult education, and for adult educators. Includes a list of institutions offering professional training in adult education classified according to type of program offered.   328

Svenson, Elwin V. "A Study of Professional Preparation
Programs for Leaders in Adult Education Offered by
Schools of Education." Ed. D. Dissertation. University
of California, Los Angeles, 1954.   329

Weinhold, Clyde E. "Proposed Standards for Teachers and
Directors of Adult Education in New Jersey." Ph. D.
Dissertation. Rutgers University, 1957.   330

White, Thurman J. "Similarity of Training Interests Among
Adult Education Leaders." Ph. D. Dissertation. University of Chicago, 1951.   331

White, Thurman J. Some Common Interests of Adult Education Leaders, In Adult Education, 6 (Spring, 1956) 155-
162. Reprinted in No. 326.
    Based on the author's doctoral dissertation (see pre-
ceding item), a study which isolated in-service training
topics in which adult education leaders have a high degree of common interest. Findings showed a high common interest in: (1) an understanding of basic educational needs of adults; (2) insight into changing interests of
adults; (3) ability to apply psychological principles of selection of objectives; (4) techniques for relating programs
to needs and interests of adults; (5) techniques for relating programs to needs of the community; (6) recognizing community needs and resources important to adult education programs; (7) methods and (8) materials suitable
for mature people; (9) procedures for keeping up with
new developments for adult education programs. Discusses
implications of findings for those concerned with development of a leadership training program, for agencies having the social responsibility for general leadership training, for planning of community leadership training programs. Findings also strengthen the concept of a field of
adult education and general recognition of adult education
as a field in the science of education.   332

8. Historical Studies

Arnold, James E. "A Study of Adult Education Through
University Extension with Special Reference to the Univer-
sity of Tennessee." Ed. D. Dissertation. University of
Tennessee, 1955.   333

Brian, D. Garron. "Adult Education in the Church of Jesus
Christ of Latter Day Saints." Ph. D. Dissertation. University of Chicago, 1956.   334

Burrell, John A. "A History of Adult Education at Columbia
University, University Extension and the School of General
Studies." New York: Columbia University Press, 1954.
111 pp.
    This volume forms a part of the bicentennial history of
Columbia University. The first chapter traces the early
history of extension teaching at Columbia beginning with
the plans drawn up in 1830 by the Board of Columbia College for a literary and scientific course in extension.
The first director of Extension Teaching was appointed in
July, 1904. During its first six years Extension Teaching
was fostered by Teachers College, but the administrative
board included officers from other parts of the University.
The second chapter gives the history of the Institute of
Arts and Sciences established in 1913 for popular education in literature, art, and music carried out through lectures, discussions, forums, films, concerts, and short
courses. Chapter III deals with Home Study, a branch of
Extension Teaching for correspondence instruction without
academic credit, begun in 1919 and ended in 1937. Chapter IV describes several programs which were at some
time under Extension or the School of General Studies in
business, the professions, languages, and the arts. Chapter V is mainly a listing of teachers and courses taught
throughout the history of university extension at Columbia.
Chapter VI deals with controversies concerning university
extension and criticisms and defenses of Columbia's policies. Chapter VII discusses the origin of the School of
General Studies which was established in July, 1947. It
replaced University Extension and established the program
more firmly and legitimately in the University family. The
Faculty of General Studies was created in February, 1952.
A final chapter, "Epilogue," presents further comments
on services to the urban community of Columbia's program
of adult education and points out the dual interest of degree and non-degree students and the danger of overempha-

sis on the former, and the problem of uncertainty of registration from semester to semester in the School of General Studies.   335

Elkin, Harry. "Adult Jewish Education in the United States." Ph. D. Dissertation. Dropsie College, 1954.
                                                          336

Finkelstein, Elizabeth. "A Survey of Adult Education in 296 Public Schools in the U. S. A., 1938-1947 Inclusive." Ph. D. Dissertation. Temple University, 1950.   337

Getsinger, Joseph W. "The History of Adult Education in the Public Schools of California." Ed. D. Dissertation. Stanford University, 1949.   338

Grattan, C. Hartley. "In Quest of Knowledge, a Historical Perspective on Adult Education." New York: Association Press [c1955]. 337 pp.
    A selective, historical treatise sponsored by the Fund for Adult Education. Part I defines adult education and discusses implications. Part II gives the Western European background up to the industrial revolution, with chapters on Preliterate Man, Greece, Rome, and the Middle Ages. Part III is the history of adult education in Great Britain from its beginning in the eighteenth century to the present time. Part IV, which is the focus of the book, traces the history of adult education in America from its beginnings in the Colonial Period to the 1950's, including development of the lyceum, chautauqua, university extension, vocational education in agriculture and mechanic arts, adult education in public schools, libraries, the labor movement, and societies and clubs, organizations of professional adult educators, use of mass communications, and the present status of adult education. The final chapter points out problems such as the gap between idea and reality in adult education, the need for attention to the study of the humanities, the social sciences, the arts, and science for cultural enrichment of adult education, basic problems of personnel, leadership and finance, and obstacles and challenges.   339

Grumman, Russell M. and others. "University Extension in Action." Extension Bulletin V. 26, No. 1. Chapel Hill: University of North Carolina Press, 1946. 175 pp. Also published as a University of North Carolina Sesquicentennial Publication, 1947.

Section I traces the history of extension at the University of North Carolina. Section II includes descriptions of extension class and correspondence instruction, special aspects of extra-mural in-service teacher education, post-graduate medical and dental courses, short courses and institutes, and study tours. Section III traces the history of library extension service since its beginning in 1907. Section IV describes activities in the areas of art, audio-visual education, debating, athletic and academic contests, drama, English, music, public forums, lectures, publications, radio, and recreation. Section V discusses University Extension's cooperation with state, regional, and national organizations. Section VI describes special University agencies of adult education such as Bureau of Business Services and Research, Folklore Council, Institute for Research in Social Science, Institute of Government, Inter-American Institute, and University of North Carolina Press. Section VII describes special services during the war and reconstruction period, including the Carolina Playmakers, Carolina Institute of International Relations, Southern Council on International Relations, University Center for Civilian Morale Service, Engineering, Science, and Management War Training, U.S. Armed Forces Institute, War Information Center, etc. Section VIII discusses recent developments and future trends such as the Communication Center, Workers' Education, greater participation in the cultural and recreational life of the State, the task of training leaders and teachers and developing teaching materials, development of the Division of Research Interpretation, etc.   340

Hugg, Alan E. "Informal Adult Education in the Y.M.C.A.; A Historical Study." Ph.D. Dissertation. Columbia University, 1951.   341

Jackson, George A. "A History of the Adult Education Program in the Los Angeles Public Schools." Ph.D. Dissertation. University of California, Los Angeles, 1957. 342

Kelly, Thomas. "Outside the Walls, Sixty Years of University Extension at Manchester, 1886-1946." Manchester: University of Manchester Press [1950] 124 pp.
Part I gives the history of the early development of extension work and its pioneer administrators and teachers at Victoria University at Manchester from its beginnings in 1886 to 1903, when the federal university was dissolved. Part II is an account of extension work at Manchester

University from 1903 to 1946, including work of the
W.E.A., the tutorial class movement, effects of World
War I and its aftermath, the period between the wars,
and development and expansion during World War II. Epilogue by R.D. Waller.   343

Mann, George C. and J. Wilson Getsinger. "Development of
Adult Education in California." Revised by Stanley E.
Sworder. California State Department of Education Bulletin, Vol. 26, No. 13. Sacramento: California State Department of Education, December, 1957. 99 pp.
    Part I is a summary of the history of adult education
in California from its beginning in 1856, presented in
Getsinger's doctoral dissertation (see No. 338). Part II
"Current Programs of Adult Education in California,"
deals with the philosophy, purposes, and structure of a-
dult education in California at the present time, which are
more meaningful when studied in relation to the history of
the program.   344

Rosentreter, Frederick M. "The Boundaries of the Campus,
a History of the University of Wisconsin Extension Division, 1885-1945." Madison: The University of Wisconsin Press, 1957. 210 pp. Also Ph.D. Dissertation.
University of Wisconsin, 1954.
    The book is a revision of the doctoral dissertation.
The first chapter examines the meaning of university extension and traces its early development in England and
the United States. Subsequent chapters give a detailed,
historical account of activities, problems, conflicts, and
personalities throughout the history of extension work at
the University of Wisconsin from the establishment of
Farmers' Institutes in 1885 and the formal creation of an
Extension Division in 1906 through World War II and the
post-war period. The final chapter is a summary and e-
valuation.   345

Schoenfeld, Clay. Fifty Years of Wisconsin Extension, In
School and Society, 83 (March 3, 1956) 78-80.
    The year 1906 marked the formal birth of the "Wis-
consin Idea" of partnership between people and university
which was to make the University of Wisconsin famous as
a pioneer in university extension. Individual instruction
has always been the hallmark of Wisconsin Extension enterprise, but it has been matched by broad public service
projects. Today the university extension concept is flour-
ishing as never before throughout the world, as people

recognize that foundations of peace and prosperity must
be established in the minds of men. Statistics show the
growth of the Wisconsin Extension Division in number of
students, faculty, budget and organization. The Extension
Division has become the instrument used by the university
and, in a broad sense, by the state to discover new educational needs, interpret them to the University and translate them into educational action programs in all parts of
the state. Some of the new activities and trends of the
Wisconsin Extension Division at present are: a wide
range of institutes and conferences to meet specific needs
of professional and functional groups in the state; a critical survey and experimentation in the correspondence
study program; constantly growing programs of general
adult education; use of educational television; research in
social sciences in order to capitalize on unique field facilities of the Division; analysis and realignment of field
organization; growth of off-campus graduate programs.
The University will seek in the next fifty years to be of
even greater service to the people and places of Wisconsin.   346

Stephan, A. Stephan. Backgrounds and Beginnings of University Extension in America, In Harvard Educational Review,
18 (March, 1948) 99-108.
     University extension was an English importation in the
latter part of the last century. The soil for the planting
of the extension movement in America was prepared by
previous efforts in adult education, by the cardinal position of education in American life, and by the social conditions of the times. The American Lyceum and the Chau-
tauqua were predecessors of university extension. The
first introduction of the English system of university extension was in 1887. During the 1870's and 1880's a number of related movements came into existence including
vacation schools, evening schools, social settlements,
Teachers and Parents Associations, Federation of Women's
Clubs, and farmers' institutes. Much of the extension
work of the early days was patterned after the English
system with emphasis on the lecture system and an organizational system of local extension centers. A list of
American universities is given with dates of organization
and reorganization of university extension. After a period of quiescence there was a revival of interest in university extension about 1906. In 1915 the National University Extension Association was organized, composed of extension divisions of state universities and larger private

universities. The lecture system and loose methods of
organization were replaced by a more connected form of
study in regular class work and organization of separate
administrative units. University extension in America has
continued to develop through extension classes, correspondence instruction, short courses, conferences, institutes, and a variety of service functions.   347

Stockton, Frank T. "The Pioneer Years of University Extension
at the University of Kansas. " University Extension Research
Publication. University of Kansas, April, 1956. 39 pp.
The beginning of adult education and related activities
at Kansas, tracing the course of events which led to the
organization of an Extension Division in 1909.   348

Thomas, Ralph R. "A History of the First Hundred Years
of Public School Adult Education in Buffalo, New York."
Ed. D. Dissertation. University of Buffalo, 1957.   349

Wadler, Nathan. "Adult Jewish Education in New York."
Ph. D. Dissertation. Columbia University, Teachers College, 1952.   350

Warner, Gordon. "A History of the Continuation Education
Program in California." Ed. D. Dissertation. University of California, Berkeley, 1954.   351

Wilson, William P. "The History and Development of the
Public Adult Education Program in Chicago." Ph. D.
Dissertation. University of California, Los Angeles,
1948.   352

9. Other Surveys and Studies.

Adult Education Association of the U.S.A. National Commission on Adult Education Finance. "Financing Adult Education in America's Public Schools and Community Councils," complete report by Edward B. Olds, Research Co-
ordinator. Washington, D. C.: A. E. A. [1954] 124 pp.
Report of a research study on financing of public school
adult education and coordinated adult education programs
outside the public schools. Major sections of the report
are: Financing Adult Education in Public Schools; Financing the Local Coordinative Effort; Studying the Financing
of Adult Education in Other Fields. The final section
summarizes major kinds of findings and lists fifteen recommendations with supporting conclusions based on the

study.   The appendix explains methods and sources used
in the study.   353

Allion, Helen and Robert A. Luke.   Public School Adult Education in the United States; Report of a Survey, In Adult
Education, 3 (February, 1953) 69-75.
    Report of a comprehensive survey of public school a-
dult education programs.   See No. 390 for complete report.   This article summarizes major findings under the
headings: objectives, costs, how adult education programs
are supported, the adult student, program content, trends
in enrollment in various content areas, teaching methods,
the adult school director, the adult teacher, publicity and
promotion, relating the program to the community, community services.   354

Brown, Frank R.   "Training Centers for Leadership Education."   Ph.D. Dissertation.   Columbia University,
Teachers College, 1956.   355

Campbell, George W.   "University Extension Centers in the
United States."   Ed.D. Dissertation.   Columbia University, Teachers College, 1957.   356

Clark, Burton R.   "Adult Education in Transition: A Study
of Institutional Insecurity."   Ph.D. Dissertation.   University of California, Los Angeles, 1956.   Also published as:
University of California, Publications in Sociology and Social Institutions, Vol. 1, No. 2. 1956.   202 pp.
    A sociological study of educational administration of the
adult school in California and the way it has been shaped
in the last quarter of a century as a distinct type of public school enterprise.   The study includes the historical
background of adult education in California; statewide conditions of administrative action; detailed analyses of an a-
dult school organization in Los Angeles; the impact of
state legislature and the junior college on position and
security of the adult school.   Wider implications of the
study are developed and appendixes give the methodology of
the research.   The general finding of the study is that the
adult school in California has gradually taken on a service
character, with programs adaptive to interests of students
and community groups and little affected by professionally
set goals.   This tendency stems from three basic conditions of administrative decision making: marginal status,
open-ended purpose, and pressures of enrollment economy.
                                                           357

Clark, Edwin C.   "The Upward or Outward Extension of
   Education in Burbank, California." Ed. D. Dissertation.
   Stanford University, 1955.   358

Cooper, William M.   Adult Education Programs of Negro
   Colleges and Universities, In Journal of Negro Education,
   14 (Summer, 1945) 307-311.
       Report of a survey of one hundred six Negro institu-
   tions in 1944-45 on: (1) adult education carried on by
   Negro colleges; (2) major problems encountered; (3)
   plans for future adult education programs; (4) evaluation
   and recommendations for improvements.   Offerings
   ranged from none to extensive, well-balanced programs
   providing systematic study in classes and informal and
   mass education activities.   Some of the outstanding programs are described.   Major problems are classified as:
   (1) problems within the college, and (2) problems within
   adult groups served.   Twenty institutions indicated plans
   to continue present programs and add new ones.   Evaluation indicated promising beginnings and future expansion
   despite limited resources.   Recommendations include i-
   tems on staffing, research needs, program concentration,
   and use of radio and audio-visual aids.   359

Crimi, James E.   "Adult Education in the Liberal Arts Colleges."   Notes and Essays on Education for Adults, No.
   17.   Chicago: Center for the Study of Liberal Education
   for Adults, 1957.   38 pp.   Also Ph. D. Dissertation.
   University of Chicago, 1957.
       Results of a study made in 1953 of over four hundred
   liberal arts colleges to determine: (1) whether independent liberal arts colleges of the United States are engaged
   in adult education; (2) the extent and nature of their efforts; and (3) why they have added this function.   Summary of (1) analysis of adult enrollment statistics, geographical differences, sources of control, size of college,
   size of community, trends; (2) variety, types, content,
   and typical patterns of liberal arts college adult education
   and the place of the teacher in adult work of these colleges; (3) reasons why adult education is offered in liberal arts colleges.   Concludes that the question of whether
   liberal arts colleges should engage in adult education is
   philosophical and not a matter for research.   The data
   presented in the study may assist colleges in deciding
   whether it is expedient and appropriate to examine opportunities and obligations in the field of adult education, if
   there are unmet college-level educational needs in the com-

munity, if meeting such needs would violate important institutional policy or philosophy, and if such action can
bring significant values to the college.   360

Curry, William F. "A Descriptive Study of A Continuing
Type of Short-Term Training." Ph. D. Dissertation.
Columbia University, Teachers College, 1954.   361

Dean, Leland. "A Study of the Attitudes of Adult Conference Participants Toward Three Types of Conference Experiences." Ph. D. Dissertation. Michigan State University, 1956.   362

Essert, Paul L. and Coolie Verner. Education for Active
Adult Citizenship, In Teachers College Record, 53 (October, 1951) 16-31.
    The Institute of Adult Education, Teachers College,
Columbia University undertook a program of research in
October, 1949, to explore problems and develop techniques
of education for citizenship. This program has taken the
form of two lines of inquiry: (1) a study of individuals
educating themselves for more responsible citizenship,
and (2) an investigation into the role of community institutions primarily concerned with the educational development of adults as resources in furthering the process of
self-education. The Institute undertook specific studies on individuals in their personal groups, and individuals in
their community groups, and attempted through several research projects to examine the functioning of specific institutions in terms of their operations as resources for
furthering development of effective citizenship, including
(1) an intensive study in an urban area to discover effectiveness of the impact of existing institutions upon lives of
people and their resultant responses; and (2) studies of
institutions of higher learning in regard to three potential
areas, - basic research in complexities of community life,
social services direct to the community, and training potential professional leaders; (3) studies of ways a library
might function most efficiently as sponsoring agency for
discussion of current problems through formation of
groups utilizing resources of local libraries; and (4) studies of school districts to determine means of sustaining
interest of people from all sections of a district in school
affairs. Education for citizenship is taking place but activities are too scattered and disorganized to fulfill the
need. The educator has the responsibility of developing
processes for broadening dissemination of methodology

leading to universal participation. Such studies as those
of the Institute help to clarify purposes of research in
this area and to delineate specific sectors which further
study must explore. In its essence this investigation into problems of education for active adult citizenship is
directed toward the process of equipping people with a-
bility to make adjustments to social changes and toward
evaluating these changes in terms of people's reactions to
them in directing the course which change will pursue.
To achieve an understanding of the process of citizenship
education, research and experimentation must involve
three major areas: (1) the individual in his personal
group; (2) individual and personal group relationships to
social institutions; and (3) individual, personal group,
and social institutional inter-involvement in the total community structure.   363

Essert, Paul L. Report to Teachers College on Adult Education in the United States and Its Implications to Education. See No. 43.   364

Fitchett, E. Horace. What are the Responsibilities of Negro
Colleges for the Adult Education of Negroes in the Post-
War World?, In Quarterly Review of Higher Education A-
mong Negroes, 13 (April, 1945) 94-112.
    If the Negro college has a special responsibility for
the education of the adult Negro, that assumption must be
based on the supposition that: (1) the Negro has a special
set of problems which no other agencies can or will undertake to solve; (2) these problems can be solved by the
colleges; and (3) the Negro adult population is not only
educable but it is accessible. In order to articulate the
dynamic movements, emerging problems, and unfolding
plans of this period of crisis, the writer explored the following sources of information: Questionnaires were sent
to fifty-one Negro colleges and universities in fifteen states
and the District of Columbia requesting information on:
areas in which they thought the most difficult problems
would develop for the Negro in the post-war world; groups
of people for which their programs were designed; courses
offered to meet the needs envisaged; and methods employed for instructional purposes. The second approach
was to solicit statements from leaders in areas in which
needs of the adult Negro are most eminent. A third
source was questionnaires sent to three hundred service
men and women to ascertain what they considered difficult
problems they would meet on return to civilian life. Re-

turns from this source were received too late to be included. Findings are presented, including tabular information, for each area of inquiry in the first questionnaire.
Conclusions are that the spheres constituting greatest difficulty and need are: (1) labor and economic adjustment,
(2) civic and political participation, (3) mental and physical health, (4) parenthood and family relationships. The
study shows a glaring inadequacy in present offerings for
preparation to cope with anticipated problems. However,
many institutions are using methods of instruction which
will be valuable in developing a more effective program
of adult education. Experience of the national government
will cause it to give support to such endeavors. Educators will not seriously undertake a plan for adult education until they develop a sound philosophy. The writer
cites the recommendations of the Survey of Higher Education of Negroes as a tenable point of view.   365

Freeman, Samuel. "Adult Education in the Jewish Community Center." Ph.D. Dissertation. Columbia University,
1953.   366

Hutchinson, E.M. Liberal Education in a Technical Age, In
Adult Education, 6 (Summer, 1956) 195-201.
An article on the report of the National Institute by the
same title, published in 1955. (See No. 386). Discusses
the central question of the report, scope, background, and
findings, with a summary of conclusions and recommendations, and next steps for the National Institute in order to
expand the initial impulse which the report provided. 367

Jenkins, Thomas S. "Correspondence Course Instruction and
Investigation of Practices, Regulation, and Course Syllabi
as Developed in State Teachers Colleges." Ph.D. Dissertation. University of Oregon, 1953.   368

Kempfer, Homer H. "Adult Education Activities of the Public
Schools; Report of a Survey, 1947-48." U.S. Office of
Education. Pamphlet 107. Washington, D.C.: Government Printing Office, 1949. 21 pp.
An inquiry was sent to 3,613 school districts in communities having a 1940 census population of 2,500 or
more. Checklists included thirty-seven types of education
for adults and out-of-school youth; twenty-two categories
of subject matter; three levels of study (elementary,
secondary, college); eight types of places in which adult
education activities are conducted; enrollment; whether or

not there was a lay advisory committee council.   Detailed
results are given in tabular form.   Conclusions drawn
from the results are that adult education is relatively
highly developed in a number of individual schools and in
a few states.   The limited number of adults served by
most public schools in light of the widespread and growing
interest in adult education suggests that a great many
districts are providing too little opportunity for continuing
education.   369

Kempfer, Homer H.   How Much Adult Education Do 444
   School Programs Provide?, In School and Society, 75
   (January 12, 1952) 26-27.
      A report on the amount of adult education provided by
   four hundred forty-four public schools during 1948-49 and
   1949-50 school years, as measured by the "clock-hour
   index," which shows the relationship between amount of
   time spent in educational activities and the total adult population of a community.   370

Kempfer, Homer and Grace S. Wright.   "100 Evening
   Schools."   U.S. Office of Education.   Bulletin 1949, No.
   4.   Washington, D.C.:   Government Printing Office, 1949.
   71 pp.
      A study of one hundred representative public adult
   evening schools in thirty-six states.   Information, which
   was collected by a combination of methods, is divided into
   sections on: programs of evening schools, schedules,
   administrative and instructional staffs, supervision, lay
   advisory committees, housing, finance, promotion methods.
   Conclusions cite a wide range of change.   Instead of limiting its emphasis to individual self-improvement, the trend
   of the evening school is toward developing a broader con-
   sciousness of its responsibility to the whole community.
   Activities and methods which break with traditional patterns have been widely introduced.   The evening school is
   becoming a part of the total community program of adult
   education sponsored by the public schools.   Evening
   schools are looking beyond ranks of professional teachers
   for leadership.   They are recognizing the necessity of adequate publicity.   State aid has a marked bearing on development of evening schools.   Appendix lists schools
   studied.   371

King, William H.   "The Administration and Function of An
   Adult Center of Education."   Ph.D. Dissertation.   Columbia University, 1951.   372

Laidlaw, Alexander F. "The Campus and the Community."
Ed. D. Dissertation. University of Toronto, Ontario College of Education, 1956.   373

Laird, Bryon F. "A Survey of the Certificate and Terminal
Curricular Offerings of University Extensions and Evening
Colleges." Ph. D. Dissertation. Indiana University,
1954.   374

Larson, Vernon C. "A Survey of Short Courses in the
United States and Canada." Ph. D. Dissertation. Michigan State University, 1955.   375

Levine, Herbert. "The Union Leadership Academy, a Un-
ion-University Experiment in Labor Education." Ed. D.
Dissertation. Columbia University, Teachers College,
1957.   376

Liveright, Alexander A. "Lay Leaders in Adult Education."
Ph. D. Dissertation. University of Chicago, 1956.   377

Malamud, Daniel I. "A Participant-Observer Approach to
the Teaching of Human Relations." Notes and Essays in
Education for Adults, No. 10. Chicago: Center for the
Study of Liberal Education for Adults, 1955. 35 pp.
   The writer summarizes his experience with the discussion method of teaching courses in the psychology of personality and interpersonal relations, and presents techniques found useful in teaching an adult education course
at New York University. The teacher attempts to (1) ex-
cite the student's curiosity about aspects of behavior hither-
to overlooked, taken for granted, or considered insignificant; (2) motivate him to discover his own insights; and
(3) help him to absorb these insights in a personal-emo-
tional way rather than to accumulate them as psychological
facts. The students' classroom experiences and reactions
become the major subject matter of the course. Student
evaluations indicate the high degree of success with which
the workshop met their needs.   378

Martorana, Sebastian V. Problems in Adult Education in the
Junior College, In Junior College Journal, 18 (November,
1947) 115-123.
   An investigation by the Committee on Curriculum and
Adult Education and the Research Office of the American
Association of Junior Colleges was made in 1947 to gather
information in two major areas: (1) problems in inaugu-

ration and expansion of adult education programs that junior college administrators consider are in need of detailed study; and (2) present extent of activity in the field of adult education in junior colleges. This article presents findings concerning problems confronting adult education programs in junior colleges. Inquiries were sent to six hundred forty-eight junior colleges, with three hundred thirty-seven or 52 percent responding. Respondents rated thirteen problems listed on inquiry form and added and rated additional problems. Ratings of public junior colleges, of private junior colleges and of all junior colleges are given in tabular form. It is recommended on the basis of findings that the Association's Committee on Research and Service should consider these questions: (1) bases for determining need for courses in adult education; (2) problems of instructional staff; (3) scope of the program; (4) financing; (5) coordination with adult education programs of other agencies and integration with other units in the school system. It is suggested that the proper starting point would be to seek a clear and acceptable definition of adult education and its relationship to junior colleges in America.   379

Martorana, Sebastian V. Status of Adult Education in Junior Colleges, In Junior College Journal, 18 (February, 1948) 322-331.

This article summarizes the findings of the second part of the inquiry by the Research Office of the American Association of Junior Colleges. Findings are given in tabular form on: number of colleges offering adult education programs; enrollment of regular students and of students in adult education programs; composition of enrollment; distribution according to date of inauguration of adult education program; percentages of junior colleges offering adult education courses in various areas or curriculums. Conclusions are that junior colleges have begun to give emphasis to adult education services at comparatively recent dates, but have progressed so that almost half offer programs with responsibility for meeting needs of adults particularly evident among public junior colleges. Major emphasis is on vocational subjects, with courses in cultural subjects, citizenship, homemaking, and recreational areas following in that order. It is recommended that junior colleges give more attention to the last two fields.   380

Mather, Louis K. "The New American School for Adults."

Washington, D. C.: National Education Association, Division of Adult Service [1955]. 39 pp.

This report is a summary and rewriting, in less statistical style, of the original study of adult education activities in city public schools (See No. 385) covering a general survey, participants in adult study, courses studied, teachers of adults, teaching methods, education in public affairs, aims of adult education, agencies of adult education, financing adult education, and administrative problems. 381

Morrison, Duncan G. "Relation of the Public Library to Adult Education in the State of Washington." Ph.D. Dissertation. University of Washington, 1949. 382

Mumma, Richard A. Public School Administrators and Adult Education, In Adult Education, 1 (October, 1950) 12-18.

Report of a survey made in April, 1950, of adult education activities in public schools of Delaware, Maryland, New Jersey, New York, and Pennsylvania. Questionnaires were sent to school superintendents in 765 cities with 651 responding. A summary of replies revealed: (1) 81.9 per cent of administrators expressed belief that public school systems should include adult education; 3.2 per cent opposed the idea. (2) 37.5 per cent of school boards have stated a policy on adult education in recent years. (3) A small part of total budgets was spent for adult education. There is almost no relationship between size of city and percentage spent. (4) Only 30 per cent of the administrators claimed membership in one or more adult education associations or groups; fewer than 9 per cent in more than one. There is a relationship between such membership and size of school system; the larger the system the greater the percentage of administrators holding membership. (5) Within the last year 51.8 per cent of respondents had attended a convention which considered adult education; 19.4 per cent had attended more than one. There is a relationship between attendance at conventions and size of school system. 383

Mumma, Richard A. Trends in Adult Education Offerings in Region II, In Adult Education Bulletin, 14 (August, 1950) 180-186.

The first of three reports of a survey of the status of adult education in the public schools of Region II of NEA Department of Adult Education (comprised of Delaware,

Maryland, New Jersey, New York, and Pennsylvania).
The purpose of the survey was to focus attention of administrators on problems of adult education, to shed light
on trends in adult education offerings, interest and leadership of public school administrators in promoting adult education, and barriers to development of adult education
programs. A questionnaire was sent to superintendents of
public schools in 765 cities with populations of 2,500 or
more in the five states. Usable replies were received
from 85.1 per cent of administrators. Findings: (1) Of
those responding, 67.9 per cent indicated an adult education program of some type. There was a relationship between the size of the community and the existence of a
program. (2) There was a marked increase in the past
year over the preceding year in the number of cities offering classes for adults, with the greatest increase in
crafts and homemaking, and the least in academic subjects. (3) 45.9 per cent of cities with programs reported
activities other than classes and 65.8 per cent reported
cooperation with other organizations in offering programs.
                                                        384

National Education Association. Division of Adult Education
  Service. "A Study of Urban Public School Adult Programs of the United States." Washington, D.C.: N.E.A.,
  1952. 171 pp.
  A comprehensive survey of public school adult education programs in communities of 2500 and over, undertaken in 1952 by the N.E.A. Division of Adult Education
with the assistance of the N.E.A. Research Division
through a grant from the Fund for Adult Education. The
three sections of the study are: Report of the Questionnaire Study of Adult Education in Urban Public School Systems; Report of the Community Self Studies of Public
School Adult Education; Continuing Education for Adults in
the Public Junior Colleges. The appendix includes the
questionnaires used for the study. General findings and
implications are summarized in the introduction, including
growth of public school adult education problems, goals,
financial support, methods, teachers, relationship to the
community, cooperation with groups and organizations,
publicity, leadership, administration, and the role of the
junior college.   385

National Institute of Adult Education. "Liberal Education in
  a Technical Age; A Survey of the Relationship of Vocational and Non-Vocational Further Education and Training."

London: M. Parrish, 1955.   128 pp.   Distributed in the
U.S.A. by the Center for the Study of Liberal Education
for Adults.
A study sponsored by the National Institute of Adult
Education covering Professional and Examining Bodies,
Technical Institutes and Art Colleges, Teachers and Students in Technical Institutes, Mail Courses, University Extra-Mural Departments, Residential Colleges and Centers.
Summary and conclusions state responsibility of educational institutions for liberal education and present suggestions for liberalizing technical studies and technical institutions.   386

National University Extension Association.   "Adult Education
in the Modern University," a Preliminary Report by a
Special Committee of N.U.E.A.   Ann Arbor: University
of Michigan Press, 1949.   46 pp.
A preliminary report based upon response to a questionnaire sent to members of the N.U.E.A., covering types
of adult education activities offered, proportion of extension enrollment in adult education (non-credit) courses,
administration of adult education within the university,
attitude of faculty and administrative officers toward adult
education, frontiers of service, and the role of the university in the field of adult education.   387

National University Extension Association. "University Extension in the United States;" a Study by the N.U.E.A.   John
R. Morton, Director.   University, Alabama: University
of Alabama Press, 1953.   144 pp.   Summary: Adult Education, 4 (September, 1954) 207-214.
Report of a survey covering origins and development of
university extension, its functions and administrative arrangements, facilities used, staffs, users, financing,
principal subject areas, and methods   of development and
instruction, in the group of seventy-six universities holding membership in the National University Extension Association.   Made under the auspices of N.U.E.A. with funds
from the Fund for Adult Education.   388

Neuffer, Frank R.   "Administrative Policies and Practices
of Evening Colleges, 1953; a Report."   Chicago: Center
for the Study of Liberal Education for Adults, 1953.   25 pp.
Report of a survey of eighty-four university evening divisions on policies and administrative practices, including
relationship of the evening division to the university, financial policies, faculty, administrative staff, public re-

lations, admission, guidance, tuition and fees, certificate
programs, non-credit courses, courses via television.
Includes tabular information. Appendix lists the institutions surveyed.   389

Nichols, Charles H. "A Study of the Educational Activities
of Selected Industrial, Commercial, and Professional
Foundations." Ph. D. Dissertation. Northwestern University, 1954.   390

Olds, Edward B.   A. E. A.'s Finance Study, In Adult Education, 4 (February, 1954) 109-115.
A research study by the National Commission on Adult
Education Finance of the A. E. A. focusing on three areas:
the financing of public school adult education; the financing of community adult education councils; the designing of a broader finance study. The study is designed to
serve as a starting point for additional research in adult
education and to broaden the use of research in solving
other problems of adult education. See No. 353 for complete report.   391

Partridge, Deborah C.   Adult Education Projects Sponsored
by Negro College Fraternities and Sororities, In Journal
of Negro Education, 14 (Summer, 1945) 374-380.
Questionnaires on nature of adult education project,
methods and materials, staff, relationship of project to
other organizations, size and nature of group served, were
sent to sixty-four Negro colleges, and a similar questionnaire to national offices of the fraternities and sororities.
Findings indicate that a small percentage of college fraternities and sororities sponsor adult education projects.
Projects directed toward better citizenship and vocational
education are most frequent. Discussions, forums, lectures, and mass media are methods most widely used.
Projects serve community and campus groups as well as
members of sponsoring organizations. A majority of projects are addressed to urban population.   392

"Patterns of Liberal Education in the Evening College, A
Case Study of Nine Institutions." Chicago: Center for
the Study of Liberal Education for Adults [c1952]. 82 pp.
A study of the evening divisions of nine institutions--
Akron, Chicago, Cincinnati, Detroit, Louisville, New York,
Northwestern, Southern California, and Western Reserve--
representative of general types of evening colleges, of un-
usual approaches to the philosophy or methods of evening

college work, and of a broad geographical distribution.
Data were obtained by observation and interviewing by
field workers who visited each institution.   Problems per-
ceived reflect important needs of the evening colleges:
(1) need to establish satisfactory procedures for modify-
ing the college and its policies as the result of constant
reevaluation; (2) need to arrive at a clear definition of
the relationship between the day and evening college in
terms understood and accepted by both administration and
faculty; (3) the need to achieve a unified and interested
faculty informed about its own activities and about the
relevant needs and attitudes of administration and students; (4) the need to attract a satisfactory number of
students; and (5) the need to satisfy enough students with
what goes on in the classroom.   Problems and issues
under these categories are discussed from four points of
view, represented by the first four sections of the report:
I The Evening College and the University;   II Faculty
Relationships; III Sources of Student Satisfaction; and IV
The Study of Attitude.   The fifth section looks at the five
problem areas in the context of the whole report and suggests how other problems can be approached in this light.
Appendix gives interview schedules used in the case studies.   393

Polley, John W.   "A Plan for the Activities of a Pilot Pro-
ject in Cooperative Educational Development Among the
Public Schools of a Large City."   Ph. D. Dissertation.
Columbia University, Teachers College, 1950.   394

Reals, Willis H.   The Education of the Aging in Institutions
of Higher Learning, In School and Society, 79 (June 12,
1954) 177-184.
Report of a survey of one hundred thirty-six colleges
and universities, members of AUEC, NUEA, or the Association of Urban Universities, on four questions: (1) In
what divisions or departments is education for the aging
being given; (2) nature of the program; (3) whether or not
those over fifty were encouraged to enroll in undergraduate daytime courses; (4) whether or not they employed
professors retired from other institutions.   The following
is a brief summary of the ninety-nine questionnaires re-
turned: sixty-three have no program; thirty-six offer
courses, institutes, or conferences; four have had radio
or TV programs; two have provided free tuition to those
over sixty-five and one plans to do so; two have "Golden
Years Clubs;" seven employ professors emeriti.   Con-

clusions drawn from the study are: (1) Universities and
colleges have been providing special programs for older
adults only since 1948.   (2) Courses offered follow four
general patterns: (a) those dealing with health, living
arrangements, religion, creative activities, and legal
problems; (b) those including social and recreational activities; (c) workshop type courses on important problems
of older people; (d) short courses on television with supplementary materials.   (3) Institutes have been of a general nature, but there is a recent tendency to limit the
area to problems of the older worker, family, etc. (4)
Courses for credit are natural developments of non-credit
courses and will expand rapidly.   395

Redd, George N.   Adult Education for Negroes Under Public
School Auspices, In Journal of Negro Education, 14 (Summer, 1945) 312-321.
     A survey of nineteen states which maintain by law
separate schools for Negroes on the following questions:
(1) How are adult education programs under public school
auspices administered?   (2) To what extent do Negroes
participate in them?   (3) What are the types of programs
available to Negroes?   (4) What are the main features of
representative programs?   Conclusions drawn from the
study are: (1) Although state education authorities have
legal authority to organize and administer adult education
programs for both racial groups, there has been very
little activity outside Federally-aided programs in vocational education.   (2) Programs of public school systems
of cities are organized chiefly around evening school
classes and most are inadequate to meet educational needs
of Negroes in urban centers.   (3) The tendency is to con-
fine programs to literacy and vocational skills; broad areas of learning are generally   lacking.   (4) State or city
sponsored programs for Negroes are inferior in quantity
and quality to those for Whites except in Washington, D.C.
where identical programs are reported.   (5) Quality of
adult education programs for Negroes is best in large centers of Negro population in border cities.   396

Rochte, Newton C.   "A State Program of Tax Supported A-
dult Education in Ohio."   Ph.D. Dissertation.   Ohio University, Athens, Ohio, 1951.   397

Rohrer, Wayne C.   "The Nature of Large-Scale Farmers'
Organizations and Their Relationship to Non-Vocational A-
dult Education Programs."   Ph.D. Dissertation.   Michi-

gan State University, 1955.   398

Scott, Marshall L.   "A Proposal for Strengthening Presby-
terian Churches of Industrial Communities Through the
Use of Adult Education."   Ph.D. Dissertation.   Columbia
University, 1953.   399

Shanner, William M.   Industry and Education, In Elementary
School Journal, 50 (December, 1949) 183-187.
   Describes the five year contractual agreement between
International Harvester Company and the University of
Chicago, which had the immediate objective of revitalizing Harvester's training programs, and also the aim of
developing an integrated, long-run program of industrial
training and education and making a meaningful contribution to existing knowledge on adult education.   Research
studies have been conducted by the University in six major areas of adult education: (1) evaluation of teacher-
training methods used in an adult education program;   (2)
employees' problems as related to interest in an off-hour
education program;   (3) an evaluation of the factors affecting development and coordination of field training programs;   (4) evaluation of general education in industry;
(5) development of testing and rating techniques for use at
Harvester's Central School;   (6) development of instructional material for use in basic courses.   400

Sillars, Robertson.   Education for International Understanding; A Report of a Survey, In Adult Education Journal, 8
(April, 1949) 91-98.
   Report of a survey made at the request of the Committee on International Relations of the American Association
for Adult Education and the Adult Education Panel of the
U.S. National Commission for UNESCO, November, 1948-
January, 1949 to determine how well American adult education is meeting responsibility for education in international relations and other public affairs, methods used,
and problems encountered.   Based on reports from two
hundred fifty agencies typifying the better developed and
more active public affairs programs conducted by recognized adult education agencies in the United States.   A
summary of findings gives percentages for: topics or subjects; principal methods used; types of materials; agency
goals; reasons for participation; problems encountered.
Agricultural groups ranked first in programs of international affairs, and also in programs of community-related
topics.   Discussion and lecture were the methods most

Smith, Helen L.   143

frequently used, with pamphlets and films ranking highest
in types of materials. Farm groups favored discussion
over lectures to a greater extent than other groups. A
comparison of findings with respect to agency goals and
reasons for participation indicate that frequently adult educators and clients are working at cross purposes and
that too many agencies give clients what the agencies
think they need, not what they want. This results in public apathy ranking highest in problems encountered. It is
concluded that programs in the public relations field are
weak in content and that the paramount need in educational
method is adjusting agency goals to educational needs of
clients which in the public relations field are rooted in
their economic, social, and psychological relationships to
local, national, and world communities.   401

Smith, Helen L. "Adult Education Activities in Public Libraries; A Report on the A. L. A. Survey of Adult Education Activities in Public Libraries and State Library Extension Agencies in the United States." Chicago: American Library Association, 1954. 128 pp.
   A comprehensive report of the A. L. A. Survey giving
detailed information on the findings as reported in questionnaires and interviews. Summarizes chief services of
public libraries and reasons for lack of certain services;
facts related to adult education agencies and community
groups; library adult education programs and personnel.
The final chapter contains conclusions and recommendations. Appendices include a listing of libraries visited;
instructions for the interviewer; a copy of the questionnaire; and a selected bibliography.   402

Spence, John A. "A Study of the Need for the Extension
and Improvement of the Adult Education Services of Ohio
State University." Ph. D. Dissertation. Ohio State University, 1956.   403

Stanfield, John M. "Extending Secondary Education to Meet
and Further Educational Needs of Ohio Rural Youths and
Adults." Ph. D. Dissertation. Ohio State University,
1955.   404

Study of Adult Education in Rural Areas. "Rural Social Sys-
tems and Adult Education;" A Committee Report by
Charles A. Loomis and others. [East Lansing] Michigan
State College Press, 1953. 392 pp.
   A study sponsored by the Association of Land Grant

Colleges and Universities and the Fund for Adult Education to: (1) determine nature and magnitude of existent
programs of adult education in rural areas in the fields
of (a) international understanding for world peace, (b)
understanding and strengthening of the economic order, and
(c) understanding of democracy, its functioning and structure; (2) to appraise current practices and methods in the
three fields, and to determine amount of time, effort and
expenditure devoted to these fields; (3) to make recommendations to the Fund for Adult Education as to programs or activities which might be encouraged or supported.   Separate chapters, written by members of the
study staff, deal with various systems and organizations
in rural areas, including public schools; cooperative extension service of the U.S.; farmers' organizations and
cooperatives; service, professional and other civic clubs;
special agencies within the Department of Agriculture;
public libraries; churches; colleges and universities;
rural local government.   Also included are international
exchange of persons and the part played by mass media
of communication in programs of adult education.   The
last chapter gives a summary of findings of the study,
with statistical tables, as to number and percentage of organizations having general education programs and programs in the three fields of interest; inter-agency communication; forms and procedures used in the best programs; mass media as channels of communication of social systems; participation of foreign persons in programs;
organizational levels suitable to the advancement of adult
education in the three fields; and overall generalizations
concerning adult education agreed to by the staff.   405

U.S. Office of Education.   "Resident, Extension, and Adult
Education Enrollment in Institutions of Higher Education:
November, 1953."   Circular No. 414.   Washington, D.C.:
Government Printing Office, 1954.   29 pp.
   A statistical report on enrollment of 1,852 institutions,
giving data for the following classes of students: I Resident Enrollment: A. undergraduate (1) full-time and (2)
part-time; B. graduate; C. total resident enrollment; II
Extension: A. enrolled for college credit; B. not enrolled for college credit; III Adult Education (non-college
credit).   Table 1 gives the data by state; Table 2, by individual institution listed by states.   Basic terms relating
to enrollment are defined.   406

U.S. Office of Education.   "Resident, Extension, and Adult

Education Enrollment in Institutions of Higher Education:
November, 1954. " Circular No. 454. Washington, D. C.:
Government Printing Office, 1955. 34 pp.

The second annual report in this series. Tables 1 and
2 give the same type of data as Tables 1 and 2 in the
first report (Circular 414). In addition, Table A gives
Resident, Extension, and Adult Education Enrollment in
Institutions of Higher Education by College-Credit and
Non-College-Credit Status, Aggregate and Continental
United States, November, 1954 and November, 1953, with
increase by number and by percentage. Analyses of findings show: (1) percentage of increase in various classi-
fications of students; (2) comparison between composition
of total enrollment in 1954 and corresponding composition
in 1953; (3) analyses of sub-categories of enrollment;
and (4) differences in enrollments among states.   407

U. S. Office of Education. "Resident and Extension Enrollment in Institutions of Higher Education: November, 1955."
Circular No. 493. Washington, D. C.: Government Printing Office, 1957. 40 pp.

The third annual report in this series. Data are presented on: I Resident Enrollment subdivided as: A.
college grade: 1. undergraduate (a) full-time and (b)
part-time; 2. graduate; B. other than college grade: 1.
terminal-occupational and 2. adult education; II Extension
Enrollment subdivided as: A. college grade; B. other
than college grade. Table 12 gives this data by state;
Table 14, by individual institution listed by states. Table
13 gives a summary of data on correspondence courses,
short courses, individual lessons; and on veterans enrolled in courses of college grade under Public Laws 13,
346, 894, and 550. Tables 1-11 show comparisons for
various categories in 1953, 1954, and 1955. A copy of
the questionnaire used in the 1955 survey, and a sheet entitled "Some Basic Definitions" which accompanied the
questionnaire, are included.   408

Williams, Stanley W. "A Study of the Organization, Ad-
ministration, and Supervision of the Curriculum in Adult
Education in the United States. " Ph. D. Dissertation.
University of Southern California, 1949.   409

Williams, Ward R. "Post-High School Education in Minnesota, 1952-1953. " Ph. D. Dissertation. University of
Minnesota, 1956.   410

Willis, Ivan L.   Industry's Concern With Adult Education, In
Institute for Administrative Officers of Higher Institutions
Proceedings. Vol. 20, "The Community Responsibilities
of Institutions of Higher Learning." Chicago: University
of Chicago Press, 1948. Pp. 24-32.
Description of a cooperative relationship between the
University of Chicago and International Harvester in developing a program of adult education for managerial employees. In addition to general assistance in the program,
the University set in motion six research projects, one of
which was an evaluation of general education in industry.
The objectives of the program were the general development of the individual for his current job, or any job, and
his personal and social growth.   The other research projects were: an evaluation of teacher training methods
used in an adult education program; employees' problems
as related to interest in an off-hour education program;
an evaluation of factors affecting development and coordination of field training programs; development of testing
and rating techniques; development of instructional materials for use in basic courses.   411

B. Bibliography

Adult Education Association of the U.S.A.   Committee on
Evaluation.   "Program Evaluation in Adult Education."
Chicago: A.E.A., 1952. Pp. 30-32.
"Selected References" contain thirty-nine items, including books, pamphlets, and periodical articles, published
1934-1952, on evaluation of educational programs, particularly in adult education.   412

Adult Education Association of the U.S.A.   National Commission on Adult Education Finance.   "Financing Adult Education in America's Public Schools and Community Councils." [complete report by] Edward B. Olds. Washington:
A.E.A., 1954. Pp. 120-124.
The bibliography includes seventy-three references to
books, government publications, periodical articles, pamphlets, and doctoral dissertations, covering the years
1923-1954.   Grouped under eight headings: Studies of Financing; Administration and Supervision; Description of
Programs; History; Coordination; Public Policy; Public
Opinion; Research Methods.   413

American Educational Research Association.   Adult Education,

In Review of Educational Research, 20 (June, 1950) 161-
249.
    Reviews the literature in this area through September,
1949, concentrating on the last five years. Bibliographies
at the end of each chapter total six hundred seven references. See No. 157 for listing of chapters.   414

American Educational Research Association. Adult Education,
In Review of Educational Research, 23 (June, 1953) 191-
283.
    Reviews the literature for the period October, 1949-
October, 1952. Bibliographies at the end of each chapter
total six hundred references. See No. 158 for listing of
chapters.   415

American Library Association. Office for Adult Education.
"Experimental Projects in Adult Education; A Report of
the A. L. A. Adult Education Subgrant Project." Chicago:
A. L. A., 1956. Pp. 35-36.
    A bibliography of forty-two references to reports and
periodical articles on the subgrant projects, arranged by
state.   416

Atkins, James A. Resource Materials and Agencies for A-
dult Education, In Journal of Negro Education, 14 (Summer, 1945) 494-508.
    A combination annotated bibliography and directory.
The bibliography consists of sixty-eight items published
between 1927 and 1944, annotated and classified under the
headings: Adult Interests, Capacities and Abilities; History and Background of Adult Education; Areas of Activity;
Principles and Methods; Instructional Aids; Accomplishments, Problems and Prospects. The directory of fifty-
four agencies includes (1) federal, (2) public and quasi-
public, and (3) commercial and industrial organizations,
with address and function of each.   417

Baron, George. "A Bibliographical Guide to the English Educational System." London: The Athlone Press, 1951.
70 pp.
    Section VIc contains a selected list of books on adult
education.   418

Besterman, Theodore. "A World Bibliography of Bibliographies and of Bibliographical Catalogues, Calendars, Abstracts, Digests, Indexes and the Like." 3d ed. N.Y.,
Scarecrow Press, Inc. [c1955]. Vol. I, pp. 1178-1179.

A classified list of separately published bibliographies,
with entries arranged chronologically under each heading.
Eighteen bibliographies on adult education, published 1905-
1954, are listed under "Education-6, Adult Education,"
Vol. 1, pp. 1178-1179.   419

"Bibliographic Index." New York: H.W. Wilson, 1945 to
date.
A listing by subject of bibliographies published separately, and of bibliographies in books and periodicals, including foreign publications. Each issue contains a listing under "Education of Adults." Published quarterly with
cumulations.   420

Bittner, Walton S. Adult Education, In Walter S. Monroe,
"Encyclopedia of Educational Research." New York:
Macmillan, 1950. Pp. 31-32.
A bibliography of sixty-two references, including books,
reports, bulletins, and association proceedings, most of
which were published in the last twenty years.   421

Brickman, William W. Adult Education, In School and Society, 66 (September 27, 1947) 247-253.
A critical review of the literature of adult education
covering principally the years 1944-1947. Bibliography of
thirty-nine references p. 253.   422

Brickman, William W. Education for Adults, In School and
Society, 78 (October 31, 1953) 133-139.
A critical review of the literature of adult education for
the six year period 1948-1953. Bibliography of thirty-
three references pp. 138-139.   423

Clark, Burton R. "Adult Education in Transition; A Study
of Institutional Insecurity." University of California Publications in Sociology and Social Institutions, Vol. 1, No.
2. Berkeley and Los Angeles: University of California
Press, 1956. Pp. 195-197.
A bibliography of seventy references including books,
periodical articles, bulletins, and reports on adult education, covering a period of approximately twenty years.
Major sections of the book are: Background of Adult Education in California; Pressures on a Marginal Program;
The Adult School Organization in Los Angeles; Service
and Legitimacy; Continuing Insecurities; Implications for
Theory and Policy.   424

"Cumulative Book Index." New York: H. W. Wilson,
1933 to date.
A dictionary catalog of author, title, and subject entries for publications in English from the book trade of
the United States and other countries. Entries on adult
education are listed under "Education of Adults." Published monthly with cumulations. 425

"Dissertation Abstracts." Ann Arbor, Michigan: University Microfilms, 1952 to date.
Each monthly issue contains a section on Education with
a subdivision on Adult Education. Abstracts of doctoral
dissertations which are available in complete form on
microfilm. Preceded by Microfilm Abstracts, 1938-1951.
426

Dyer, John P. "Ivory Towers in the Market Place; the
Evening College in American Education." Indianapolis:
Bobbs-Merrill [c1956]. Pp. 196-201.
A bibliography of seventy-four books and articles on
the general subject of adult education and related fields,
publications of the Center for the Study of Liberal Education for Adults, publications of the Association of University Evening Colleges, and of the Association of Urban
Universities, published 1919-1955. 427

"Education Index." New York: H.W. Wilson, 1932 to date.
An author and subject index to educational periodicals,
books, pamphlets, and government publications. Each issue contains a listing under "Adult Education" with sub-
divisions. Published monthly with cumulations. 428

Eells, Walter C. American Doctoral Dissertations on Adult
Education in Foreign Countries, In Adult Education, 6
(Winter, 1956) 117-119.
A listing by country of sixty-two dissertations concerning some aspect of adult education in foreign countries accepted by American universities, covering a period of a-
bout forty years, with approximately half during the past
seven years. 429

Essert, Paul L. "Creative Leadership of Adult Education."
New York: Prentice-Hall, 1951. Pp. 291-303.
"Selected References" listed by chapter total one hundred eighty-eight references to books, periodical articles,
and government publications, published 1921-1950. Major
divisions of the book are: Goals of Creative Leadership

of Adult Education; Criteria Applied to Adult Study for
Personal Objectives; Criteria Applied to Adult Study for
Community Development; Discussion Guide for Practical
Education of Creative Leadership.   430

Great Britain.   British Information Services.   Reference Division.   "Adult Education in Britain."   1D579. Rev. ed.
London: The Services, 1951.   Pp. 13-15.
A bibliography of twenty-three books and pamphlets,
published 1913-1950; and fifteen government publications,
published 1919-1947.   431

"Guide to Studies in Adult Education." See Kelly, Thomas,
ed. "A Select Bibliography of Adult Education in Great
Britain Including Works Published to the End of the Year
1950." No. 438.

Hand, Samuel E.   "A Review of Physiological and Psychological Changes in Aging and Their Implications for Teachers
of Adults." 3d ed.   Bulletin 71 G-1.   Tallahassee:
Florida State Department of Education, Division of Vocational and Adult Education, 1957.   Pp. 28-31.
A bibliography of forty-six references to books, periodical articles, proceedings of associations, and government publications, published 1927-1953.   432

"Handbook of Adult Education in the United States," edited
by Mary L. Ely.   New York: Institute of Adult Education, Teachers College, Columbia University, 1948. Pp.
515-528.
"Suggested Supplementary Readings," a bibliography of
about three hundred fifty references, classified by forty-
seven headings including various agencies, types of adult
education, methods, etc., includes books, periodical articles, proceedings, and government publications, published 1931-1947.   433

"Handlist of Studies in Adult Education."   See Kelly, Thomas,
ed.   "A Select Bibliography of Adult Education in Great
Britain Including Works Published to the End of the Year
1950." No. 438.

Hendrickson, Andrew.   "A Review of Post-War Literature
on Public School Adult Education." Columbus: Bureau of
Special and Adult Education, Ohio State University, 1951.
18, 5 pp.
The last five pages are a bibliography of sixty-six

books, periodical articles, proceedings and reports, published 1944-1950, relating to adult education and the public school system. (See also No. 163).   434

Houle, Cyril O. and others. "The Armed Services and Adult Education." Washington, D. C.: American Council on Education [c1947]. Pp. 253-257.
An annotated bibliography of thirty-eight references to periodical articles, yearbooks, proceedings, and pamphlets, published 1942-1946.   435

"Index to American Doctoral Dissertations." Ann Arbor, Michigan: University Microfilms, 1957 to date.
Annual listing of doctoral dissertations, arranged by subject, and by university under each subject. Includes a section on Education. Issued as No. 13 of "Dissertation Abstracts." Preceded by "Doctoral Dissertations Accepted by American Universities," 1936-1956.   436

"International Index; Guide to Periodical Literature in the Social Sciences and Humanities." New York: H. W. Wilson, 1907 to date.
Subject and author index to scholarly periodicals. Entries on adult education are listed under "Education of Adults." Issued quarterly with cumulations.   437

Kelly, Thomas, ed. "A Select Bibliography of Adult Education in Great Britain Including Works Published to the End of the Year 1950." London: National Institute of Adult Education, 1952. 84 pp.
A partially annotated list of eight hundred fifty-nine books, pamphlets, articles, and theses divided into four major sections: I General; II History (to 1918); III Recent and Contemporary Developments (from 1919); IV Theory. Appendix of Selected Works on Adult Education Abroad. Supplemented by annual volumes following the same classification: "Handlist of Studies in Adult Education," 1951. 31 pp. (241 annotated references); ------, 1952. 32 pp. (228 annotated references); "Guide to Studies in Adult Education," 1953. 33 pp. (261 annotated references); ------, 1954. 24 pp. (147 annotated references); ------, 1955. 40 pp. (272 annotated references); ------, 1956. 36 pp. (232 annotated references).   438

Kempfer, Homer. "Adult Education." New York: McGraw-Hill, 1955.
A list of eight general references on adult education, published 1941-1953, p. 423. "Selected References" at

the end of each of fifteen chapters total two hundred
ninety references to books, periodical articles, bulletins,
proceedings, etc. The book is of three parts: The
Task of Adult Education, Program Development, Problems of Organization and Administration.   439

Kempfer, Homer. "Checklists for Public School Adult Education Programs." U.S. Office of Education. Circular
No. 356. Washington, D.C.: Government Printing Office,
1952. P. 17.
    "Selected References" is a list of fourteen books,
pamphlets, government publications, and periodical articles, published 1936-1950, in addition to six references
in footnotes.   440

Kempfer, Homer. "Education for a Long and Useful Life."
U.S. Office of Education. Bulletin 1950, No. 6. Washington, D.C.: Government Printing Office. Reprint
1954. Pp. 30-32.
    "Selected References" include forty-four pamphlets,
periodical articles, books, and government publications,
published 1938-1950, grouped under: general, special
fields, magazines.   441

Kempfer, Homer and Grace S. Wright. "100 Evening
Schools." U.S. Office of Education. Bulletin 1949, No.
4. Washington, D.C.: Government Printing Office,
1949. Pp. 69-71.
    "Selected References" include twenty-eight books,
periodical articles, and bulletins, briefly annotated. 442

Kidd, James Roby. "Adult Education and the School."
Toronto: Canadian Association for Adult Education
[c1950]. Pp. 35-36.
    "Additional Sources of Information" list seven general
references to books and pamphlets, published 1939-1950,
five Canadian journals, and two other references, all
briefly annotated. Also listed are fifteen national organizations with their addresses.   443

Kidd, James Roby, ed. "Adult Education in Canada."
Toronto: Canadian Association for Adult Education, 1950.
Pp. 239-243.
    Bibliography includes nine books, eighteen pamphlets,
twelve special reports, and sixty-six journal articles, published 1935-1950, and a listing of six Canadian journals in
the field of adult education.   444

Kidd, James Roby. "Adult Education in the Canadian University." Toronto: Canadian Association for Adult Education, 1956. Pp. 131-137.
   A selective bibliography including seventy-five books
and pamphlets; twenty-seven periodical articles; fifty-
three reports, proceedings and extracts; twenty-one special papers, theses, and dissertations, published 1908-
1956, listed by United States, Canada, Great Britain, and
Other Countries.   445

Knowles, Malcolm S. "Informal Adult Education; a Guide
for Administrators, Leaders, and Teachers." New York:
Association Press, 1950. Pp. 255-258.
   A bibliography of forty-three books, nine pamphlets,
four periodicals, and two reports, published 1926-1950.
The book is in four parts: The Opportunity; The Methods
and the Programs; The Administration of Adult Education;
Evaluation.   446

Lowy, Louis. "Adult Education and Group Work." New
York: Whiteside and Morrow, 1955. Pp. 215-217.
   A selected bibliography of thirty-eight books and periodical articles, published 1933-1954.   Chapters of the
book are: Group Work and Adult Education; Group Work
in Liberal Adult Education; Group Work With Young A-
dults; Group Work in Parent Education; Group Work With
Older Adults; Principles of Group Work Applied in Adult
Education.   447

Luke, Robert A. "Adult Education." Vocational and Profes-
sional Monographs, No. 29. Cambridge, Mass.: Bellman
Publishing Company. [c1955]. P. 19.
   A bibliography of eleven books published 1948-1955.
                                                          448

National Association of Public School Adult Educators. "Public School Adult Education; a Guide for Administrators and
Teachers." Washington, D.C.: N.A.P.S.A.E. [c1956].
Pp. 147-151.
   A bibliography of one hundred references published
1928-1955, with a majority published since 1950, classified under the headings: Periodical Publications in the
Field of Adult Education; General References; Advisory
Committees; Counseling and Guidance; Curriculum Planning; Evaluation; Financing; In-Service Training; Methods
and Learning; Public Relations; Other Bibliographies. Emphasis is on adult education as a phase of public school

activity.   449

National University Extension Association. "University Extension in the United States;" a Study by the N. U. E. A.
John R. Morton, Director. [University, Ala.] University of Alabama Press, 1953. Pp. 142-144.
    A listing of fifty-six books, periodical articles, govern-
ment publications, publications of associations, etc., published 1910-1953.   450

Phi Delta Kappa. "Research Studies in Education; a Subject
Index of Doctoral Dissertations, Reports, and Field Studies, 1941-1951." Boulder, Colorado: Phi Delta Kappa,
1953.
    A ten-year index including dissertations, theses, re-
ports, and field studies accepted for the degrees of Doctor
of Philosophy in Education, and Doctor of Education.
Based on "Doctoral Dissertations Accepted by American
Universities." Studies are listed alphabetically by author
under thirty subject headings.   The section on Adult Education, pp. 29A 1-2, contains eighty-six entries.   Supplemented by annual volumes.   (See next entry)   451

Phi Delta Kappa. "Research Studies in Education; a Subject
Index of Doctoral Dissertations, Reports, and Field Studies; and a Research Methods Bibliography." Bloomington, Indiana: Phi Delta Kappa, 1953 to date.
    Annual supplement to preceding item, following the
same arrangement.   Each volume contains two sections on
Adult Education--"Doctoral Dissertations Completed," and
"Doctoral Dissertations Under Way."   452

"Public Affairs Information Service Bulletin." New York:
Public Affairs Information Service, 1915 to date.
    A listing by subject of current books, pamphlets, peri-
odical articles, and government publications in the field of
economics and public affairs.   Entries on adult education
are listed under "Education, Adult." Issued weekly with
cumulations.   453

Raybould, S. G. "The English Universities and Adult Education." London: The Workers' Educational Association,
1951. Pp. 167-169.
    "Bibliographical Note" consists of forty-eight refer-
ences, published over a period of fifty years, grouped under five headings: (1) Official Reports, Regulations, and
Other Papers Published by H. M. Stationery Office; (2)

The University Extension Movement; (3) University Tutorial Classes; (4) Education in H. M. Forces; (5) General.
454

Reader's Guide to Periodical Literature." New York: H. W. Wilson, 1900 to date.
Subject and author index to periodicals. Entries on adult education are listed under "Education of Adults" in some volumes, and under "Adult Education" in others. Issued semi-monthly with cumulations.   455

"Research Studies in Education." See Phi Delta Kappa, No. 451.

Scates, Alice Y. "Jointly-Sponsored Programs of College Credit Work for Employed Adults; A Report of a Project Sponsored by the Office of Naval Research." Washington, D.C.: American Council on Education, 1953. Pp. 227-233.
Bibliography of eighty references, published 1930-1953, including books, periodical articles, government publications, proceedings of associations, doctoral dissertations, and publications of the Center for the Study of Liberal Education for Adults.   456

Selected References on the Organization and Administration of Secondary Education: Adult Education. In School Review, 53 (October, 1945) 493-494; 54 (October, 1946) 492; 55 (October, 1947) 490-491; 56 (October, 1948) 490; 57 (October, 1949) 444-445; 58 (October, 1950) 423; 59 (October, 1951) 429; 60 (October, 1952) 432; 61 (October, 1953) 428; 62 (October, 1954) 427; 63 (October, 1955) 400-401; 64 (October, 1956) 324.
Annotated references principally on public school adult education. Most of the references are periodical articles, with some books, pamphlets, yearbooks and proceedings.
457

Sheats, Paul H., Clarence D. Jayne, and Ralph B. Spence. "Adult Education; the Community Approach." New York: Dryden, 1953. Pp. 507-519.
"Notes on Sources," arranged according to chapters, consist of three hundred reference to books, government publications, periodical articles, and reports, published 1935-1953. Major divisions of the book are: Scope and Purpose; Organized Programs; Ways and Means; Action Responsibilities.   458

156   Smith, Helen L.

Smith, Helen L.   "Adult Education Activities in Public Li-
    braries; a Report of the American Library Association
    Survey of Adult Education Activities in Public Libraries
    and State Library Extension Agencies of the United States."
    Chicago: A. L. A. , 1954.   Pp. 94-96.
       A selected bibliography of seventy-six references to
    books, periodical articles, theses, reports, UNESCO pub-
    lications, U. S. government publications, publications of
    universities and of associations, published 1926-1954. 459

Smith, Robert M.   Adult Education and the Library; an In-
    troduction, In Library Occurrent, 18 (March, 1956) 198-
    199, 211.
       A selected list designed to furnish background and per-
    spective on education for adults and the library's place in
    the adult education movement.   Thirty-four annotated ref-
    erences to books, periodical articles, and UNESCO publi-
    cations, published 1938-1956, are grouped in five classifi-
    cations: What Do We Mean By Adult Education; What
    Role for the Library; What Libraries Can and Are Doing;
    Other Resources for Practitioners; Training Opportunities.
                                                        460

Snow, Robert H. "Community Adult Education." New York:
    Putnam, 1955.   Pp. 163-166.
       "Selected Readings" is a bibliography of thirty-five
    books and fourteen pamphlets (including government publi-
    cations, publications of the Center for the Study of Liberal
    Education for Adults, and publications of universities and
    associations), published 1926-1953.   The book covers
    kinds of adult education services needed, resources for a-
    dult education, group leadership, supervision of activities,
    publicity and public relations, extension of adult education
    services, and program evaluation and adaptation.   461

"Study of Adult Education in Rural Areas.   Rural Social Sys-
    tems and Adult Education;" a Committee Report by Charles
    A. Loomis and others.   [East Lansing] Michigan State Col-
    lege Press, 1953.
       Bibliographies at the ends of chapters total two hundred
    twenty references, including books, periodical articles,
    government publications, publications and proceedings of
    associations, and dissertations.   Separate chapters deal
    with various systems and organizations in rural areas.
                                                        462

Thomson, Murray and Diana J. Ironside.   "A Bibliography

of Canadian Writings on Adult Education.   Toronto: Canadian Association for Adult Education, 1956. 56 pp.
   A briefly annotated bibliography of over five hundred
references published 1935-1956, classified in five major
sections: (1) Ideas and Directions; (2) Growth and Development in Canada; (3) Programmes and Interests in A-
dult Education; (4) The Adult Educators; (5) Periodicals
and Journals.   With an author index.   463

Tomlinson, Laurence E. "Adult Education; Its Vital Significance for Your Town." Portland, Oregon: Educational
Studies [c1951] Pp. 40-46.
   The bibliography contains seventy-one references to
books, government publications, and reports, published
1926-1951.   464

UNESCO.   "Adult Education, Current Trends and Practices."
Problems in Education, 2.   New York: Columbia University Press, 1949.   Pp. 141-145.
   "A Selected Reading List" is an annotated list of
twenty-five UNESCO documents and publications of interest
to adult education, grouped under the headings: Education,
Exchange of Persons; Libraries; Museums; Natural Science.   465

UNESCO.   "America's Education Press; a Classified List of
Educational Periodicals Issued in the United States of A-
merica, Together With an International List of Educational
Periodicals." Educational Press Association of America,
26th Yearbook.   Paris: UNESCO, 1957.   212 pp.
   A list of eight American periodicals on adult education
giving for each: title, editor, address, price, and beginning date, in Part II p. 151.   Part I is   a listing of educational periodicals of one hundred two countries, many of
which have a section on "Adult and Workers."   466

UNESCO.   "International Directory of Adult Education."
Paris: UNESCO, 1953.   324 pp.
   A survey of the adult education movement in major
countries of the world, with a selected bibliography of
books and periodicals published since 1935 for each country.   A bibliographical index of periodicals.   467

UNESCO.   A Preliminary Survey of Bibliographies on Adult
Education, In Education Abstracts, 6 (September, 1954)
1-26.
   An annotated list of one hundred twenty-six bibliographi-

cal works from twenty-eight countries and an international
and regional list, covering the period 1920-1954 with emphasis on current works.   468

UNESCO. "Universities in Adult Education." Problems in
Education, 4.   Paris: UNESCO [c1952]. Pp. 169-172.
   A bibliography of forty references to books, periodicals,
and annual reports, published 1887-1951, grouped under
Great Britain, Canada, and U.S.A.   469

U.S. Library of Congress.   "Subject Catalog; A Cumulative
List of Works Represented by Library of Congress Printed
Cards."   Washington, D.C.:   Library of Congress, 1950
to date.
   A subject listing of books, pamphlets, periodicals and
other serials, and copies made by photoreproduction. Entries on adult education are   listed under "Education of A-
dults."   Published quarterly with cumulations.   470

U.S. Office of Education.   "Adult Education References."
Washington, D.C.:   Government Printing Office, 1948-
1952.
   An occasional publication with each issue listing books
and articles on some special aspect of adult education.
No. 1. "Bibliography of Bibliographies on Adult Education,"
prepared by Virginia L. Burgess and Homer Kempfer.
July, 1948, 2 pp.   No. 2.   "Bibliography of Books and
Periodical Articles on Teaching Methods, Organization and
Supervision of Classes, Evaluation of Programs of Adult
Literacy Instruction."   July, 1948.   No. 3. "Materials
for Adult Illiterates," prepared by Virginia L. Burgess
and Homer Kempfer.   August, 1948.   8 pp.   No. 4.
"Adaptations of Classics and Famous Fiction," prepared
by Virginia L. Burgess and Homer Kempfer.   August,
1948. 4 pp. No. 5.   "Adult Education Councils," prepared
by Virginia L. Burgess and Homer Kempfer.   July, 1948.
2 pp. No. 6. "Education for the Aging," prepared by
Burton W. Kreitlow and his students at the University of
Wisconsin.   April, 1952.   9 pp. No. 7. "Books for Program Directors."   August, 1952. 2 pp. No. 8. "Adult
Education in Rural and Village Schools," prepared by
Homer Kempfer and others.   September, 1952. 4 pp. No.
9. "Evaluating Public School Adult Education," compiled
by Homer Kempfer.   September, 1952. 3 pp.   471

Verner, Coolie.   Research-Based Publications, 1955, In A-
dult Education, 6 (Summer, 1956) 232-233.

Waller, Ross D.   159

   "List of References" includes the thirty-six books,
pamphlets, periodical articles, publications of the Center
for the Study of Liberal Education for Adults, bulletins,
and government publications reviewed in the article pp.
226-232.   472

Waller, Ross D.   "Learning to Live; a Short and Long View
   of Adult Education."   London: Art and Educational Publishers, 1946.   Pp. 61-63.
   "Select Bibliography" includes forty-four references,
published 1851-1945, classified in four groups: I Periodicals; II Histories, and Other General Studies; III Studies
of Particular Sections or Aspects; IV Books on the Danish
Folk High School.   473

III. The Roles of Universities and Colleges

A. United States

Adolfson, Lorentz H.   The University's Role in Adult Education, In Adult Education, 5 (Summer, 1955) 231-232.
Two broad categories of activities which most universities consider within the scope of their adult education programs are: (1) extending regular undergraduate and graduate credit work through off-campus classes and correspondence study; (2) engaging in a wide variety of informal educational activities that meet professional, cultural, vocational and civic needs of individuals, groups and communities.   The essential role of the university in adult education is to bring its reservoir of talent, resources, and facilities within reach of its adult constituency.   University adult education has the task of discovering off-campus educational needs, interpreting those needs to the university, and meeting the needs with action programs.   474

Adult Education and the Universities, In Food for Thought, 8 (April, 1948) 19-22, 24.
An excerpt from the Report of the President's Commission on Higher Education.   See Nos. 624 and 625.   475

Anikeef, Alexis M.   Scholastic Achievement of Extension and Regular College Students.   See No. 239.   476

Arnold, James E.   "A Study of Adult Education Through University Extension with Special Reference to the University of Tennessee."   Ed. D. Dissertation.   University of Tennessee, 1955.   477

Banta, Clarence O.   We Can Afford Adult Education, In Junior College Journal, 25 (January, 1955) 279-282.
Any junior college can afford an adult education program and few can afford not to provide educational opportunity to adults of the community.   Financial support depends upon organizational type of the junior college, whether state, municipal, or county junior colleges.   Federal funds are

available in states in which adult education is organized
under the state department of education.   Many states
provide state aid.   Experts in public school finance believe education is largely a responsibility of the state.
Some junior college administrators believe that as many
sources of income as possible should be used to ease the
burden on any one source.   The writer does not agree
with some adult education leaders who believe that adults
should pay no course fees.   In courses for which fees
are paid, adult attendance is better, interest is higher,
and students place more value on the course.   A table
shows sources of income for public junior colleges of
Colorado, giving average per cent, per cent range, and
recommended range for each source.   Responsibility for
education should be shared by local community, state and
nation.   In states where no favorable legislation for state
aid for adult education exists, junior college administrators should press for such legislation.   478

Barbash, Jack.   "Universities and Unions in Workers' Education." New York: Harper [c1955].   206 pp.
A report and evaluation of an experiment by the Inter-
University Labor Education Committee, a corporation established by a grant from the Fund for Adult Education to
encourage extension of workers' education in international
affairs, economic understanding, and community participation by eight universities: Cornell, Rutgers, Pennsylvania
State, Illinois, Chicago, Roosevelt, Wisconsin, and University of California at Los Angeles.   This report serves
four purposes: (1) to make available an historical record
of a unique enterprise in university-labor movement collaboration; (2) to describe skills and insights developed in
the course of carrying on specific programs; (3) to determine the extent of fulfillment of the purposes of the
Fund for Adult Education and also of IULEC's own objectives; (4) to consider the broad effect of the programs on
the unions and on the universities.   Projects are described
as the sponsoring universities reported them, supplemented
by the author's field visits.   Part I of the book gives the
background of workers' education in the United States and
trends in university workers' education.   Part II describes
types of workers' education programs in the participating
universities in the following areas: (1) institutes and discussions in international affairs, community participation,
and economic understanding; (2) educational materials in
world affairs; workers' education councils; the "county a-
gent" in workers' education; labor health council; labor

participation in community affairs; integrating workers'
education into the local union; programs for union women;
review of the total program of each participating university and examination of extent of realization of goals.
Part III discusses the administration of IULEC as a national enterprise and the way the individual universities
administered their IULEC grants. Part IV is given to
general evaluation of the program, and recommendations,
and a discussion of the program's significance for workers'
education generally. Appendix A is a selected bibliography on workers' education in the United States. Appendix B is a briefly annotated list of publications issued by
participating universities in connection with IULEC activities. Appendix C is a list of officers of IULEC by university or labor organization represented.   479

Barden, John P. and others. The Theory of the Basic Arts
    Program, In Adult Education Journal, 8 (October, 1949)
    237-243.
        The Basic Arts Program, begun by the School of Gen-
    eral Studies at Cleveland College of Western Reserve Uni-
    versity in 1948-49, is addressed to the need of adult A-
    mericans to make responsible decisions in an era charac-
    terized by accelerating intellectual and social confusion.
    The program intends to provide tools for making justifi-
    able choices in all areas where significant choices can be
    made. The basic arts are those by which we extract theo-
    retical knowledge, practical knowledge, and productive or
    artistic knowledge from experience. Development of tech-
    nical facility in reading, listening, observing, talking and
    writing is a preliminary objective. Methods which lead to
    responsible decisions can profitably be studied in six
    areas: natural science, history and social science, writ-
    ing, visual arts, music and philosophy. The seminar
    method is used with credit given toward the degree of As-
    sociate in Philosophy. Non-credit participants are also
    admitted. No previous educational qualifications are re-
    quired for admission.   480

Benezet, Louis T. General Education For the Adult in Con-
    temporary Society, In Journal of General Education, 2
    (July, 1948) 336-340.
        The definition of what a university college ought to be
    and do lies in the character and needs of the students.
    The extent to which college education for adults can suc-
    ceed depends on understanding of its special nature and the

extent to which it differs from other types of college education. The writer proposes a program of adult education
characterized by flexibility in admissions, in policy on
prerequisites, and in curriculum. Admission would be
based upon a high school diploma or aptitude tests, with
specific subject requirements having little place. Students
would not be compressed into any particular discipline,
and majors in the conventional sense need not be offered
to the adult degree student. Courses for specialized
training would be available as electives, but the core of
the university college degree program would be general
education in contemporary society, which might be presented in two sections. In the first two academic years
a program of courses would be offered which introduce
focal problems of four areas: (1) communication, (2)
economics, (3) government, (4) human organics and personality. The last two years' study might be narrowed
to a study of one or two of the world's geographic and
cultural units. In addition to the responsibility to meet
the needs of its adult students, the university has the responsibility to teach its adult students their obligations to
society. In a true program of general education the two
objectives are concentric and coextensive.   481

Benne, Kenneth D.   Adult Education in the University, In
Journal of Higher Education, 27 (November, 1956) 413-
418; (December, 1956) 467-470.
The first part of this paper discusses the organization
of the American university as a social system. The second part discusses the role of adult education in university affairs. The university is a complexly organized activity, set off from other social systems by more or less
clear-cut boundaries. The central region of the university is in the departments of the college of arts and sciences and of the graduate school. The more peripheral
regions are occupied by the professional schools and extension activities of various kinds. The virtue of the center is to maintain precise, accurate, sufficiently qualified
statements and generalization about a number of things.
The virtue of the periphery is that it is closer to interests, concerns, and maintenance and growth requirements
of other parts of society, brings the wider society to the
university, and mediates between the two. Tension and
conflict between the central and peripheral regions of the
university can be used by the administration so that the
university can both keep alive to categories of social im-

portance and urgency, and maintain standards of intellectual rigor.   This tension and conflict is especially evident
in the university's adult education activities.   Adults want
help from the university in meeting demands of personal,
civic, and organizational concerns.   The proper goal of a-
dult teaching in the university is not so much to solve social or personal problems of adults in terms of the university's resources of knowledge or method, as to infuse
into personal and social situations where practical choices
are made some of the knowledge seeker's intellectual
functions, standards of precise and refined statement, and
urge to be accurate and intellectually responsible.   Three
reasons why there is a coincidence between the welfare of
the social system of the university and participation of its
residents in adult education are: (1) The adult group or
class provides an opportunity to study and experiment with
the application of knowledge to practical questions.   (2)
The adult student can provide the professor with insights
regarding gaps in existing knowledge and deficiencies in
communication among the disciplines and departments of
the university.   (3) One of the best ways of becoming a
better teacher is to go through the process of trying to
teach adults effectively.   The art of creative university administration is not to smooth over or erase conflict and
tension between the center and the periphery of the university, but to channel it into collaborative activity, with the
aim that society may become more intellectually responsible and that the university can become more socially responsive and relevant.   482

Beran, D. L.   A University Serves Its Community, In Adult
     Education, 2 (February, 1952) 108-112.
     Describes services of Drake University's extension pro-
gram as an example of services which schools can render
the community.   In addition to regular classes in Community College, other services are the Institute for Workers,
institutes for industrial and business groups, and a leadership training series held in cooperation with the Des
Moines P. T. A. Council.   The school or university has the
responsibility of making known to the community its services and its willingness to give assistance.   483

Bethel, Lawrence L.   The Satisfaction of Needs in Adult Ed-
     ucation, see No. 9.   484

Bittner, Walton S.   University and College Extension, In
     Handbook of Adult Education in the United States, edited

by Mary L. Ely.   New York: Institute of Adult Education,
Teachers College, Columbia University, 1948.   Pp. 214-
221; 465-478.

Discusses the meaning of the term "university extension," historical development, functions, scope, ages and
occupations of students, types of classes, evaluation as
to unity and integration, diversity of services and significant developments.   Descriptive notes on extension programs of a selected, representative list of educational institutions are given.   485

Bittner, Walton S.   University Teaching by Correspondence,
In Handbook of Adult Education in the United States, edited
by Mary L. Ely.   New York: Institute of Adult Education, Teachers College, Columbia University, 1948.   Pp.
222-224; 465-478.

Describes the origin and growth of correspondence
teaching; the U.S. Armed Forces Institute program as an
important development in correspondence teaching, and
cooperation of colleges and universities with the Institute;
evaluation of correspondence teaching as to quality of instruction, value of credits, and achievement of students.
Notes on university extension programs include information about correspondence courses offered by colleges and
universities.   486

Blakely, Robert J.   Freedom, the University, and Adult
Education, In National University Extension Association
Proceedings.   Thirty-Eighth Annual Meeting, East Lansing,
Michigan, May 3-6, 1953.   Vol. 36.   Pp. 20-29.

The writer criticizes a statement issued by the Association of American Universities, March 30, 1953, on
"The Rights and Responsibilities of Universities and Their
Faculties," the purpose of which was to defend intellectual
freedom within the university.   The statement makes no
mention of the change in climate of opinion which is inimi-
cal to freedom, and reflects no awareness of the extent of
the threat to academic freedom.   The fate of academic
freedom depends upon the fate of freedom in the national
culture.   The statement does not assert the power to influence the course of events which the university has
wielded in generations of greatness.   Preservation and advancement of freedom depend upon wisdom of decisions
and responsibility of actions of the general adult population.   This means that the most important level of education is adult education and the most important kind of a-
dult education is that aimed at fulfillment of individual per-

sonality and responsible exercise of citizenship, which is
liberal adult education.   The A. A. U.'s statement lists
only two functions of the university, research and teaching.   Extension workers must endeavor to establish dissemination of knowledge through adult education as a function of the university on an equal plane with and related
integrally to teaching and research.   Some administrators
and scholars believe that adult education is not properly
the role of the university.   There is a natural relationship between the university and the adult learner.   The
challenge of adult education is not merely to the extension
division, but to every college, school, department and resource of the university.   University extension should be
the projection of the entire university into the entire society.   Millions of adults wish to improve themselves as
persons and citizens; thousands of organizations feel the
need to enrich their services to their membership; many
specialists realize they must relate themselves and their
specialties to the general life of the community.   In this
situation will the university serve as an agency of unification, and decisively influence events of the time?   487

Blakely, Robert J.   The Relationship Between National Organizations, Foundations, and Universities in the General
Education of Adults, In   Peter E. Siegle, ed., The University's Responsibility for the General Education of A-
dults, Conference Report.   Chicago: Center for the Study
of Liberal Education for Adults, 1955.   Pp. 70-87.
    Discusses the meaning of general education, the lack of
liberal   or general education in the curriculum of the
modern university and in the programs of foundations, and
sketches seventeen areas in which universities, with the
help of foundations, can advance the general education of
adults: (1) self study by a university; (2) centers such as
C. S. L. E. A. ; (3) alumni working with the community; (4)
economic organizations such as business and labor; (5)
professional organizations; (6) learned societies; (7) self
government, especially on state and local levels; (8) liberal arts colleges and junior colleges; (9) voluntary organizations; (10) institutes and workshops; (11) the local community; (12) research in adult education; (13) mass media;
(14) the aging population; (15) parenthood; (16) development of leadership; (17) synthesizing ideas and analysis.
                                                     488 ⁄

Bower, Warren.   The Liberal Arts in Adult Education,
In National University Extension Association Proceedings.

Thirty-Ninth Annual Meeting, Gatlinburg, Tennessee, May
9-12, 1954. Vol. 37. Pp. 58-63.

Discusses the unique features of the Division of General Education of New York University and how they have
affected its programming and philosophy of adult education. Only non-credit evening courses are offered by the
Division. Courses for credit are offered by evening divisions within other colleges of New York University. The
Division of General Studies is an autonomous school,
headed by a Dean, with its own faculty and full authority
and academic competence to originate courses and curricula proper for needs of students. The philosophy and practice of adult education in New York University is based
upon belief in the effectiveness of liberal arts in the continuing education of adults. The Division also offers vocational courses, services to industry and management,
and services for many specialized needs. Central to the
Division's theory and practice in adult education is that
no hard and fast line can be drawn between vocational and
cultural courses. An effort is made to encourage teaching that opens up meaning and implications beyond immediate purposes of the courses. Teachers are not taken primarily from the University faculty. Many are recruited
among non-academic men of talent and reputation in their
own fields. The big task of re-molding men and society
through continuing education should be a partnership of all
means and devices that adult education has been able to
devise and use.   489

Bradley, Phillips. University's Role in Workers' Education,
In Adult Education Journal, 8 (April, 1949), 81-90.

Discusses the right of workers groups to university adult education, problems in developing a university workers' education program, joint educational participation with
labor groups, policy considerations, and goals of workers'
education. In addition to education related directly to immediate interests of labor unions, university workers' education services have a broader goal of education for understanding of economic, political, and social institutions.
This predominant objective in the current concern of labor
to broaden it s educational base is identical with that of
organized education itself.   490

Broady, Knute O., Betty B. Dimmit, and Russell Grumman.
"Three Arts Go On Tour." N.U.E.A. Studies in University Extension Education, No. 6. Bloomington, Indiana:
National University Extension Association, November,

1951.   13 pp.
A description of three projects as experiments in art
extension sponsored by N. U. E. A. member institutions.
Contents: "Nebraska's Traveling Art Galleries, " by K. O.
Broady; "The Touring Theatre of the University of Wash-
ington, " by Betty B. Dimmit; and "The North Carolina
Symphony Orchestra, " by Russell Grumman.   491

Brown, Giles T.   Two Minutes Are Not Enough, In Junior
College Journal, 25 (October, 1954) 75-82.
Lack of interest and ignorance in world affairs constitute   an opportunity and challenge to adult education in
this field.   Describes a course at Orange Coast College,
Costa Mesa, California, as an example of an adult education program in international affairs, including type of
students enrolled, reasons for enrollment, content, and
methods used.   Makes suggestions for such a course, resulting from experience with this particular program, as
to student response, qualifications of teachers, informality
in presentation, student interest, and values of the course.
                                                     492

Burrell, John A.   "A History of Adult Education at Columbia University, University Extension and the School of
General Studies. "   See No. 335.   493

Campbell, George W.   "University Extension Centers in the
United States. " Ed. D. Dissertation.   Columbia University,
Teachers College, 1957.   494

Campbell, George W.   University Extension Centers in
Higher Education, In Teachers College Record, 59 (December, 1957) 156-62.
University extension centers are defined as "off-campus locations at which universities provide physical facilities, some full-time personnel, and selected educational
programs for persons not utilizing campus resources. "
These centers have grown rapidly in recent years and will
probably continue to increase in importance as they are
used to relieve enrollment pressures.   The writer discusses the centers' responsibilities for providing lower-
division education of the junior college type, upper division education, and graduate study, for distributing, ex-
plaining and popularizing research, for offering programs
of community development, and responsibility of extension
personnel for organization, development, and operation of
well-rounded off-campus programs.   Extension centers

have a special responsibility in higher education which is
to minimize the gap between educational needs and available resources. This gap is now greatest at the community college level, but will probably shift to a higher level.
Because of connections with universities, ability to provide services of all types and levels, and adaptability to
changing conditions, extension centers are particularly
well suited to this task.   495

Carson, J. O.   Meeting Community Needs Through the
Community College, In   Association for Higher Education, Current Trends in Higher Education, 1949.   Official
Group Reports of the Fourth Annual National Conference
on Higher Education, Chicago, Illinois, April 4-7, 1949.
Washington, D.C.: National Education Association, Department of Higher Education, 1949. Pp. 90-98.
     The community college attempts to meet the post high
school educational needs of youth of college age, and also
to serve higher education needs of adults in the community.   While drawing on community resources and talents
for its program, the community college should provide
service and facilities for enriching the cultural life of the
community through educational experiences appropriate to
vocational, educational and cultural interests of adults.
Types of institutional organization, advantages of the community college as a form of higher education organization,
and determinants in establishing a community college are
discussed.   Well-rounded terminal curricula interrelate
two major functions, provision of a core of general education and offering vocational training.   In adult programs
most community colleges find that courses providing vocational or personal development are most popular and
courses pertaining to avocational skills and recreation are
second in popularity.   Demand for cultural courses has
often been disappointing.   Community colleges also render
valuable adult education services through staff members
who act as consultants in community planning.   Mature
teachers who can relate courses, whether general or vocational, to the world of work are most successful in dealing with adults and terminal students.   Administration of
adult education requires special ability in identifying need.
The community college offers challenging new educational
horizons and frontiers.   496

Center for the Study of Liberal Education for Adults. "A
Review of 1956, a Report of Center Activities During the
Past Year, and a Look Ahead." Chicago: C.S.L.E.A.,

1957. 45 pp.

An introductory section, "Some Observations and Hypotheses," underlines some insights about the Center's operation and hypotheses about its activity based upon experience of past years, and identifies several points of emphasis in program direction. Activities and projects of the Center are viewed as falling into five distinct categories, each described in a section of the report: (1) strengthening associations in the field of university adult education; (2) improving relationships between divisions of adult education and the total university; (3) strengthening leadership and faculty in university liberal education for adults; (4) clarifying relationships between universities and their communities; (5) experimentation with new approaches to programming in liberal education. Projects and activities in these areas include sponsorship of conferences, seminars and institutes, sponsorship of research studies and projects, cooperation with associations and voluntary organizations, experimental programs, development of materials for improving classroom instruction, field work and consultation, and publications. The last section, "Future Directions," describes seven major tasks which should dominate Center activity during the coming year: (1) experimental programs, (2) cooperation with associations, (3) improving relations between divisions of adult education and the total university, (4) strengthening leadership and faculty in university adult education, (5) clarifying relations of universities to their communities, (6) expanding field work and consultation, (7) communication and publication.   497

Colwell, Ernest C.   The University Serving Its Community and the Nation Through a Program of Adult Education, In National University Extension Association Proceedings, Thirty-Third Annual Meeting, Chicago, 1948.   Vol. 31. Pp. 67-69.

The task of adult education in America is too extensive for universities to do all that is needed, but if the job is to be done on a national scale, universities and colleges must take the lead in planning this program. Adult education should not be remedial or supplementary, but a distinct part of the total program for education of all citizens.   The primary task of adult education is to continue education for citizenship begun in formal schools.   Society can educate its citizens in the most important areas only by providing education for them as adults.   Universities and colleges are especially fitted to experiment with methods and contents of adult education.   498

Conley, William H.   The Adult Education Program in the
Catholic College, In National Catholic Educational Association Bulletin, 54 (August, 1957) 371-375.
    Discusses responsibility of the Catholic college for a-
dult education, and some guiding principles in developing
and carrying out a successful program. At present most
urban Catholic collegiate institutions offer some type of
program for adults consisting of courses identical with
day courses, courses provided solely for evening students,
graduate programs, non-credit courses, workshops, and
laboratory programs. Forces causing colleges to expand
adult work are: (1) administrators being continuously
made aware of the college's responsibility for adult education, (2) pressure by different community groups to offer
specified courses; (3) faculty members seeing a felt need
for courses they are qualified to teach; (4) financial re-
turns. Three principles are suggested for use in evaluating present programs and in serving as a guide in introduction of future offerings: (1) Adult education programs
should be in harmony with stated objectives of the institution. This principle restricts offerings to those areas in
which there is intellectual content. Two other areas appropriate to the university are development of leaders for
adult education and research.   (2) Directing learning activities of adults is different from directing that of later
adolescents. (3) Organization for adult education depends
on local conditions. Types of organization include the
separate administrative unit called university college; the
evening college or evening division which may or may not
be autonomous units; the organization in which the day
dean or deans control the adult program.   Evaluation of
existing structure or planning of the future organization
should include careful consideration of local conditions and
judgment on which type of organization can achieve desired
goals.   499

Conley, William H.   The University's Role in Adult Education, In Journal of Higher Education, 26 (January, 1955)
14-17.
    Discusses multiple functions of the university in adult
education: (1) to provide regular degree programs to
persons who have delayed their education and wish to have
a unified program, and a certificate or diploma program
for those interested in a limited area; (2) to provide a
continuation of education for those who have degrees or

some college work; (3) to meet vocational and professional needs in harmony with objectives of the university; (4)
to develop leaders in adult education; (5) to carry on research in adult education. Although there are pressures
to expand into other fields, the university can perform its
greatest service by adhering to activities in harmony with
its objectives.   500

Cooper, William M. Adult Education Programs of Negro
    Colleges and Universities. See No. 359.   501

Cousins, Norman. Where Higher Education Begins, In New
    York State Education, 37 (October, 1949) 11-14+; same
    condensed under title, The Whole Man, In National Edu-
    cation Association Journal, 39 (April, 1950) 264-265.
       Due to the vast expansion of human experience and
    knowledge, a program for true undergraduate higher edu-
    cation requires extension beyond the traditional four years.
    What form an extension of college training may take will
    be open to considerable disagreement. It is a fruitful
    field for pioneering by colleges and universities. A great
    opportunity faces colleges and universities in the field of
    adult education. This has two aspects: (1) the field of
    general knowledge and the arts, and (2) the field of those
    professions closely related to public welfare. By "adult
    education" is meant the need for a coordinated national
    program for continued education for college graduates.
    The plan here described is for the development of the
    whole man, one who will have an understanding of inter-
    connections and interrelationships within the entire province
    of organized knowledge. The individual requires both spe-
    cialization and general study. Over and above specialized
    training, there is a vast area to be cultivated in making a
    new science of integration, built on interdependence of
    knowledge. Since we live in an interdependent world, we
    must educate for interdependent living. The transcendent
    goal of education today is preparation for world citizen-
    ship under freedom.   502

Crimi, James E. "Adult Education in the Liberal Arts
    Colleges." See No. 360.   503

Darden, Colgate W., Jr. The Most Pressing Question, In
    Adult Education Journal, 7 (January, 1948) 14-15.
       The President of the University of Virginia, in his in-
    augural address, October 1, 1947, made a plea for greater
    emphasis on adult education by the University. The most

pressing question is what is to be done for the seventy-
five per cent of high school graduates who go to work,
not to college. Given the opportunity, they can supply a
larger number of able citizens than are supplied by colleges and universities. The resources of the University
should be mobilized behind a carefully prepared program
of adult education. The day will come when adult education will eclipse in effectiveness anything ever done with
children. The adult can profit more from learning because of life experience. Experiments of the Danes in
this field are of great value. It is hoped that the University of Virginia will be able to carry on experiments a-
mong the people of Virginia. Through adult education it
may be possible to solve the enigma of how to build a society which will endure.   504

Davis, George E.   What Will Be the Changing Responsi-
    bilities of the Colleges and Universities to Adult Educa-
    tion, In   Association for Higher Education, Current Is-
    sues in Higher Education, 1957.   Proceedings of the
    Twelfth Annual National Conference on Higher Education,
    Chicago, Illinois, March 3-6, 1957.   Edited by G. Kerry
    Smith.   Washington, D.C.:   National Education Associa-
    tion, Association for Higher Education [c1957]. Pp. 105-
    107.
        Currently the interest in liberal education for adults
    has gained eminence. It represents an area which all ad-
    ministrators of adult education programs increasingly
    need to develop. However, there are needs that will not
    be completely served by expansion of liberal education
    programs as currently conceived. Colleges and univer-
    sities must be increasingly involved in semi-professional
    programs relating to particular occupational areas. A re-
    view of problems will indicate areas in which the college
    and university can analyze needs and suggest ways of
    meeting them, and will also indicate areas better handled
    by representatives of industry. No college or university
    can administer a complete adult education program, but
    those responsible for adult education activities can work
    through public schools, libraries, churches and other cul-
    tural agencies. The greatest service the college or uni-
    versity can perform is to keep informed about new develop-
    ments in the field and new opportunities for service, and
    acquaint heads of community agencies with what they are.
    Through excellent adult education programs these commu-
    nity agencies can gain needed community support. Adult
    education needs to offer retraining programs in technical

fields, and also education for increasing leisure, including liberal education, hobby interests, and civic activities leading to community development and improvement. Colleges and universities should take the lead in encouraging studies of problems of aging, in preparing individuals for changes of retirement, and in collecting and disseminating facts concerning successful programs in this area. There is need for research programs in adult education in the areas of health, employment, standards of living, educational needs, recreation, spiritual needs and approaches to solving problems in these areas. Through research and increased involvement of staffs of colleges and universities in solution of adult education problems will come a more complete comprehension of the magnitude of the field and a better appreciation of the contributions college and university staff members may make to solution of these problems.   505

Demarest, G. Stuart. The Evening College at Rutgers, In New Directions for University Adult Education: Institution Centered. Notes and Essays on Education for Adults, No. 11. Chicago: Center for the Study of Liberal Education for Adults, 1955. Pp. 1-24.

The purpose of the paper is "to show the advantages of a complete, full-time evening college faculty and staff concerned exclusively with education of adults as it is now operating in University College of Rutgers University, and to consider how such a plan fits into the present state of university adult education." Includes historical development of University College of Rutgers University; characteristics of organization of the College; academic departments; part-time faculty; financial problems; integration with the University; entrance requirements; academic standards; characteristics of students; curriculum.   506

Dickerman, Watson, Adult Education Through University Extension, In California Journal of Secondary Education, 21 (November, 1946) 310-312.

Describes services of the University of California Extension, particularly for veterans, in the reconversion period. It is the responsibility of adult education in the reconversion period to provide three significant types of services: (1) education, retraining, and guidance for veterans and war workers; (2) education for responsible international and community citizenship; (3) opportunities for cultivation of personal interests. This is similar to the responsibilities of adult education in normal times to

provide education for occupational improvement, more responsible citizenship, and personal growth. The University finds these needs can be met through adaptation and
expansion of existing services of its five major departments: classes, correspondence courses, institutes, lectures, and visual services.   507

Diekhoff, John S. Alumni University, In Journal of Higher
    Education, 28 (October, 1957) 353-360; 407.
    Urges universities to provide programs of adult educa-
tion for college graduates to bring them up to date in
changing fields such as natural sciences and social sciences, and to provide general education from which the a-
dult college graduate can benefit more in his maturity
than as an undergraduate.   508

Diekhoff, John S. From the Cradle to the Grave, In Journal
    of Higher Education, 26 (January, 1955) 10-12.
    It is never too late to start school, but it is easy to
depend on school too long. The important adult education
functions of the evening college are in a sense remedial
education: (1) to provide special instruction in subjects
within the purview of the university; (2) to provide vocational or professional up-grade training; (3) to provide
educational programs designed to foster the qualities that
make an educated man. None of these activities should be
interminable. Liberal education ends with intellectual maturity, which includes independence of schools, teachers,
and school programs. The measure of success of an
evening college should not be in terms of those who keep
coming back, but in terms of those who stop coming with
"unfelt needs" satisfied and a felt need to keep learning
still unsatisfied.   509

Diekhoff, John S. "Schooling for Maturity." Notes and Es-
    says on Education for Adults, No. 13. Chicago: Center
    for the Study of Liberal Education for Adults, 1955. 19 pp.
    An expansion of the remarks made by the author under
the title, "From the Cradle to the Grave." See No. 509.
                                                        510

Diekhoff, John S. Time Off for Good Behavior, In Journal
    of General Education, 7 (October, 1952) 41-47.
    The college degree program for adolescents, based on
certain specified courses and amassing a certain number
of credits, is not appropriate for adults. The replica of
the day program is the most common liberal arts activity

of evening colleges.   There is a significant difference between day and evening college students even when the age
difference is only a few years, because of job and family
responsibilities, experience, attitudes, needs and understanding.   The type of adult program consisting of various
courses, referred to as the "evening cafeteria," often includes many things that are not education in the sense
that they form or cultivate the intellect.   Certificate programs or "associate degrees" for adults are steps in the
right direction, but they do not solve the problem because
they are also awarded on the basis of credits amassed,
and are considered inferior to the Bachelor's degree.
What adults need is an opportunity to plan their formal
schooling and to earn degrees in terms of what they know
and what they can do.   The College of the University of
Chicago has such a plan for undergraduates, in which both
admission and graduation are determined by examinations
constructed to test accomplishments of students.   Three
important differences between this program and those of
other colleges are: (1) the policy of stating requirements
for graduation in terms of comprehensive examinations
rather than time served in class, and use of placement
tests to determine what portion of the college program the
student had mastered before beginning his work in the College; (2) giving of primacy to discussion as a method of
teaching and learning; (3) subordination of the textbook to
primary sources as material to be studied.   Far-sighted
evening colleges can establish an appropriate integrated
program of liberal education, proposing the degree for that
program only after its merit has been demonstrated.   At-
tacks against "standards" can be met by challenges to
make comparative studies of achievement of day and evening students. Such a program would establish far reaching
precedents in adult education and contribute to improvement of higher education generally.   511

Douglass, Harl R.   Adult Education--an Impressive Challenge
    for the Community College, In Junior College Journal, 25
    (April, 1955) 448-452.
        Early junior colleges were largely college preparatory.
    In the 1930's and 1940's terminal programs spread widely.
    More recently junior colleges have begun to develop cur-
    riculum courses of the semi-professional and technical
    type.   The community college concept includes not only
    teaching along lines of community needs and resources,
    but also reaching a larger number of adults with educa-
    tional programs.   Among the many types of adult educa-

tion courses and programs are: (1) vocational courses,
(2) courses related to opportunities for education for leisure; (3) cultural study courses; (4) courses on various
aspects of parenthood. Improvement of public relations
and development of good will is important in the program
of adult education. Organization of courses and methods
of teaching should be different for adults than for college
students. Rarely should there be credits or examinations.
Materials should be carefully selected to meet needs and
interests of adults. Teachers should be carefully selected
and be aware of the necessity of planning and teaching in
a manner suitable for adults.   512

Durham, Elizabeth W.   Alumni Education, In Handbook of
Adult Education in the United States, edited by Mary L.
Ely. New York: Institute of Adult Education, Teachers
College, Columbia University, 1948. Pp. 225-227; 320-
325.
    Alumni education dates from the end of World War I
when there was spreading recognition by colleges of the
possibilities inherent in well organized alumni bodies. The
challenge has been met first in liberal arts colleges with
two general types of programs, the first centered in books
and reading lists, the second centered in group activity,
designated variously as alumni lectures, conferences, forums, institutes, or as "alumni colleges." Many programs
of both types ended with World War II. A survey in 1946
sent to two hundred members of the American Alumni
Council found that fifty-nine institutions were carrying on
some type of post-collegiate education for their graduates
and former students. Urban universities have found it
easy to establish programs of alumni education because of
large groups of alumni in their vicinities. Since the war
there has been an increase in interest which may be
traced to the return to civilian life of alumni who were
matured by military service and by the realization of the
importance of higher education. Brief descriptions of
thirty-one programs representing various types of alumni
education, listed alphabetically by names of colleges and
universities, are given.   513

Dyer, John P. "Ivory Towers in the Market Place; the
Evening College in American Education." Indianapolis:
Bobbs-Merrill [c1956]. 205 pp.
    "A report on the university evening college, its nature,
its practices, and its problems, and a suggestion of what
its role probably should be in our contemporary society."

Based upon extensive research conducted under the auspices of the Center for the Study of Liberal Education for Adults. Chapters are: "The Evening College Student;" "Development of the Evening College;" "The Evening College and the Community;" "The Curriculum--Real and Imaginary;" "Dean and Faculty;" "A Role for the Evening College;" "Liberal Education."   514

Dyer, John P.   Should Our Colleges and Universities Rethink Their Objectives in Adult Education? In   Association for Higher Education, Current Issues in Higher Education, 1954.   Proceedings of the Ninth Annual National Conference on Higher Education, Chicago, Illinois, March 4-6, 1954. Edited by G. Kerry Smith. Washington, D.C., National Education Association, Association for Higher Education [c1954]. Pp. 239-242.
     The fact that many colleges and universities have some form of a program for adults does not mean that there has been any really basic thinking done about these programs. The college or university is youth-centered, and adult departments are treated as appendages not vital to educational progress.   Basic thinking on adult education must include the following: (1) There must be a basic frame of mind or fundamental credo that education must be based on a belief in true democratic processes, and that education is for people, not just for youngsters in the daytime. (2) This credo must be translated into terms not only of the individual, but of the community and its needs.   (3) There must be enough flexibility to examine critically teachers and curricula in terms of adult needs and capacities.   (4) An institution must decide its goals for an adult program and the foci of effort.   (5) The administrative relationship between the adult education division and the other divisions must be clearly defined and understood. Adult education is a vital force which requires earnest thinking, objective and constructive criticism, and sustained attention.   515

Eells, Walter C.   The Community's College, In Adult Education Journal, 4 (January, 1945) 13-17.
     Statistics are given for the total enrollment of junior colleges, the adult student enrollment, and percentage of adult students in the total enrollment for 1936-1944. These figures show that the junior college is a rapidly growing phase of American education and that the most rapid junior college growth is in the field of adult education.   This increase is due to the fact that the junior col-

lege, particularly the local, publicly controlled junior
college, is increasingly being thought of by its leaders
and supporters as a community institution with the opportunity and obligation to meet the educational needs at the
college level of all the community's citizens.   In many
cases the junior college can organize and operate a complete adult education service more effectively, convenient-
ly, and economically than any other agency.   Courses offered include both those designed to develop vocational
competence and those designed to raise the general cultural level of the community and to develop more intelligent citizenship.   Several examples are given of types of
work given in widely scattered institutions to suggest the
varied ways in which progressive junior colleges are attempting to meet the needs of their communities.   Every
indication points to a still wider and more vigorous response to this educational opportunity in the decade ahead.
                                                          516

Eisenhower, Milton.   Responsibility of the University for
   Adult Education,   In National University Extension Association Proceedings, Fortieth Annual Meeting, Pennsylvania
   State University, May 1-4, 1955. Vol. 38. Pp. 78-84.
   The need for extension services of an institution of
higher education is as critical as that for on-campus instruction and research.   The extension function should be
regarded as equal with the other two in the development
of the institution's total educational program.   Five major
problems facing the American people that pinpoint the
critical need for strengthening and expanding university-
related adult education programs are: (1) displacement of
hand labor by an accelerating technology and the consequent requirement for many levels of training in various
occupations and professions; (2) the need of continuing
liberal adult education for people of all levels of education
in an age of extreme specialization; (3) the problem of
how best to meet social, economic, and cultural needs of
an aging population; (4) the problem of how to develop motivation and opportunity for constructive use of leisure
time; (5) need of developing among all citizens the capacity to think in global, as well as local and national
terms, understanding of world problems, and an appreciation of basic moral values of a free society.   517

Essert, Paul L.   "Report to Teachers College on Adult Education in the United States and Its Implications to Education." See No. 43.   518

"Evaluating the Evening College as a Teaching Institution."
Report of the Southern Regional Faculty Seminar, New Orleans, Louisiana, November 10-13, 1955. See No. 286.
                                                      519

Fitchett, E. Horace. "What Are the Responsibilities of Negro Colleges for the Adult Education of Negroes in the
Post-War World?" See No. 365.   520

Georgia. West Georgia College. "College in the Country,
a Program of Education for Adults." Carrollton,
Georgia: The College, 1955. 29 pp.
    "College in the Country" is a program of adult educa-
tion in fourteen communities near West Georgia College,
a unit of the University System of Georgia. The program
has also spread to other centers. A Policy Committee,
made up of administrative officers of West Georgia College, considers all requests for assistance to College in
the Country groups and for new projects in terms of staff
time, consultants and leaders available. No set pattern
for the program has been developed; dissimilarities in
communities are taken into account and the program and
leaders profit from experiences with different community
groups. Leaders are found among professional educators,
semi-professional and lay people. Potential leaders e-
merge as members participate in discussion meetings, and
form a Planning Committee or Conversation Team which
contributes to the program of studies. Special consultants
and resource leaders are brought in from time to time.
West Georgia College cooperates with agencies requesting
study programs. Subjects studied have been concerned
with history, world affairs, lives of great men, family
life and understanding children, cultural and scientific subjects. Some techniques used are informal study-discus-
sion groups, films, speakers followed by audience discussion, role playing, panel-symposiums, forums, buzz sessions, studycades and field trips, and surveys. Through
the College in the Country programs there has been a
deepening of insights, awareness of opportunities for learning, feeling of togetherness, better understanding of other
peoples, and appreciation of opinions of others. Leadership has been developed and community welfare has been
advanced.   521

Getsinger, Joseph W. Adult Education, a Separate Major
Division of Education, In School and Society, 63 (April 27,
1946) 314-316.

A reply to an article by Maurice Matloff (see No. 568)
who proposed that colleges undertake a major role in
post-war adult education. Getsinger points out that colleges can do only a small part of the job of adult education. He describes adult education as a major division of
education, just as elementary, secondary, and higher education.   522

Gillen, Wilfred D.   The Institute of Humanistic Studies for
Executives: an Experiment in Adult Education, In   Fund
for Adult Education, Liberal Adult Education.   White
Plains, N. Y. :   F. A. E. , 1956.   Pp. 15-27.
A description of the University of Pennsylvania Institute of Humanistic Studies, developed with the cooperation
of and for the American Telephone and Telegraph Company. The Company has had training courses both technical and non-technical, but a program was needed which
would "sharpen the individual's creative insight, widen his
frame of reference to many fields of human behavior, and
provide him with some techniques with which he could test
the logic and consistency of his own thinking. " The administration of this program has been in the hands of a
committee of five faculty members of the University of
Pennsylvania, two representatives of the Telephone Company, with the provost of the University as chairman. Objectives are: (1) to enable a potential future executive to
understand and interpret social, political and economic
changes, national and worldwide, which will influence problems of corporate management increasingly in the future;
(2) to indicate the importance, impact and use of history,
science, philosophy, and the arts, particularly as they influence large groups of people such as employees, cus-
tomers, and stockholders; (3) to motivate participants in
the program to accept the concept of intellectual activity
as a never-ending process to be continued through life;
(4) to balance with a humanistic background the almost
complete attention generally given by younger men to technical knowledge and competence; (5) to offset a tendency
to over-conformity which occurs in a business which is
highly specialized and which promotes from within the organization. Men are selected from middle management
groups on the basis of past performance and expected potential for progression in the business. Their educational
backgrounds are varied, and in each group there have been
some non-college men. The permanent faculty is drawn
primarily from the University of Pennsylvania, with some
from Swarthmore and Bryn Mawr, and additional guest

lecturers. Subjects are grouped in four major fields:
history, science, philosophy, and the arts. Teaching
methods include lectures, discussions, seminars, and
field trips. There are no marks or examinations, and
no reports about individual students to the Company. E-
valuation of the program by means of psychological tests
has given valuable information about the curriculum and
has pointed the way toward modifications. Some of the
results of the experiment are summarized: (1) Participants were enthusiastic and indicated they have increased
personal identity and self-realization. (2) They have
greater intellectual curiosity and self-confidence and are
better able to express ideas. (3) It has made them better
family men, better citizens in their communities, and
better individuals. Results have encouraged the Company
to plan additional experimental programs at Williams,
Dartmouth, and Swarthmore College.   523

Goldwin, Robert A., ed. "Toward the Liberally Educated
Executive." White Plains, N.Y.: Fund for Adult Education, 1957. 111 pp.
   A collection of articles designed to illustrate three
propositions fundamental to an understanding of the education of executives: (1) Tasks executives face, arising out
of economic and social roles of corporations, are of a
magnitude that cannot be grasped and dealt with except by
men with "big" minds. (2) In terms of education, the
best way to cultivate the requisite "bigness" of mind is
through liberal studies. (3) Since the needs for understanding and insight are never wholly met, liberal education should be continuous throughout life. Selections include: "Introduction," by C. Scott Fletcher; "Specific
Needs for Leadership in Management," by Gilbert W.
Chapman; "A Lifetime of Learning," by Francis H. Horn;
"Bell Telephone's Experiment in Education," by E. Digby
Baltzell; "Why Should a Company Spend Money in This
Way?" by Wilfred D. Gillen; "The Big Job of the Mo-
ment," by Frank W. Abrams; "When Is Education Liberal?" by Ralph B. Perry; "Aims of Education," by Alfred
N. Whitehead; "Liberal Arts as Training for Executives,"
by Frederick E. Pamp, Jr.; "Importance of Language,"
by Peter F. Drucker; "An Ulcer, Gentlemen, Is an Un-
written Poem," by John Ciardi; "Communications and
Distribution," by Frederick R. Gamble; "Labor, Leisure,
and Liberal Education," by Mortimer J. Adler; "Liberal
Education for Business Leadership," by J. Roby Kidd;
"Social Innovation," by Peter F. Drucker; "The Free In-

dividual and the Free Society," by Robert J. Blakely;
"The Cultivation of the Mind," by Clarence B. Randall.
                                                    524

Gordon, Morton, ed. "New Dimensions of University Responsibility for the Liberal Education of Adults;" a Report of the Daytona Beach Conference of Urban University
Presidents, Daytona Beach, Florida, May 3-6, 1956.
Chicago: Center for the Study of Liberal Education for A-
dults, 1956. 44 p.
    Report of a seminar co-sponsored by the Association of
Urban Universities and C. S. L. E. A. to (1) provide a national forum in which educators could exchange views concerning the urban university's pioneering mission for liberal education of adults; (2) enhance participants' awareness
of important new trends in university adult education; and
(3) produce a statement of policy for guidance of the Center and of deans and directors of adult education in further
exploration of the theme of the seminar. Areas of activity and purposes of C. S. L. E. A. are defined in the introduction. The report contains "A Policy Statement;" the
keynote address, "The Urban Environment's Challenge to
the University," by George D. Stoddard (see no. 616);
and a list of five experimental programs (Brooklyn College
Experimental Degree Program, Basic Program of Liberal
Education for Adults at University of Chicago, Queens
College Seminars for Adults, Master's Degree in General
or Liberal Education, and Laboratory College for Adults)
with the principle illustrated by each, and a discussion of
participants' reaction to these models. Appended are the
Seminar Agenda, Roster of Participants, and Seminar
Staff.   525

Gordon, Morton. "The Role of Liberal Arts in the University Evening College Curriculum," a Report of a Conference of Liberal Arts Deans Held at Pinebrook, New York,
October 14-17, 1954. Chicago: Center for the Study of
Liberal Education for Adults [1955] 15 pp.
    Objectives of the Conference were: (1) to provide a na-
tional forum in which prominent deans of liberal arts
could exchange views; (2) to enhance the deans' awareness
of the importance of university-level adult education; (3)
to sharpen basic issues and problems amenable to research
and experimentation by the Center and by deans and directors of the Association of University Evening Colleges.
Problems discussed were: the role of the university in
adult education, how the liberal arts can be adapted to the

interests, experiences, and special abilities and disabili-
ties of adults, academic standards, special problems of
non-credit liberal arts programs for adults, and merchandizing liberal arts programs. Impressions and conclusions drawn were that the tenor of comments indicated
a need for the Center or some other agency to communi-
cate to liberal arts deans information about adult education
in general and about the evening college movement; and
that a greater liaison between day and evening deans is
required for exchange of views concerning objectives and
methods of the evening college to establish a basis for
working out problems to the satisfaction of both day and
evening divisions. As a result of the Conference, at
least some of the deans became more aware that university-level adult education is a serious and legitimate field,
that problems of this field are complex and that "respectable" research can contribute to their understanding and
solution, and that there are many kinds of evening colleges
and many kinds of relationships between day and evening
colleges. In view of these impressions and conclusions,
alternative next steps open to the Center seem to be:
(1) a conference of evening deans to explore methods of
improving relations with day divisions; (2) a conference
of pairs of evening and day deans to discuss mutual problems; (3) a conference of evening deans, day deans, and
faculty to accomplish purposes stated in (1) and (2). 526

Graney, Maurice. General Extension Courses, Their Place
in Publicly Supported Institutions of Higher Education, In
Journal of Higher Education, 28 (January, 1957) 10-14,
57-58.
      The general extension program in higher education is of
value because it is oriented toward purposes, wishes, and
welfare of a large segment of the citizens in a democracy.
An examination of general extension activities of modern
universities reveals four clear-cut purposes: (1) Expansion of resources and services to individuals and institutions within the culture which supports the university.
This service directs attention to those persons desiring
formal collegiate instruction, and embraces almost every
subject area.   (2) Opportunity for any learning important
to problems and lives of the people served.   This is a-
chieved by instruction in two major categories, non-credit
courses of college grade and courses of less than college
grade specialized to meet real needs and demands.   (3)
Promotion of understanding of educational and research
processes so that these processes will be supported by the

community. (4) Conduct of exploratory and developmental work to determine areas of university activity in a dynamic society. Extension service is the "present" of a structure of which the instruction is the "past" and research is the "future." Increasing acceptance of extension service is reflected in statistics of enrollment, staffs and budgets. Almost every subject matter field is covered with about half of the instruction given in the arts and sciences. Any institution of higher education should consider carefully its general extension activity as an instrument of over-all institutional policy, especially publicly supported institutions such as state universities and land grant colleges.   527

Grumman, Russell M. and others. "University Extension in Action." See No. 340.   528

Guzzetta, D. J. A Three-Pronged University Program, In Adult Leadership, 6 (September, 1957) 78-80.
Adult education services of the University of Akron are in three clearly defined areas of responsibility, the Evening College, The Community College, and the Institute for Civic Education. The Evening College offers courses for certificates and degrees, and has a traditional, academic character. The Community College has a program designed to meet specific community needs with shorter, non-credit courses. This area also serves as an experimental phase of operation for varying classroom type courses. It often co-sponsors series and courses with other agencies. The Institute for Civic Education provides special services and programs to groups in a variety of fields, such as conferences and workshops, information for group or organizational meetings and informal programs in the general area of liberal adult education. This three-pronged program of the University of Akron and similar programs are evidence that our universities can effectively expand into "non-traditional" channels and meet a variety of needs without sacrificing educational stature.
529

Hammarberg, Helen V. "Informal Adult Education Programs." N.U.E.A. Studies in University Extension Education, No. 9. Bloomington, Indiana: National University Extension Association, 1953. 16 pp.
A description of the administration and operation of informal programs such as lectures, institutes, conferences, forums, short courses, workshops, tours, etc., at Pennsyl-

vania State College, University of Chicago, and University
of California.   530

Harrison, R. Wendell.   The Community Responsibilities of
    Institutions of Higher Learning, In Institute for Admini-
    strative Officers of Higher Institutions Proceedings, Vol.
    20, The Community Responsibilities of Institutions of
    Higher Learning.   Chicago: University of Chicago Press,
    1948.   Pp. 1-4.
        The first responsibility of a college to the community
    is to do its own work well.   The second responsibility is
    to assist in the general improving of the quality of higher
    education.   But the college must also be alert to the pos-
    sibilities of contributions to the community.   It must take
    the lead in planning the adult education program.   It must
    explore community needs and problems and find means of
    meeting them.   531

Horn, Francis H.   The Community Responsibilities of In-
    stitutions of Higher Education, In Association for Higher
    Education, Current Issues in Higher Education, 1950.
    Major Addresses, Official Group Reports, and Resolutions
    of the Fifth Annual National Conference on Higher Educa-
    tion, Chicago, Illinois, April 17-19, 1950.   Edited by R.
    W. McDonald and R. C. Maul.   Washington, D. C.:   Na-
    tional Education Association of the U.S., Department of
    Higher Education [c1951] 168-173.
        Every institution of higher education has some responsi-
    bility to its community.   Expansion of educational oppor-
    tunity for youth of the community through full-time, day
    programs is one of the major responsibilities.   The sec-
    ond broad category of community responsibility comprises
    educational services which supplement and extend regular
    programs, and which include courses comparable to those
    of the undergraduate program, degree programs not con-
    fined to duplication of daytime courses, courses for voca-
    tional and professional advancement as well as for per-
    sonal and cultural development, non-degree programs lead-
    ing to a certificate, isolated courses with or without aca-
    demic credit, consultant and advisory services, clinics
    and testing laboratories, audio-visual materials, and re-
    search and analysis studies.   Which services a college or
    university will render will depend first upon institutional
    factors of basic objectives, size and tradition, and re-
    sources, and second, upon the nature and needs of the'
    community.   In these critical times requiring an informed
    and educated citizenry, every college and university must

contribute to the continuing education of adults in its community. In many institutions of higher education the adult
education program will be the most important service they
render to the local community.   532

Horn, Francis H.   International Understanding, the Lament
of a Discouraged Adult Educator, In Adult Education Journal, 9 (July, 1950) 109-118.
    The Dean of McCoy College of Johns Hopkins Univer-
sity describes his efforts to develop a program of adult
education for more effective citizenship in the world community, which he considers the most important goal of a-
dult education.   He expresses disappointment and dis-
couragement at the lack of interest in courses on international affairs and offers some explanations and invites suggestions of other adult educators for making this type of
program more successful.   The article is followed by comments of Wilbur C. Hallenbeck, John P. Barden, Maria
Rogers, and Shepherd L. Witman.   533

Houle, Cyril O.   The American University and Adult Education, In Educational Record, 36 (October, 1955) 336-345.
    A paper originally presented to a national conference of
university administrators, sponsored by the Center for the
Study of Liberal Education for Adults.   University adult
education in the United States has existed for a century
and a half, but all stages of its development may still be
seen in existing programs.   In the education of adults,
our generation sees the goal of creating a better society
by giving all men the opportunity to continue to learn
throughout life.   Early patterns were good to the extent
that they provided immediate gratification and awakened desire for further knowledge.   In moving toward broader
goals and a more comprehensive program, deans of adult
education have discovered that the new dimension of lifelong learning has changed their perspective toward traditional ends of university education.   Three conclusions are
of major importance: (1) Adult education restores to liberal education an older and broader interpretation than
customarily provided on our campuses.   Mature adults are
more concerned with and more competent to handle deeper
and less precise subjects than undergraduates.   (2) Professional education of adults must have different and more
complex goals than professional education offered to young
people.   Its task is one of in-service education which goes
on through a life-time.   (3) There are other ends of education which are coordinate with and perhaps equally im-

portant to liberal and professional education. They are
concerned with practical but non-vocational responsibilities
of adults related to their personal and social lives. A
fourth broad goal is recreative education. The four goals
are intertwined in real life. Extension and evening college deans must demonstrate the importance of building
new programs concerned with the nature, needs, and interests of adults, and of the development of an adequate
system of administration which achieves both flexibility
and coordination. Deans of adult education operate under
several disadvantages not shared by fellow deans: (1)
lack of a single, all-embracing goal, and the necessity of
playing many roles; (2) lack of any recognized area of
content as their own; (3) lack of cooperation from colleagues from departments or schools within the university
in building extension programs; (4) problems arising from
having or not having their own faculties; (5) uniqueness of
the evening college or extension division which makes it
impossible to fit into a rigid scheme. A period of further
growth of university adult education is required before issues become clear and an acceptable pattern emerges.

534

Houle, Cyril O. "Community Educational Services as an
    Emerging Function of Higher Education," in Institute for
    Administrative Officers of Higher Institutions Proceedings,
    Vol. 20, The Community Responsibilities of Institutions of
    Higher Learning. Chicago: University of Chicago Press,
    1948. Pp. 5-13.
    Some changes have taken place in colleges and univer-
sities due to internal adaptation to the world, but the
greatest changes in the future will come from the motion
outward to provide community services to the adult public.
Included will be: changes in undergraduate and graduate
curriculums; vitalization of teaching methods; change in
organizational structure of colleges and universities; community education services will help to support colleges and
universities. Colleges and universities have a great future
in the field of adult education if they rise to the challenge.

535

Houle, Cyril O. Education for Adult Leadership, In Adult
    Education, 8 (Autumn, 1957) 3-17.
    The development of continuing education has added a
new dimension to the work of universities. The central
function of the university in continuing education is to develop and serve mature self-educating leaders who can

guide the social change of the future. A second broad
task is to put the knowledge of its faculty at the service
of those who have already developed a strong habit of self
education, for example, in programs to help people advance in their professions, meet new tasks which adulthood brings, aid in enlargement of understanding and appreciation of life through liberal education. A third task
of the university in this field is to study its implications
for the operation of the whole institution, in its organization and in its cooperation with other agencies. In the
future, universities will do more research on the psychology of adult learning in order better to educate adult educators.   536

Houle, Cyril O. "The Evening College: Its Purposes and
Its Relationships Within the University." Detroit: Association of Urban Universities, Wayne University, 1953.
12 pp.   Same in Association of Urban Universities Proceedings.   Thirty-Ninth Annual Meeting, St. Louis, October 18-19, 1953.   Pp. 91-108.   Same condensed:
Journal of Higher Education, 25 (October, 1954) 362-372;
398-399.
    Discusses, through description of an imaginary institu-
tion as illustration, the growth and development of the
university evening college, its functions, objectives, areas
of activity, programs, methods of instruction, administration, faculty, finance, relationships within the university,
relationships with the community, collaboration with other
institutions of higher education, success, and potentialities.   537

Houle, Cyril O. and Charles A. Nelson. "The University,
the Citizen, and World Affairs." Washington, D.C.:
American Council on Education, 1956.   179 pp.
    Co-sponsored by the Carnegie Endowment for Interna-
tional Peace, the Adult Education Association, the Association of University Evening Colleges, and the National University Extension Association, this comprehensive treatment of the university's role in educating adults about
world affairs considers both the present scope and future
development of this work.   The ten chapters discuss the
goal and methods of teaching understanding of world affairs as the responsibility of the adult educator; public
opinion and foreign affairs; principles which define the
role of the university in the field of adult education; an
analysis of the kinds of adult education activities which
universities now sponsor and the organization of these services within the university; the kinds of education suitable

for each of four major groups of citizens--the inattentive
citizen, the attentive citizen, the actively concerned citizen, and the specialist; and a general summary of the
main themes of the book with a program of action based
upon ends desired, means available, the distinctive role
of the university and ways of overcoming deterrents to
further development of education in world affairs.   538

Hudson, Robert B.   Extension of the Campus, In Adult Education Journal, 4 (April, 1945) 55-58.
   Emphasizes the need for college and university administrators and teachers to make adjustments to meet their
responsibilities toward adult education. Colleges and universities are the best equipped of all agencies to undertake education of adults because of their accumulated
knowledge and their scholars, teachers and research
workers.   But they are so rigidly bound to habit and tradition that they are not fulfilling the responsibility that is
their potentially greatest service to democratic society.
Adult education in colleges and universities should be a
recognized arm of the administration and the Extension
Division should be an Administrative Service Office, with
prime responsibility for off campus teaching in subject
matter schools and departments. If other less qualified
agencies take adult education away from colleges, it is because teachers and administrators are unwilling or unable
to adjust themselves, their routines, and their thinking to
the real challenge of society.   539

Hunsaker, Herbert C.   The Urban University Provides Community Educational Services, In Institute for Administrative Officers of Higher Institutions Proceedings, Vol. 20,
The Community Responsibility of Institutions of Higher
Learning.   Chicago: University of Chicago Press, 1948.
Pp. 78-88.
   Institutions of higher learning must accept adult education as an integral part of their responsibility. Describes
community adult education services of Western Reserve
University as illustrations: consultative services of the
faculty, for example in the steel industry; research in the
medical, pharmaceutical, and chemical fields; cooperation
with social welfare agencies; Personnel Research Institute;
television research; city planning; Cleveland College
School of General Studies; short-course programs; lecture
series.   Future developments for urban universities are
to sell the idea of adult education, study the characteristics and needs of students, study community needs for

curriculum development, study materials and methods,
widen areas of service and cooperate with other community agencies, in-service training of professional people,
use of mass media, better physical facilities, expansion
of extension work especially in urban areas.   540

Hunsaker, Herbert C.   What Are the Responsibilities of
Higher Education for the Continuing Education of Adults?
In Association for Higher Education, Current Issues in
Higher Education, 1955.   Proceedings of the Tenth Annual
National Conference on Higher Education, Chicago, Illinois,
February 28--March 2, 1955.   Edited by G. Kerry Smith.
Washington, D.C.:   National Education Association, Association for Higher Education [c1955].   Pp. 85-90.
    It is imperative that institutions of higher education now
engaged in or planning to expand adult education programs
arrive at a precise definition of their responsibilities.
The same factors that will contribute to an anticipated increase in college enrollment will also contribute to an
increase in the number of adults wishing to continue their
education.   The problems of planning for full time college
students and for adult students are closely related and
should be considered at the same time.   Failure to meet
the demand for adult education will prove detrimental to
colleges and universities and to the local and national
community.   Adult education has become so major a
phase of the total operation of many colleges and universities that many institutions are questioning how much of
what is being done is central to their objectives and appropriate to their total responsibilities.   We cannot hope
to secure understanding and support for adult education
until faculty, administration, and community leaders com-
prehend its vital role in our society and the responsibility
of colleges and universities for leadership in this field.
More and more colleges are sponsoring community improvement and development programs.   They are discovering rich resources for research and teaching available in
the community, the educational values for faculty and students who participate in community projects, and better
understanding and support for higher and adult education
resulting from community development.   To achieve institutional communication and coordination, a central administrative unit is needed to serve all divisions engaged in a-
dult education and related community services.   In considering responsibilities of higher education for continuing
education of adults, some crucial questions are: (1)
Should subject matter and standards for mature adults be

the same as for youth? (2) How can experience gained
by teaching adults and rendering service to the community be integrated into graduate and undergraduate instruction and research activities? (3) What kind of cooperative relations should be developed with other colleges and
cultural agencies? (4) To what extent should adult education be expected to pay for itself? (5) Is there need for
reappraisal of objectives and functions of institutions of
higher learning? If so, how should it be undertaken and
by whom?   541

Hutchinson, Robert M.   A Program in Adult Education, In
School Review, 54 (October, 1946) 446-447.
      Announcement of the basic program of liberal education
offered by the University College of the University of Chicago, beginning with the autumn quarter, 1946.   The an-
nouncement defines liberal education, discusses its concern with adults, and states the purpose of the Basic Program.   542

Ingraham, Mary S.   "Development of Evening Programs."
See No. 77.   543

Jenkins, Thomas S.   "Correspondence Course Instruction
and Investigation of Practices, Regulations, and Course
Syllabi as Developed in State Teachers Colleges." Ph.D.
Dissertation.   University of Oregon, 1953.   544

Johnson, Eugene I.   Variations on a Theme, In Adult Leadership, 3 (January, 1955) 10-12, 25.
      The article describes a youth and family life program
to illustrate a new approach to liberal education called
"thematic coordination," identifies basic principles on
which this kind of coordination rests, and concludes with
a statement of reasons for describing it as liberal education.   The core program revolves around seventy-six discussion groups, based on a radio series, "The Years Between," which presents questions and issues arising in
families with teenagers.   The Community Education Project at San Bernardino (California) Valley College acts as
a service center providing the radio programs, newspaper
articles to publicize them, reading materials, bibliographies, a resource persons bureau, and counseling services for the discussion groups.   Each phase of the program represents coordination of talents and services of
the community around a central theme.   Three of the
principles governing the development of thematic coordina-

tion seem of special significance: (1) The total community needs to be involved. (2) Modern mass media techniques need to be given a chance to work in ways which strengthen the values of a free society, and prevent creation of a mass mind by providing active and thoughtful reactions rather than passive acceptance of material presented. (3) Adult educators must learn how to relate education to organizational forms which people of a community spontaneously evolve, such as families, friendship groups, and work cliques. Factors that make this program liberal education are: (1) The entire program emphasizes the discussion method which has values for liberating the mind of man. (2) Emphasis has been placed on resolving great issues of human relationships that have always been of concern to thoughtful men. Objectives are to enlarge knowledge, deepen understanding, increase sensitivity to enduring values, and to lead people into creative response to the confusion of modern life. (3) A major aim of thematic coordination is to produce documents which are modern in terms of technique and valid as vehicles for liberal education.   545

Kempfer, Homer H.   Adult Education in the Community College, In Junior College Journal, 21 (September, 1950) 18-25.
     Defines a community college as a junior college with a comprehensive community program of adult education serving three major groups: (1) twelfth grade graduates pursuing studies in preparation for college or professional school; (2) students with or without twelfth grade diploma pursuing occupational, citizenship, or cultural courses; (3) part-time students of any age, any educational level, and any employment status, in both credit and non-credit courses. The third group is the major challenge to the community college. Discusses principles or policies for the community college in attempting to serve adults, such as selection of staff leaders for their competence, flexibility of schedules, location of activities close to the people, use of non-traditional methods, influence through community organizations, cooperation with other agencies and organizations, comprehensiveness of the adult education program of the community college, and utilization of many approaches. Suggests that community college adult educators work together with social scientists in improving community life.   546

Kempfer, Homer H.   Community College and Adult Educa-

tion, In Adult Education Bulletin, 14 (August, 1950) 166-
172.

The community college is defined as "a composite of
educational opportunities extended by the local public school
system free to all persons who, having passed the normal
age for completing the twelfth grade, need or want to continue their education." Groups served by the community
college should be those included within the present junior
colleges plus the total adult population. Therefore its
program should include: (1) full-time credit carrying
curriculums based upon twelfth grade graduation for young
adults and others planning to transfer to institutions of
higher education; (2) full-time curriculums in occupations,
homemaking, and general education for those who want to
attend full-time for two years or less; (3) part-time activities for adults above the normal high school graduation
age, from illiterate to college graduate. If the community college program is thus broadly defined, it can include most of the total adult education program. The
community college can provide education for mate selection, marriage, child-rearing, home management, occupations, civic and social responsibility, leisure-time activities, and health and adjustment to age. Schedules will be
flexible. Among educational approaches upon which the
community college might draw in an effort to assist
larger population segments are: (1) community surveys,
studies, and improvement projects; (2) supervised participation in community organizations; (3) educational services to community organizations; (4) work-study programs; (5) camping experiences; (6) excursions and hos-
teling; (7) voter induction program; (8) organized volun-
teers for health, welfare and other social and civic services; (9) supervised individual service such as correspondence study, tutoring, counseling, etc.; (10) production
programs in creative and performance arts; (11) large and
small group meetings; and (12) mass media. Integrating
adult education into the community college presents risks
as well as rewards. Since there is a trend toward community colleges, adult educators should help develop a
concept broad enough to include adult education in all its
future possibilities.   547

Ketcham, Charles B.   The Liberal Arts College Serves its
    Community, In Institute for Administrative Officers of
    Higher Institutions Proceedings, Vol. 20, The Community
    Responsibilities of Institions of Higher Learning. Chicago:
    University of Chicago Press, 1948. Pp. 53-62.

Mount Union College in Alliance, Ohio has served its
community through wartime civilian defense activities,
services to churches, college courses and one-day institutes for adults, help on social problems, forums for
high school teachers and students, and assistance to community institutions.   In these fields the liberal arts college can make a significant contribution to the life of the
community, and the college benefits by development of
better student morale, better teaching, and a more up-to-
date curriculum.   548

Kinnell, Galway.   The Basic Program of Liberal Education
   for Adults, In New Directions for University Adult Education: Institution Centered.   Notes and Essays on Education for Adults, No. 11.   Chicago: Center for the
   Study of Liberal Education for Adults, 1955. Pp. 25-47.
   Description of the Basic Program offered by University
College of the University of Chicago, a four-year program
of liberal education for adults, begun in 1946, meeting six
hours a week for nine months, with no formal admission
requirements, no examinations, and no grades other than
pass or fail, with the Certificate in the Liberal Arts a-
warded on completion.   Liberal education is defined as
knowledge in the areas of the natural sciences, the social
sciences, and the humanities.   For the sake of the wholeness of liberal education and the accurate study of the
disciplines within it, it is important to establish the dis-
tinctions and connections among the three areas.   The
curriculum of the Basic Program is divided according to
these three areas with tutorial classes in each, and a
fourth inter-disciplinary class called the Seminar.   The
content and method of each course is described.   Except
for a formal lecture once a month, all classes are taught
by the discussion method.   Diversity of background of the
students is a challenge to the abilities of the teacher and
forces the class to move in a liberal direction on a high
level of inquiry.   Teachers selected must be liberally educated, although it is inevitable and probably desirable
that they be specialists in some field.   Students are recruited by four techniques: (1) word-of-mouth publicity
by students and alumni, (2) aid of persons in advisory
capacities, (3) promotional literature, (4) full commitment
of the adult education agency of which the Program is a
part.   Counseling and social activities outside of class
help to maintain students' interest.   Four considerations
generally applicable to a program such as the Basic Program are: (1) A program need not be large to be effec-

tive. (2) Adults should not be treated as if they were inferior to adolescents. Courses designed for special,
preparatory under-graduate use are not appropriate for
liberal adult education. (3) It is difficult either to over-
estimate or underestimate the adult student. A course
designed with the idea that adults are intelligent will attract intelligent students. (4) To interest adults in general education, an approach through vocational or special
interest topics is not necessary, as argued by some adult
educators. The obligation is to teach the classics in such
a way that they enlist and reward the student's labor, as
living statements of insight, beauty and wisdom.   549

Laird, Bryon F. "A Survey of the Certificate and Terminal
Curricular Offerings of University Extensions and Evening
Colleges." Ph. D. Dissertation. Indiana University,
1954.   550

Lear, Elmer N. Solvents and Cements in Adult Extension
Education, In Progressive Education, 31 (February,
1954) 113-116.
The conflict between imparting information to the student and contributing to the satisfaction of the student's
personality needs is a pedagogical problem particularly
acute in adult extension education because of two characteristics of this program: (1) the voluntary nature of the
program with student attendance depending on instructors'
holding power, and (2) extreme heterogeneity of students
as to educational level and maturity of personality. Discusses problem situations such as those caused by irrelevant discussion and by brighter students, with suggested
solutions. The instructor also has the problem of integration of diverging motivations and purposes of students.
He must try to lead them from limited interest in specific
issues to an appreciation of more fundamental knowledge
and generalized understandings. It is necessary to recognize social needs of students as distinguished from intellectual needs. For successful teaching in adult extension education, the instructor should have a non-rigid personality,
be sensitive to personality needs of students, have a flexible lesson plan that permits departures without losing
sense of direction, and employ informal group procedures.
                                                        551

Leonard, Olen E. and Sheldon G. Lowry. Continuation Education in Colleges and Universities, In Study of Adult
Education in Rural Areas, Rural Social Systems and Adult

Education, a Committee Report by Charles Loomis and others. [East Lansing] Michigan State College Press, 1953. Pp. 230-243.

Continuation education, in existence for over a century, and for a long period concerned with extension of formal campus courses, has broadened its objectives to educating for changing social, economic, and political conditions of the twentieth century. A recent study of a particular program revealed that students in university continuation education are predominantly male, in the younger age brackets (20-35), of a high level of formal education, mostly in high income levels, and attend classes principally to improve their economic positions and increase their incomes. It is estimated that more than half of the institutions of higher education in the United States have continuation programs. Most programs are limited to credit courses by correspondence but non-credit courses are increasingly being offered by means of panels, discussions, and conferences. The trend in methods appears to be away from formal lectures to a more personalized approach through group and informal instruction. Most programs of continuation education are designed for urban people, but progress is being made in reaching more rural adults. A majority of colleges and universities with departments of continuation education are conducting programs in the three fields of interest in this study, international understanding for peace, strengthening of democracy, and understanding and strengthening of the economy. Regionally these programs are concentrated in the West and North Central states and are found most frequently in larger metropolitan institutions. Work in the three fields is mostly conducted through conferences, workshops, and public meetings, and is often administered in cooperation with public schools and local civic organizations. There is evidence of some association between size of centers in which the institutions are located and the extent and nature of educational programs in the three fields.   552

Leys, Wayne A. R. The Two Roles of the University in Adult Education, In Journal of Higher Education, 26 (January, 1955) 12-14.

The two roles are defined in terms of degree and non-degree education. The purpose of non-credit programs is not accurately described by the phrase "adult education." "Education" is used by universities to refer to production of scientists, scholars, and skilled practitioners by way of formal courses. Adult interests are for more immedi-

ate and more practical purposes, for the solution of problems of the individual and of society, not scholarship.
Professional educators want to evaluate "adult education"
by measuring what specifically has been learned. Leys
proposes applying the term "civic religion" to non-credit
activities, which are "a struggle with passion, a practical deliberation, a consultation."   553

"Liberal Education; Summary of a Discussion by the Trustees of the Carnegie Foundation for the Advancement of
Teaching, and Implications for University Adult Education." Notes and Essays on Education for Adults, No. 18.
Chicago: Center for the Study of Liberal Education for
Adults, 1957. 29 pp.
The three parts of the pamphlet are an introductory
statement of the problem of liberal and specialized education; a summary of the central themes of the discussion
by the Trustees of the Carnegie Foundation for the Advancement of Teaching on the subject of liberal education; a commentary by the staff of the Center for the
Study of Liberal Education for Adults, giving implications
for making liberal education an integral part of university
programs for continuing education of adults. In the Pro-
logue it is stated that the question today is how and within what time period it is possible to give students a general and liberal education and at the same time give them
competence in a vocational or professional field. Continuing education throughout life is a possible solution. In the
summary of the Trustees' discussion, it is stated that demands for specialized skills have led to the neglect of
liberal education. Liberal arts education is under pressures and competition from graduate professional schools,
undergraduate special schools, and from within liberal arts
departments themselves. Such pressures upon liberal education have led to vigorous efforts to counteract specialization. The discussion includes a definition of objectives
of a liberal education in terms of kinds of knowledge,
skills or competences, and attitudes, values and habits of
mind; need for liberal education in high schools and junior
colleges; content versus method; the timing of general education in colleges; and liberal education in graduate and
professional schools. It is concluded that one obstacle to
success of attempts to strengthen liberal education is the
misconception that liberal education is incompatible with
specialization. The Center staff agrees with the Trustees' statement of imbalance and suggests adult education
for the undereducated among college graduates. The task

of adult education is two-fold: remedial for those whose
education has been overbalanced by technical or professional content, and supportive for those whose undergraduate preparation was well balanced and who need continuing education.   It is the university's responsibility to provide
both liberal and technical continuing education.   The trustees suggest that for everyone to have a liberal education it
must become part of pre-college education in high schools
and junior colleges.   The Center staff agrees but doubts if
this will solve the problem since high schools and junior colleges are more subject than universities to community and
social pressures to meet vocational and recreational needs.
For the college graduate who has had essentially professional
education, general education should come after specialized
education, beyond graduation.   Universities, in some cases
in cooperation with industry, are making special efforts to a-
dapt programs to the character of the adult audience.   These
programs are of two types, those based on need to redress
imbalance of an earlier, overspecialized education, and those
which fill the more general need for continuing liberal education.   Examples of each type are given.   554

Littlefield, Henry W.   Connecticut Junior Colleges Serve A-
    dult-Education Needs, In School and Society, 63 (January
    26, 1946) 69-70.
      The large enrollment of adults in non-degree and short
    term programs is responsible for the development of a
    type of institution described as a junior university or com-
    munity college.   Four commonly accepted functions of the
    junior college are: (1) to provide locally the first two
    years of college training in preparation for admission to
    junior year of a senior college or university; (2) to pro-
    vide post-secondary training of a terminal character in the
    semi-professions, general education, and in the personal
    and civic areas; (3) to provide opportunities for training
    at the college level to increase vocational, civic, cultural,
    and personal efficiency; (4) to provide specialized short-
    term training in areas which will meet needs of various
    community groups.   In Connecticut several junior colleges
    are organizing and operating adult education services more
    effectively, conveniently, and economically than any other
    agency.   They have developed a strong rapport between
    the community and the college.   The community is looking
    to the junior college more and more to meet its adult edu-
    cation needs at the higher levels.   555

Liveright, A. A.   "The Place of a Center-Type Agency in

Liberalizing Adult Education; a Special Report." Chicago: Center for the Study of Liberal Education for Adults [1956]. 33 pp.

The report assesses the impact of the Center for the Study of Liberal Education for Adults on the field of adult education in evening colleges and universities. This impact has been primarily in terms of identifying and encouraging imaginative individuals and new ideas, in raising the status and acceptance of adult education in colleges and universities, and in increasing professionalization in the field and improving communication between persons interested in adult education.   Factors responsible for the effectiveness of the Center are identified and analyzed, including relationships with the Association of University Evening Colleges and the Fund for Adult Education, and techniques and methods, including conferences and seminars, grants for specific projects and close collaboration in developing projects, working primarily with agents of adult education rather than ultimate consumers, use of committees, use of consultants and experts, a flexible and varied publication program, effective administration and a competent and varied staff.   Another section of the report describes what a Center-type agency is organizationally and operationally, and describes operations and relationships which a Center-type organization can perform which a foundation cannot, and operations which such an organization should not be expected to perform.   The final section identifies major kinds of forces and associations influencing adult education, and the factors considered in determining their scope and readiness for Center-type activity, and includes an illustrative list of forces and organizations in the college and university, secondary school, and voluntary organization and professional fields.   556

Love, Robert A.   "Purposes of Evening Colleges and Relations With the Rest of the University." Detroit: Association of Urban Universities, Wayne University, 1953. 13 pp.   Same in Association of Urban Universities Proceedings.   Thirty-Ninth Annual Meeting, St. Louis, October 18-19, 1953.   Pp. 108-127.

An address to the Association of Urban Universities discussing the social and economic changes of the last century which have affected the functions of the university; the increase in potential clientele oi university adult education; current receptiveness to adult education; the failure of universities to meet the needs of adult education; the role of the evening college as a principal agency of

the university in its effort to meet the educational needs
of adults; problems of internal relationship between the
evening college and the rest of the university; and a plea
for united effort on common problems and overall objectives of university adult education.   557

McCoy, Dean H.   The Modern University and Adult Education, In Association of Governing Boards of State Universities and Allied Institutions Proceedings.   Twenty-
Seventh Annual Meeting, Denver, Colorado and University
of Colorado at Boulder, Colorado, October 5-9, 1949.
Pp. 100-105.
     The tremendous growth of adult education has presented
educators, particularly those in universities, with a problem so gigantic as to be termed a crisis in American education.   There is need to re-examine the basic concepts,
programs, and future of adult education from an entirely
new point of view.   The people of this country feel a
need for broader objectives than in the past, a new type
of programming, and much wider horizons in adult education.   Today's crisis in adult education arises not so
much from numbers as from objectives of those desiring
adult education. Events are providing a challenge which,
if not met by universities, may divorce adult education
from university leadership, which would be dangerous both
for the adult education program and for universities.   Increasing awareness of the value of education will force a
wholesome expansion of university participation.   Efforts
of progressive universities to bridge the gap made by the
older attitude is the most encouraging development in the
present adult education set-up.   Objectives of general education as outlined by the President's Committee indicate
that universal participation in constant re-education is essential to fulfillment of man's destiny.   We need to study
the potentialities of inter-relations between universities
and adult education programs with a view to mutual advantages, ways to use growth of adult education in keeping
colleges and universities growing, new ways of keeping
freedom growing in our society, and ways of using our
own growth to foster growth of freedom in the world. 558

McGhee, Paul A.   Adult Education and Community Action.
See No. 104.   559

McGhee, Paul A.   Higher Education and Adult Education:
Four Questions, In Association for Higher Education,
Current Issues in Higher Education, 1953.   Proceedings

of the Eighth Annual National Conference on Higher Education, Chicago, Illinois, March 5-7, 1953. Edited by
Francis H. Horn. Washington, D. C.: National Education Association, Association for Higher Education [c1953].
Pp. 196-206. Same in McGhee, Paul A. A School for
Optimists. Notes and Essays on Education for Adults,
No. 6. Chicago: Center for the Study of Liberal Education for Adults, 1953. Pp. 5-17; same condensed: A-
dult Education, 4 (January, 1954) 67-75.

Since general agreement as to relations between higher
education and adult education are lacking, the writer re-
examines basic propositions which require decision before
there can be any forward movement with a common front.
The first question is: What is the point of impact of a-
dult education on higher education? Adult education, if
higher education is to relate to it, must mean education
as the process of acquiring liberalizing methods and concepts that provide unity and direction for an individual's
thinking and acting. Colleges and universities should be
chiefly concerned with continuing education of adults in
these terms, not with methods of community organization
or group leadership. The second question is: Will it
make any difference in our institutional fortunes whether
we accept or disclaim any responsibility in adult education? If a college neglects the educational interests of a-
dults in its community, other agencies will organize programs on what appears to be "college level" and both
college and community are the losers. The third question
is: What could we do that other institutions or agencies
can not do as well? If colleges do not accept their responsibility and society undertakes to meet its own continuing education needs, the community will not be served by
its best trained teachers and scholars, and the content of
adult education may be something not truly education.
Also a concept of separation of interest between college
and community develops. The fourth question is: If
higher education accepts the challenge of adult education,
what changes will be called for in institutional attitudes
and administrative organization? The evening college or
extension division must be given rank and autonomous status equal to that of other schools of the institution. It
should organize a special program of studies for adults
based upon their concern with functions rather than growth,
their insistence that their study be continuously meaningful, and their requirement for the best and most mature
teachers. Colleges should be organized to give sanction
to a type of teaching which applies the values of humane

culture to the daily life of the ordinary man. Since the
largest number of adults are reached through community
oriented programs centered in public schools, higher education must relate itself to these programs, cooperate
with them and influence them so that they, too, will offer
true education for adults.   560

McGhee, Paul A. "A School for Optimists." Notes and Essays on Education for Adults, No. 6. Chicago: Center
for the Study of Liberal Education for Adults, 1953. 25
pp.
     Composed of three papers. The first, "A School for
Optimists," is an extract from Dean McGhee's 1951-52
Annual Report to the Chancellor of New York University,
and is developed from the theme that the college or university can make a unique contribution to adult education
by training the individual for democratic leadership. The
second paper, "Higher Education and Adult Education:
Four Questions," is based on an address presented at the
Eighth National Conference on Higher Education at Chicago,
March 6, 1953. See No. 560 for annotation. In the third
paper, "Dean George Spelvin on 'Groupmanship,' or Let's
Keep Some Education in Adult Education," the writer dis-
tinguishes between education and its application, between
adult education that is continuing education of adults and
community dynamics. The main province of adult education is the training and education of the individual, and
"groupmanship" is an adjunct of adult education.   561

McGhee, Paul A. Three Dimensions of Adult Education, In
Educational Record, 35 (April, 1954) 119-130.
     Discusses three aspects of adult education toward which
higher education must take a stand and formulate some
policy regarding its relationship or responsibility: (1)
the adult education "movement;" (2) degree programs of
the evening college, university college, or extension division; (3) non-degree programs of varied character. The
adult education movement is concerned with the importance
of participation by the individual in small groups as the
most effective instrument for maintaining a democratic society. Its advocates propose community action programs
in place of formal classes, and "leaders" in place of
teachers. Many universities and colleges are taking
part in this movement through services to community
groups through extension directors and teachers. Some
prefer to consider it a program of training for citizenship, for revitalizing and preserving democracy rather

than adult education. Such programs are appropriate for universities because the object of education is the improvement of society. Among the problems which arise concerning degree programs are the question of independence or identity, the question of purpose, and the relationship of the evening college to the adult education "movement." Until the evening college is conceived by the university as a college in its own right with its own function and its own specialists, it will not have full vitality. The evening college has the responsibility of approaching the problem of formulating its purposes pragmatically and empirically. In defining conditions under which it can do its most effective work, the evening college should examine and experiment with all aspects of the academic tradition. Higher education should be related to non-credit, non-degree programs, long or short courses, institutes, conferences, or any other type of educational undertaking organized by the university as a response to needs and interests of the community. Weaknesses of adult education at the university level are due to a mimicry of traditional curricula, lack of imagination, infrequency of inspired teaching, and lack of academic respectability. If universities and colleges do not develop patterns of sensible and constructive education for the "after-school age" of our society, other agencies will take over the role of educational planning with resulting loss of influence, leadership and support of universities.   562

Malamud, Daniel I. "A Participant Observer Approach to the Teaching of Human Relations." See No. 378.   563

Martorana, Sebastian V. Problems in Adult Education in the Junior College. See No. 379.   564

Martorana, Sebastian V. Status of Adult Education in Junior Colleges. See No. 380.   565

Masley, John W. Adult Education in the Community College, In Junior College Journal, 20 (October, 1949) 75-81.
     Discusses the scope of the adult education program in community colleges as related to a functional philosophy of education; the basis for determination of need for courses; problems of instructional staff in adult education, financing the program, coordination of the adult education program of the community college with adult education programs of other agencies and integrating it with other units of the school system.   566

Mathews, Mildred Van Deusen. Education at Their Door-
step, In Library Journal, 70 (January, 1, 1945) 13-14.
Describes a program of evening classes for adults
given by City College of New York, with classes held for
students' convenience in branches of the New York Public
Library, a school, and a studio, as well as at City College.   567

Matloff, Maurice. Role of the College in Post War Adult
Education and Community Leadership, In School and Society, 62 (October 13, 1945) 225-227.
Proposes that colleges, especially municipal colleges,
have the opportunity and responsibility for developing a
program of adult education and community leadership. Offers reasons why colleges have not played a more active
role in adult education, and submits six proposals as
steps that colleges may adopt in order to furnish this program: (1) creation of a faculty Committee on Community
Education and Leadership to be in charge of the program;
(2) cooperation of the college with other community organizations to eradicate illiteracy; (3) a series of informal lectures and discussion groups on a wide variety of
subjects of interest to adults in the community; (4) a series of discussions and lectures on current events; (5) supervision of training of regular college students in community responsibility and practical citizenship, coordinating studies and research with community problems; (6)
organization of a pool of students to work with community groups to help eradicate illiteracy, prejudices and
misinformation.   568

Mead, Margaret. Wellesley School of Community Affairs,
In Progressive Education, 22 (February, 1945) 4-8.
Description of a six weeks summer course inaugurated
at Wellesley College in 1944 as a three year experiment in
adult education. The theme, "Cultural Differences in the
United States," was developed in three two-week units
with a change of membership and leadership. In the first
unit emphasis was placed on group techniques as the medium within which increased understanding of cultural difference would be developed. In the second unit cultural differences were set within the structure of industry, and
emphasis was placed upon techniques of human relationships adapted to industry. In the third unit emphasis was
placed upon community discussion techniques. Many techniques were used in all units with stress upon different
types of learning. In addition to familiar techniques such

as the panel, lecture and group discussion, a variety of
less well-known techniques were used including the socio-
drama, the "informant method," case method and counseling method. Specific findings about intercultural schools
of the Wellesley type are: (1) It is advantageous to have
as heterogeneous a group as possible in respect to race,
religion, nationality, class, occupation, education, sex,
age, and intelligence. (2) It is of great value for a
school of crusading values to be operated in close association with groups unconcerned with the particular crusade.
(3) A team of leaders rather than a single leader is necessary, with one supplementing the skills of the other.
(4) Emphasis on experimentation was differently valued by
different types of membership. The research emphasis
guarantees the diversity among the leaders which is essential. Useful principles of conducting intercultural discussions are explained.   569

Meder, Albert E., Jr.   The University Providing Service
to the People in an Industrial State, In   National University Extension Association Proceedings, Thirty-Third Annual Meeting, Chicago, 1948.   Pp. 82-93.
    Describes extension services of Rutgers University,
early development, agricultural extension, the credit, non-
credit and graduate programs of University Extension,
special programs for industry and labor, and other work.
Also discussed are values of extension work as a public
relations force, extension influence on the campus, extension benefits to individuals, and social benefits of extension.   570

Miller, Harry L.   "Evaluating Courses, Not Students, an
Evening College Experiment with Objective Devices." See
No. 299.   571

Mire, Joseph.   The University and the Union in Workers'
Education, In Adult Education, 5 (Summer, 1955) 232-236.
    Educational needs of the labor movement arise in three
ways: (1) need for general education by members who
lack formal schooling; (2) a concern of the labor movement about the kind of education given to regular university students concerning the labor movement; (3) needs of
workers for knowledge and skills arising out of their participation in the labor movement. Labor should offer
"bread and butter" courses on the core functions of labor,
and also be responsible for administration of union educational programs. Universities should assist labor in es-

tablishing its organization for workers' education, and offer education on broader issues in public relations, economic policies, health and welfare, foreign affairs, international trade, atomic energy, etc. Universities should
also offer education that has to do with growth and development of people. Another field appropriate for university labor education is experimenting with new teaching
techniques and materials.   572

Mosier, Jean. Problems and Policies of the University
    Evening College, In Adult Education Bulletin, 13 (June,
    1949) 140-144.
    A discussion of the ten topics included in a survey,
conducted by Frank R. Neuffer, of administrative problems and policies of member institutions of the Association of University Evening Colleges in order to provide a
measuring device in formulating and unifying policies in
evening college administration. Included are: general
administrative practice; degree and certificate programs
and academic credit; registration, admission and guidance;
tuition and fees; drop out students; faculty; financial policies and problems; publicity and public relations; student
activities; looking ahead.   573

National University Extension Association. "Adult Education
    in the Modern University." See No. 387.   574

National University Extension Association. "University Ex-
    tension in the United States; a Study by the N.U.E.A."
    See No. 388.   575

Navin, Robert B. Adult Education, In National Catholic Edu-
    cational Association Bulletin, 53 (August, 1956) 143-144.
    Discusses briefly the question of whether the adult edu-
cation program of Catholic colleges and universities should
consist only of formal courses for credit, or should also
include non-credit courses, and whether the courses
should cover vocational and recreational needs or be
limited to courses directly related to the purpose of the
college. The author favors limitation to courses closely
related to Catholic philosophy and theology, which is the
policy followed at St. John College, Cleveland, Ohio. 576

Neuffer, Frank R. "Administrative Policies and Practices
    of Evening Colleges, 1953; a Report." See No. 389.
                                                       577

"New Directions for University Adult Education: Institution
        Centered." Notes and Essays on Education for Adults,
    No. 11. Chicago: Center for the Study of Liberal Edu-
    cation for Adults, 1955. 47 pp.
        Contains "Faculty Organization at Rutgers," by G.
    Stuart Demarest, pp. 1-24; and "The Basic Program of
    Liberal Education for Adults," by Galway Kinnell, pp.
    25-47. See No. 506 and No. 549 for annotations.   578

Nolte, J. M. The Role of State Universities in Adult Edu-
    cation, In National Association of State Universities in
    the U.S.A.   Transactions and Proceedings. Annual Meet-
    ing, Minneapolis, Minnesota, April 30 - May 1, 1952.
    Vol. 50, 1952. Pp. 57-70.
        Considers various concepts of adult education and pro-
    poses to discuss it according to the historical definition
    to which most universities and colleges are committed.
    The obligation of the university to meet needs of adults
    must be understood within a complex of limitations as to
    facilities, funds, staff time, scope of curriculum and rela-
    tive urgency of needs, and in the light of what the univer-
    sity can do well. A pattern of general university exten-
    sion services has developed in most states, including
    credit and non-credit, on-campus and correspondence
    courses covering cultural, vocational and recreational sub-
    jects, and also other services in various aspects of social
    welfare activity and community planning, and supplemen-
    tary obligations such as development and application of new
    educational devices. The modern state university is re-
    quired to extend its facilities and services to all parts of
    the state in teaching, research, and informational report-
    ing, not only for the individual benefit of the citizen, but
    also for the community and the state itself; to establish
    and maintain such all-state services as will be of value
    for the public good; and to essay the role of leader and
    guide in connection with consideration and formation of
    judgment on cultural, philosophical, and political questions.
    Universities must be responsive to wishes of the popula-
    tion, but they must be responsive also to true needs and
    have and use facility in discerning them. The greatest
    task of adult education and the greatest obligation of the
    state university is to restate the cultural and political i-
    deals of America and to emphasize the dignity, sacred-
    ness, and human necessity of individual free will and self
    control. Intellectual discipline is inextricably involved in
    the process.   579

O'Malley, Comerford J.   Why Catholic Adult Education?, In
National Catholic Educational Association Bulletin, 53
(August, 1956) 145-146.
     States the responsibility of Catholic colleges along with
other institutions for adult education, and states the aim
of the Catholic college program as presenting Catholic
principles in the areas of the humanities, fine and communication arts, physical and social sciences, and theology, which will be translated into daily action and develop
leadership.   580

Osman, John.   Liberal Education for Adults and the Liberal
Arts College, In Association of American Colleges Bulletin, 39 (March, 1953) 70-79.
     Democracy requires liberal education, and liberal arts
colleges have a responsibility for the liberal education of
adults.   To carry out this obligation the liberal arts college should inform itself about the program of the Fund
for Adult Education for supporting liberal adult education
programs; establish liaison with international, national,
regional and state adult education organizations; join the
local adult education council; inaugurate an extension program in liberal education; employ the discussion group
method in teaching adults; create appropriate materials
for the mature mind;   utilize new arts of communication;
provide a successful director and teachers for the program for adults.   581

Parkinson, G. A.   Patterns of Development in the University Evening College, In Association of University Evening Colleges Proceedings, Eighteenth Annual Meeting, New
York, 1956.   Pp. 32-41.
     Cites contemporary developments affecting programs of
evening colleges: (1) development of vocational and social centers, adult education function of libraries, and numerous agencies engaged in more or less formal instructional activities; (2) radio and television; (3) development
of training courses for personnel by business and industry;
(4) training in the armed services.   Other more deep-
seated problems are those of desegregation, of an aging
population, and of the effects of atomic energy.   Discusses
two qualities of education as applied to the evening college: (1) Loss of personal relationships between faculty
and students.   This relationship has been retained to a
greater degree in the evening college than in day school
institutions.   (2) Research and development in education.
Evening college classes, faculty, and students are often

more closely related to research than those of the day
school, since many are engaged in professional research
as distinguished from amateur research of many university faculty people. Some patterns of development which
may be anticipated are: a boldly conceived, general liberal arts curriculum for evening school students; development of a general liberal arts master's degree in the
field of professional education; application of mass communication to the educational process.   582

"Patterns of Liberal Education in the Evening College, a
    Case Study of Nine Institutions." See No. 393.   583

Penney, James F. The Community College and the World
    Community, In Teachers College Record, 53 (March,
    1952) 323-326.
        The community college is uniquely suited to play a part
    in the area of world community living for several rea-
    sons.   (1) Its primary task is to educate great numbers
    of Americans for whom higher education is unavailable.
    (2) The community college is in a position to institute a
    strong, realistic, dynamic movement for world commu-
    nity living, challenging to a student body at the best age
    to profit by it.   (3) An integral part of the community
    college is the inclusion of programs of adult education to
    awaken a realization of possibilities for personality growth
    and personal responsibility for affairs of the community.
    (4) The community college by nature and concept is dedi-
    cated to study and service of community needs.   Many
    community resources for an international education pro-
    gram are available to the college.   (5) The community
    college is also uniquely suited to educate for world com-
    munity living because it is a new and dynamic force on the
    educational scene, not bound by tradition or established
    curriculum and free to explore, experiment and pioneer.
                                                            584

Pitkin, Royce S. "The Residential School in American A-
    dult Education." Notes and Essays on Education for A-
    dults, No. 14. Chicago: Center for the Study of Liberal
    Education for Adults, 1956. 45 pp.
        The residential college and the boarding school have ex-
    isted in the United States for many years, but the resi-
    dential adult school is relatively new. As developed in
    this country it is a place where adults live in small groups
    for short periods for the purpose of learning, free from
    encumbrances of grades, academic standing, credits, ex-

aminations and degrees.   There is variation in subjects
dealt with, in students in attendance, and in procedures.
Most American and Canadian residential schools are located in the country where there are few distractions.
The residential adult school takes account of the fact that
learning involves the whole person, and makes provision
for the inherent need of human beings for self-fulfillment
and for creation and expression of ideas.   The residential
school is especially useful in meeting needs of individuals
and of society because of the intimacy of small groups in
residence, favorable learning conditions, feeling of freedom in discussion and expression, close relationship between teachers and students, and an atmosphere of relax-
ation and informality.   Some limitations on the effectiveness of the residential school are discussed.   (1) Because
of the small size of the schools, a very large number
would be required to reach a large fraction of the adult
population.   (2) Because of demands of their jobs most
people are unable to pursue such a long range program of
study at a residential school as easily as they can through
evening or extension courses.   (3) The residential school
is limited by a scarcity of teachers who can work in the
intimate manner necessary for its successful operation.
(4) Another limitation is the lack of familiarity with the
residential idea among adults and among adult educators.
Despite these problems, the residential school is sound,
timely, and "as a complement to existing forms of adult
education its potential is limitless."   The residential idea
has been utilized by business and labor organizations, universities, governmental agencies, group dynamics training laboratories, churches, and others.   An appendix
gives brief descriptions of nineteen residential schools in
the United States and Canada, based on a survey by the
Committee on Residential Adult Schools of the Adult Education Association.   585

Pritchard, J. Carson.   College in the Country, In   U.S.
Office of Education, Education for Better Living.   Bulletin 1956, No. 9.   Washington, D.C.:   Government Printing Office, 1956.   Pp. 231-239.
   "College in the Country" is a movement composed of
many rural groups of adults in Georgia who meet when-
ever and wherever they want to meet to study whatever
they want to study.   Local organizations co-sponsor with
a college their own study series.   A total of 1,476 persons have been involved in the program which began in
1949 at West Georgia College and has spread to other cen-

ters.   Institutions involved in the movement call on their
own faculties as a first source of teachers.   To lead
special subjects they also call on other colleges and universities and local, state, regional, and national agencies.   "Faculty Associates" is a name given to a group
of lay teachers who have special abilities and are willing
to participate.   "Conversation Teams" of from three to
eight members volunteer to lead series of studies as a
team through informal discussion.   To assist the emerging leadership, "College in the Country" is emphasizing
leadership improvement through conferences and workshops and in-service training of lay adults.   There is no
imposed pattern in the program of "College in the Country."   Adults plan for themselves the experiences they
need and want.   Staff members from the college are part
of the planning group and are free to make suggestions,
to clarify, and to amplify.   Illustrations are given of the
great variety in the programs.   "College in the Country"
is an expression of the outward movement of the college
into the community.   586

Pugh, David B.   "The Role of Extension Centers in a State-
    Wide Program."   N.U.E.A. Studies in University Exten-
    sion Education, No. 10.   Bloomington, Indiana: National
    University Extension Association, September, 1953. 16 pp.
       A report on the establishment and operation of exten-
    sion centers throughout the state of Pennsylvania by Penn-
    sylvania State College.   Most of these centers offer a
    junior college curriculum with the addition of miscellane-
    ous extension classes, informal programs and other types
    of services to adults.   Some offer part time or full time
    technical institute programs.   Discusses history and de-
    velopment, policy and procedures, administration, rela-
    tion to the main campus, finances, credits, etc.   587

Reals, Willis H.   The Education of the Aging in Institutions
    of Higher Learning.   See No. 395.   588

Reals, Willis H.   The Evening College As I See It, In
    Association of University Evening Colleges Proceedings.
    Sixteenth Annual Meeting, Milwaukee, 1954.   Pp. 48-55.
       The evening college has had to support itself financially
    and fight for acceptance.   Lack of acceptance is due more
    to lack of understanding than to academic prejudice. Eve-
    ning college directors have the responsibility of convincing
    that adult education is not only important, but indispensa-
    ble.   The evening college should be concerned with qual-

ity of achievement. Increase in numbers of students per
se is not a criterion of success. The future of the evening college is contingent upon realization of obligations
and responsibilities, determination of purposes and functions, and development of understanding of the importance
of the evening division and its relations as an independent
and co-equal unit with other divisions of the university.
Within the next few years the evening college will keep
within its proper function and cooperate rather than com-
pete with other agencies; it will extend its services in the
college field and become an adult college with the evening
operation only a small aspect of the total operation; it
will occupy a central position in the university family and
have a voice in shaping university policy.   589

Rosentreter, Frederick M. "The Boundaries of the Campus,
a History of the University of Wisconsin Extension Division, 1885-1945." See No. 345.   590

Rowbotham, Alice. "Correspondence Instruction." N. U. E. A.
Studies in University Extension Education, No. 8. Bloomington, Indiana: National University Extension Association, July, 1953. 16 pp.
     A comparison of programs and methods of operation of
correspondence departments at University of California,
Pennsylvania State College, and University of Chicago.
                                                   591

Rushing, Joe B. "A Critical Analysis of Adult Education in
Junior Colleges in the United States." Ph. D. Dissertation.
University of Texas, 1952.   592

Ruthven, Alexander G. "The Role of the College in Adult
Education, in New York (City),' College of the City of
New York, Centennial Addresses, 1847-1947, edited by
Samuel M. Middlebrook. New York: City College Press,
1950. Pp. 102-104. Discussion by Lyman Bryson, Eduard C. Lindeman, and Walter A. Knittle, pp. 104-114.
     In a sense all students in institutions of higher learning
are adults, and the aim of higher education is to teach
them how to develop their intellects and how to behave as
intelligent human beings, and also to prepare them in
techniques of earning a livelihood. In graduate and professional schools, and often in undergraduate study, specialized training is increasingly emphasized and narrowed,
and education in the best sense is neglected. The university's responsibilities extend to those who do not go to col-

lege and to those who do not return to college after graduation. In attempting to provide a profusion of subjects
for these groups, there is danger that shallowness will be
the result. The university should provide the stimulus for
education that is formation of the intellect. Off-campus
instruction should not be primarily vocational. It should
be designed to impart knowledge that forms an inward endowment, to develop reasoning powers, and to inculcate
intellectual honesty. In the discussions following this address, Lyman Bryson expresses agreement with Ruthven's
ideas and emphasizes the point that colleges should educate their students in such a way that they will desire to
continue learning after leaving college. Eduard Lindeman
agrees with Ruthven in regard to current overemphasis
upon vocational education and warns against artificial separation of vocational and liberal education as dangerous to
democracy. Colleges and universities should strive to
lessen confusion existing in the public mind and to aid
citizens in understanding basic trends of the time. Walter
Knittle disagrees with Ruthven as to the type of adult education the college or university should offer. As much
provision as possible should be made for all who seek a-
dult education, not only to develop individuals' capacities
but also to enrich the entire community by citizens' activities. Universities should not abandon academic and
traditional purposes, but they should not restrict their offerings in adult education. Their role in the future may
be not merely to educate leaders of democracy but also
to raise the educational level of the entire body politic.

                                                         593

Scates, Alice Yeomans. "Jointly-Sponsored Programs of Col-
    lege Credit Work for Employed Adults; Report of a Pro-
    ject Sponsored by the Office of Naval Research." Washing-
    ton, D.C.:   American Council on Education, 1953.   233
    pp.
    Report of a study by the Office of Naval Research un-
der contract with the American Council on Education.
The study deals with college-credit programs offered for
the professional development of a group of adults through
a cooperative arrangement between a university and their
employing firm or agency. Part 1, "Descriptions of
Jointly Sponsored Programs," includes purpose and procedure, framework of jointly sponsored programs, descriptions of three small and three large jointly sponsored
programs. Part 2 describes problems involved in operating jointly sponsored programs, problems of organization

and administration, instruction, and quality of work offered.   594

Schacht, Robert H. "Residential Adult Education--an A-
nalysis and Interpretation." Ph.D. Dissertation. University of Wisconsin, 1957. 401 pp.   595

Schoenfeld, Clay. Fifty Years of Wisconsin Extension. See
No. 346.   596

Schueler, Herbert. Keynote Address, In Association of University Evening Colleges Proceedings. Eighteenth Annual
Meeting, New York, 1956. Pp. 24-31.
    Discusses current themes in the creative programming
of university evening colleges: (1) experimentation in
education of the individual by identifying individual need
and building it into curriculum and method of the program;
(2) building the community into adult programs; (3) diversity in methods of instruction; (4) proposed Laboratory
College for Adults in which the living community is used
as both subject matter and method. Expresses the hope
that the evening college will assume the mission of ever
developing and improving creative programming in the
service of continuing adult education and will resist com-
placency and institutionalization.   597

Schwertman, John B. "Continuing Education and the Problem of Excellence." Papers on Adult Education, No. 3.
University of Washington, Division of Adult Education and
Extension Services, 1955. 11 pp.
    A university should be a social institution that stands
for excellence. Three questions are discussed: (1) What
is meant by the term "excellence?" (2) How do we spec-
ify excellence for educational activity at the university
level? (3) In terms of continuing education, what specifically does excellence demand of the subject matter specialist? Each area of human activity has its own excellence, which is made up of a number of things, usually related. Different human activities have different kinds of
excellence. University faculty members tend to judge all
adult education activity in terms derived from and applied
to the regular degree-oriented course sequence in the graduate and undergraduate programs. Continuing education
has the right to be judged in its own terms. This point
is crucial when applied to obvious differences between
formal classroom activity on the campus, and other activities in the continuing education program. The three gen-

eral purposes of the university, teaching, research, and
specialized services to society, are operative in continuing education. In the function of providing specialized
services to the community is the greatest need to evolve
criteria for excellence. Seven questions are suggested as
criteria in selecting what the university ought and ought
not to do. These criteria concern the ability of other a-
gencies to provide educational activities, ability of the
university to do the best possible job, complexity of subject matter, extent of concern for intellectual development,
possibilities for opening up major vistas of social, spiritual, and esthetic experience, possibilities for the university to gain new insights and knowledge, and development
of community leadership. Excellence demands of the subject matter specialist that he realize that continuing education is for him too. In the academic world, our continuing education should be in two directions: we must
continue to grow deeply in the area of our own subject
matter competence, and we should constantly open new
and major vistas of experience for ourselves. Excellence
also demands of the adult teacher, as well as of the
learner, the discipline to undertake new experiences that
are difficult.   598

Schwertman, John B. Explicitly for Adults, In Association
   of University Evening Colleges Proceedings. Sixteenth
   Annual Meeting, Milwaukee, Wisconsin, 1954. Pp. 57-62.
      In answering the question of what differences should be
   recognized as explicitly pertaining to liberal education for
   adults, the key clue is in the word "experience." Three
   things distinguish adulthood from the age periods preceding it: (1) Adults have more experience. (2) They have
   different kinds of experience. (3) Their experiences are
   organized differently. Planning education for adults must
   be done in terms of experience. Education "explicitly for
   adults" is based upon a primary concern with the total
   condition under which adults most effectively learn. Eight
   ideal characteristics of a University for Adults are listed:
   (1) individuality of the learner is the first priority; (2)
   no clear status distinction between teachers and learners;
   (3) freedom for each individual to learn at his own rate
   of speed; (4) authority and discipline derived not from
   course grades and credit sequences, but from the atmosphere of the community of learners, with each area of
   subject matter demanding its own standards, set by
   teachers and learners; (5) a physically pleasant place with
   a climate of intellectual challenge; (6) an atmosphere pri-

marily of inquiry; (7) recognition of social experience as
a 'crucial factor in any learning process; (8) provision of
some formal recognition or degree to which society will
lend prestige.   599

Schwertman, John B.   "A Fourth Level of Learning." Reprint from Oberlin Alumni Magazine, January, 1956.
Distributed by the Center for the Study of Liberal Education for Adults.

Discusses the increasing trend toward adult education,
especially in the non-urban, liberal arts college, and proposes three types of adult education programs by which
liberal arts colleges such as Oberlin may meet their responsibilities for adult education: (1) programs for adult
groups with specialized interests; (2) a Master's degree
program in general education for adults; (3) programs for
liberal arts faculty members.   600

Schwertman, John B.   New Concepts of the University's Role,
In Journal of Higher Education, 26 (January, 1955) 17-20.
Same condensed under title Some Current Concepts, In
Adult Leadership, 3 (January, 1955) 26.

The great unrealized potential for adult education in the
university lies in new and bold concepts which differ in
many ways from regular graduate and undergraduate programs, as typified by the "night-school concept." The
university must move beyond the night school or remedial
concept of adult education.   Ten adult programs that have
moved beyond the regular graduate and undergraduate programs are described briefly: (1) the basic-program concept which operates in University College of University of
Chicago, a four-year program based on semi-weekly seminar discussions; (2) the elaborate non-credit concept, an
operation of the Division of General Education of New
York University, which rejects discrimination between liberal and vocational education, disregards the credit system as inappropriate for adult needs, and is concerned
with development of individual excellence; (3) the commu-
nity-service concept, operating in the program of the Community College of University of Akron and the Neighborhood College of University of Louisville, which is concerned with translation of knowledge for general or popular consumption, and has service to the community as its
aim rather than scholarship or research; (4) the commu-
nity-development concept, which has had its most spectacular success at University of Washington and is now in
operation at Southern Illinois University, which puts the

university's resources at the disposal of groups of citizens who want to solve their own social problems; (5)
the university-extension concept, a familiar phenomenon
of the American state university system, based upon the
philosophic assumption that the boundaries of the university campus are co-extensive with the boundaries of the
state; (6) the concept of residential adult education, relatively new to America, exemplified by the Continuing Education Center at University of Georgia, the Philadelphia
Junto's week-end college, some of the labor union institutes, several Canadian projects for Scandinavian ethnic
groups, and some of the Harvard University residential
projects such as the Advanced Management Program; (7)
the cognitive therapy concept, whose basic notion is to
provide at the university level something which might be
called intellectual therapy for adults.   Its nearest example
in American higher education is the Sarah Lawrence undergraduate program; (8) the senior-citizen concept, based
on the university's concern with the problem of the aging
in our society. Program ideas are being worked out,
based on several experimental projects, such as one at
Cleveland College of Western Reserve University; (9) the
concept of educational mass media, which presents the
university with a new adult education responsibility because of widespread availability of mass media, especially television; (10) the concept of a liberal-arts degree
program especially for adults, taking into account life experience of the adult, such as the experimental program of
Brooklyn College, based upon knowledge and achievement
rather than accumulation of credits.   These new concepts
of the role of the university in adult education are justified on psychological, sociological, philosophical, and
economic bases.   Important tasks of the university in a-
dult education are: research in needs and motivations of
adults, study of educational needs in urban society, experimentation with curriculum materials and teaching methods, and training leaders and teachers in adult education.

                                                        601

Schwertman, John B.   The University Evening College, Some
   Trends in Its Development, In National Education Association Journal, 43 (January, 1954) 48-49.
      In quantitative and economic terms the influence of the
   university evening college is great.   Inner academic
   councils ask what the quality of this influence is and
   whether it is good or bad for the university.   This question points to a more basic one of what the proper func-

tions of a university are in a democratic, industrialized, urban society. This must be answered for each institution in terms of its own philosophy. There is a trend toward giving the evening college an independent administrative status, although at present the picture is confused. In the evening program the major problems lie in the area of the curriculum where questions of academic standards and credit versus non-credit creates a clash of conflicting philosophies. Older people more concerned about the meaning of life than about economic or social betterment are coming to the university in increasing numbers. There is an awakening of interest in liberal arts and humanistic studies in their own right rather than as steps toward an academic degree. Some community groups are beginning to see the university as an enormous source of intellectual and spiritual nourishment. These trends may help the evening college movement to understand and define what it is. At present the evening college is being pulled by two opposing philosophies, one of which directs attention and effort inward toward academic subject matter, and the other outward toward the community where life is lived in a full and dynamic manner. The evening college may find its purposes are best served, not by inward orientation and catering to community pressures, but by looking primarily to those adults who are attracted by desire to gain a greater understanding of life. It may be that the great opportunity or purpose of the evening college is to establish or reestablish the idea of unity between life experience and knowledge by means of its educational activities for adults. This will not happen until adult students are regarded as more than a group who didn't go to college as teenagers.   602

Sheats, Paul H. The Contribution of University Extension to Learning, In Journal of Higher Education, 20 (February, 1949) 77-82, 113-114.

Granted that university extension qualifies as adult education, has it unique or peculiar characteristics which set its work apart from that of other public or private agencies in the field? University extension shares with other agencies of adult education a commitment to the task of developing a better informed citizenry, vocationally competent and capable of assuming obligations and privileges of citizenship. It is the special responsibility of university extension to serve at the postgraduate level groups who can use and apply most fruitfully expert knowledge which can be supplied by university academic depart-

ments or professional schools. A second major purpose
of university extension is to carry on experimentation
with techniques and processes of adult education in the
light of which services of other agencies in the field can
be improved. These functions are illustrated with examples of services of University of California Extension.
University extension should encourage development of local adult school programs and cooperate in a common effort to meet community needs more fully. If university
extension is to assume and discharge the major adult education role for which it has been cast, it must channel
its energies and resources into those parts of the total
job which it is best equipped to do, and work on a team
basis with public and private agencies of adult education.

603

Sheats, Paul H., Clarence D. Jayne, and Ralph B. Spence.
  "Adult Education, the Community Approach." New York:
  Dryden Press [c1953]. Chapter 8, "Universities and
  Colleges," pp. 175-199.
    Adult education in universities and colleges is most
commonly identified as university extension which is one
of the most important adult education agencies in the
United States encompassing not only classes and lectures
but also a wide variety of additional offerings and services. This chapter discusses: (1) the unique responsibilities of university extension, nature of the present program, and people who avail themselves of its offerings;
(2) organization and administration of university extension;
and (3) program trends. Excerpts from the report of the
President's Commission on Higher Education state responsibilities of universities and colleges for adult education. Against this background of recommendations the objectives of the University of California and University of
Chicago are examined and the organization and administration of University Extension in these institutions and Pennsylvania State College are described. The pattern of administrative cooperation depends upon local conditions, but
in general the role of the university through its extension
division should be to supplement and strengthen programs
of existing agencies. Important program trends in university extension discussed are the growing recognition of
need for postgraduate extension training in professions,
growing practice of short, intensive institutes and conferences, growth of residential centers, research, development of the area of community service and community development. The Adult Education Association can perform

an important service by focusing public attention upon the
key role which universities and colleges must play in a-
dult education.   604

Siegle, Peter E.   The International Conference on Residential
Adult Education, an Interpretive Review, In Adult Education, 6 (Winter, 1956) 106-113.
A review of an international conference on residential
adult education held at Harcum Junior College, Bryn
Mawr, Pennsylvania, August 20, 1955, attended by thirty-
three adult educators representing ten countries and many
different kinds of institutions.   Interest in residential a-
dult education takes many forms and derives from many
different points of view stemming from different social,
cultural, and philosophical backgrounds.   Interests that
cut across cultural lines may be classified as social action, propagandistic, crisis-control, remedial education,
and general education.   Residential education is distinguished from education-in-residence in that the educational process in residential education is a total experience
in which academic and social activities are integrated
through a process of living together as a group.   Special
values of residential education are: reduction of fears
related to formal academic work; broadening experience,
particularly in interpersonal relations; special opportunities for deeper contact with subject matter, for inquiry,
and for changes in thought and attitude.   Although these
are values of good education in any form, residential education is superior because its unifying principle is the
factor of residence itself as related to liberal education of
the whole man.   The residential atmosphere generates a
cooperative spirit which transforms "ego-centered wants to
society-centered needs."   American residential adult education in the humanistic tradition will develop from the
existing educational pattern which differs from the European in many ways.   Due to general increase in number
of years of formal schooling in this country, the task of
adult education at higher levels is becoming more and
more important.   It is in the realm of higher adult education that European countries can learn much from British
residential colleges and American non-credit liberal programs.   Suggestions are made for further discussion and
exploration of issues concerning residential adult education, including methods, better understanding and improvement of adult learning, and relationship to workers'
movements.   605

Siegle, Peter E.   Liberal Education for Adults, In Association of American Colleges Bulletin, 43 (October, 1957)
485-490.

The purposes of the Center for the Study of Liberal
Education for Adults, established in 1951 by a grant from
the Fund for Adult Education are: (a) to provide aid and
leadership for forces that can develop the college and university into more effective instruments for liberal education of adults; (b) to encourage development for adults of
a wide range of university-level educative experiences
which do more than parallel regular degree or credit programs and which are planned on the basis of distinctive
interests, experiences, and abilities of adults.   Aside
from its publications program, field work, and consultative activities, its major projects may be traced to the
following propositions: (1) Educative experiences must
take into account the special nature of adulthood as a period of learning.   (2) In an overspecialized society, liberal
education is urgently needed particularly for groups whose
education has been intensive but narrow.   (3) Appropriate
programming for adults requires "retreading" of people
in academic life who develop and teach in the programs.
(4) If individuals are to operate effectively, the entire
institution must be engaged.   (5) Liberal education programs have a beneficient effect on college-community relationships.   (6) A Center-type agency has a profound obligation to serve the intellectual community through its
consultation and field-work services.   The Center is in a
position to acquire knowledge and understanding of programs of liberal education and has a sense of responsibility to spread this information to colleges and universities expanding their programs in the direction of liberal
adult education.   606

Siegle, Peter E., ed.   "The University's Responsibility for
the General Education of Adults," Conference Report.
Chicago: Center for the Study of Liberal Education for
Adults, 1955.   75 pp.

Report of a national conference held in Chicago March
3-5, 1955, sponsored by A. U. E. C., N. U. E. A., and the
Center for the Study of Liberal Education for Adults.
Preface of the Report is "The Observer's Report," by
J. Roby Kidd.   Part I explains common problems of the
Association of University Evening Colleges and National
University Extension Association, and how the two organ-
izations differ; and states the purposes of the conference
which may be summarized as more effective cooperation

between the two organizations in the interest of university
adult education.   Part II is a report of a discussion of
"Current Social Trends," their significance for institutions and national organizations concerned with the general education of adults.   Part III is "Analysis and Interpretation of Recommendations for N. U. E. A. --A. U. E. C. Action by Special Interest Groups," by John B. Schwertman.
Recommendations relate to five problems: (1) relationship with other divisions of the university; (2) effectiveness of teaching; (3) courses and curricula; (4) relations
to community; (5) increasing drawing power of liberal
arts programs.   Part IV--Appendices.   Appendix A is an
address delivered at the Conference by Robert Blakely.
(See No. 488.)   Appendix B--Agenda of the Conference.
Appendix C--Roster.   607

Siegle, Peter E. and James B. Whipple.   "New Directions
in Programming for University Adult Education." See
No. 274.   608

Spence, John A.   "A Study of the Need for the Extension
and Improvement of the Adult Education Services of Ohio
State University."   Ph. D. Dissertation.   Ohio State University, 1956.   274 pp.   609

Spengler, Edwin H.   College Life Begins at 40, In Association of University Evening Colleges Proceedings.   Sixteenth Annual Meeting, Milwaukee, 1954.   Pp. 68-73.
    A progress report on the "Brooklyn College Experi-
ment," started in the Spring of 1954, financed by a grant
from the Fund for Adult Education through the Center for
the Study of Liberal Education for Adults, and designed
to determine whether a liberal education can be acquired
by mature adults by means other than traditional attendance in regular college classes.   Includes discussion of
aims and objectives, the pilot study, faculty sanction of
the project, preliminary cost estimates, accomplishments
to date, problems and implications for the future.   610

Steiner, Celestin J.   Our Catholic Colleges and Adult Education, In National Catholic Educational Association Bulletin, 53 (August, 1956) 147-148.
    Summary of a paper presented at the fifty-third annual
meeting of the Association at St. Louis, April 3-6, 1956.
Includes a brief statement of some of the aspects and
meanings of adult education; two principles for the responsibilities and opportunities of Catholic colleges in the

field of adult education: (1) high quality, regular credit
undergraduate and graduate programs, (2) emphasis on
ideas and philosophies rather than training in skills; the
opportunity for adult education provided by radio and television with a brief description of the program at the University of Detroit; the value of a board of citizens to
interpret the University of Detroit to the community and
to tell the university how it can serve the community.
                                                        611

Stephan, A. Stephan.   Backgrounds and Beginnings of Uni-
    versity Extension in America.   See No. 347.   612

Stern, Bernard H.   "How Much Does Adult Experience
    Count?   A Report of the Brooklyn College Experimental
    Degree Project."   Chicago: Center for the Study of
    Liberal Education for Adults, 1955.   23 pp.
        Description of an experimental project in liberal adult
    education at Brooklyn College enabling a selected number
    of mature people to earn an A.B. degree partly on the
    basis of their background and experience rather than the
    accumulation of college credits.   Describes the plan; the
    students; problems of screening and selecting students,
    expressing equivalence of adult experience, standardizing
    adult experience, instruction, and evaluation; results and
    observations.   613

Stern, Bernhard H.   "Adults Grow in Brooklyn, Report No.
    2;   The Brooklyn College Experimental Degree Project
    for Adults."   Chicago: Center for the Study of Liberal
    Education for Adults, 1955.   51 pp.
        A second report on the Experimental Degree Project at
    Brooklyn College describing the manner in which the Col-
    lege attempted to solve the major problems of academic
    credit and instruction.   Sections are: The Project;
    What Does Academic Credit Mean?; Working Within the
    Tradition; Problems of Admission and Classification;
    Problems of Instruction--tutorial groups, discussion tech-
    nique, course assignments, study questions, evaluation;
    Goals of Liberal Education; Planning a Degree Curriculum
    for Adults.   614

Stockton, Frank T.   "The Pioneer Years of University Ex-
    tension at the University of Kansas."   See No. 348. 615

Stoddard, George D.   "The Urban Environment's Challenge
    to the University," in Morton Gordon, New Dimensions

of University Responsibility for the Liberal Education of
Adults, a Report of the Daytona Beach Conference of Urban University Presidents, Daytona Beach, Florida, May,
1956. Chicago: Center for the Study of Liberal Education for Adults [1956]. Pp. 17-35.
    The concept of metropolitan education is discussed with
enumeration and comment on some services which the
city may expect from a university, such as influence of a
university for fulfillment of the city's economic, political
and cultural roles; appropriate intellectual and artistic
resources for technical, professional and liberal education; academic assistance in such matters as architec-
ture, city planning, finance, government, recreation,
health, etc.; assistance in problems of international affairs; in problems of human adjustment and happiness;
opportunities for personal fulfillment through learning in
groups and through coordinated study. The following questions concerning the role of metropolitan universities are
considered: (1) How can the city and the city-located college or university be brought into a meaningful partnership? (2) Is loneliness a necessary condition of city
life? (3) Does liberal education of adults imply a further
report among the concepts "vocational," "cultural" and
"recreational?" (4) Which is the dominant "community"
in the modern city--the geographic complex, the vocational interest, or the recreational interest? (5) What part
of city life nourishes and is nourished by a university's
program in adult education? The writer points out a need
for more attention to liberal education in science and art.
He suggest that some valid measures of adult capabilities,
interests, status in a discipline, maturity in a discussion,
and rate of progress could be helpful in advancing liberal
education. City universities need constantly to reshape
their offerings and methods. It is the business of education for learners of all ages to encourage straight thinking
and to improve human relations.   616

Stratton, Burton E. and Lawrence Lipsett. An Extension
    Division Evaluates Its Program, In Adult Education Bulle-
    tin, 13 (December, 1948) pp. 240-244. See No. 258.
                                                          617

Tidwell, R. E. The University Participates in Adult Educa-
    tion for Better Living in a Dynamic Society, In National
    University Extension Association Proceedings. Thirty-
    Third Annual Meeting, Chicago, 1948. Vol. 31. Pp. 22-30.
        Traces the development of education, especially of adult

education in the last century; discusses the job of adult education in present day society; how problems of adult education are related to the individual and his community and how service agencies are involved; the role of university extension in identifying fields of activity in which adults may participate and which give promise of better living, the building of a competent extension staff, developing suitable materials, programs for training adult education leaders, and research.   618

"Tradition and Innovation in University Adult Education," Conference Report, Swampscott, Mass., October 22-24, 1954. Chicago: Center for the Study of Liberal Education for Adults [1954] 22 pp.

Summaries of addresses and discussions: "Explicitly for Adults," by John B. Schwertman; "University Adult Education for New England: a Look to the Future," by J. Paul Mather; "How the Adult Student Is Different," by Raymond Kuhlen; "What This Suggests for Adult Education--For the Traditionalists" (discussion); "What This Suggests for Adult Education--For Innovation" (discussion); "Social Problems and Adult Learning," by Kenneth Benne; commentary by Stephen G. Burke; "What This Suggests for Adult Education--For the Traditionalists" (discussion); "What This Suggests for Adult Education--For Innovation" (discussion); "An Example of Progress Through Innovation," by Paul A. McGhee; "An Example of Progress Within the Tradition," by Bernard H. Stern.   619

UNESCO. "Universities in Adult Education." Problems in Education, 4. Paris: UNESCO, 1952. 172 pp.

Comprehensive reports on the university extension movements in Great Britain, by S. E. Raybould; in Canada, by E. A. Corbett; and in the United States by Baldwin Woods and Helen Hammarberg. Introduction by Cyril O. Houle. See Nos. 681, 643, and 636 for annotations of sections.   620

U.S. Office of Education. "Resident, Extension, and Adult Education Enrollment in Institutions of Higher Education: November, 1953." See No. 406.   621

U.S. Office of Education. "Resident, Extension, and Adult Education Enrollment in Institutions of Higher Education: November, 1954." See No. 407.   622

U.S. Office of Education. "Resident And Extension Enroll-

ment in Institutions of Higher Education: November,
1955."   See No. 408.   623

U.S. President's Commission on Higher Education. "Higher
Education for American Democracy." Vol. I, Establishing
the Goals.   Washington, D.C.:   Government Printing Office, 1947.   Chapter IV, "Education Adjusted to Needs--
Adult Education."   Pp. 96-100.

An expanded program of adult education must be added
to the task of the colleges.   This is a vital and immediate need because crucial decisions of our time will have
to be made in the near future.   Colleges and universities
are the best equipped of all agencies to undertake the
major part of the job of adult education.   The present
status of university extension makes it clear that they do
not recognize adult education as their potentially greatest
service to democratic society.   They should elevate adult
education to a position of equal importance with any other
of their functions.   Adult education should be the responsibility of every department or college of the university.
The principal obstacle to acceptance of the program is the
limited concept that higher education holds of its role in
a democratic society.   It must broaden its concept and
take the university to the people.   The program must be
fitted in content, method, and aims to the adult student
as he is.   Vigorous experimentation with new methods is
called for.   The Commission recommends establishment
of a continuing committee devoted to study, development,
and utilization of technical aids to learning in higher education.   Such a committee should deal with four major
areas of responsibility; (1) provide facilities for coordinating information on existing materials and develop a plan
for interchange of materials among institutions; (2) arrange for continued study of special devices developed by
the Armed Services to discover possible applications for
civilian instruction; (3) stimulate individual institutions or
groups of institutions in a   program of integrated effort at
developing further basic-training aids; (4) assume responsibility for wide publicity on advantages and objectives
of technical aids in higher education.   University owned
and operated radio stations are another agency for adult
education whose possibilities are too seldom exploited.
The adult program is not an additional objective of the
college; it is one of the means by which the college can
achieve its general objective.   Higher education will not
play its social role in American democracy and in international affairs successfully unless it assumes responsi-

bility for a program of adult education reaching far beyond the campus and classroom.   624

U.S. President's Commission on Higher Education. "Higher Education for American Democracy." Vol. II, Equalizing and Expanding Individual Opportunity. Washington, D.C.: Government Printing Office, 1947. Chapter V, "Equalizing Opportunity Through Adult Education." Pp. 59-66.
The responsibility of institutions of higher education is not to youth of college age alone; it extends to all adults. The college can enrich the life of the individual and the community; round out education provided by elementary and secondary schools and other types of institutions; advance the individual in essential knowledge and skills; provide facilities for self-expression and appreciation in the arts; disseminate information on recent developments in government, economics, and science; provide opportunity for discussion of issues vital to national life and international relations; and give to both the older and younger generations a more adequate basis for mutual understanding. Rightly conceived and promoted adult education would help bring order into the spiritual chaos of today and create a democracy with enhanced material, moral, and intellectual strength. Many social factors make a broad program of adult education essential for national well-being. Present adult education programs in various types of institutions of higher education are reviewed briefly, especially as to extent, including programs of community colleges, extension services, correspondence courses, resident centers, programs in cooperation with federal agencies, and of technical institutes. Current developments in adult education are failing to meet needs and demands of adults in the United States. The magnitude of the task elevates it to a problem of top priority in national educational policy with requirements which should be viewed under the guidance and counsel of the U.S. Office of Education. The Commission recommends: assumption of greater responsibility for adult education by universities and colleges; leadership in developing and utilizing new techniques and methods; adequate appropriations by the institution and by state and federal governments to provide for essential developments in adult education; and systematic preparation of teachers and discussion leaders.   625

The University's Role in Adult Education; a Symposium, In Journal of Higher Education, 26 (January, 1955) 10-20,

56.
   Consists of four articles: "From the Cradle to the
Grave," by John S. Diekhoff; "The Two Roles of the
University in Adult Education," by Wayne A. R. Leys;
"The University's Role in Adult Education," by William
H. Conley; and "New Concepts of the University's Role,"
by John B. Schwertman. See Nos. 509, 553, 500 and
601.   626

Vaughan, Marilyn. "The Vassar Institute for Women in
   Business, a Report." Chicago: Center for the Study of
   Liberal Education for Adults, 1957. 46 pp.
   A report on the Vassar Institute for Women in Business
held August 5-19, 1956, sponsored by the National Secre-
taries Association, Center for the Study of Liberal Education for Adults, and Vassar College. The Institute was
a residential experiment in teaching liberal arts to highly
trained and experienced specialists. A curriculum was
planned in three subject areas: Public Issues, Man and
His Behavior, and Creative Arts. Observer's report describes activities of the Institute, impact of these activities on participants and evaluation, with a cost analysis.
Appendix lists suggested readings in each of the three subject areas.   627

Waters, John.   Evening Colleges, In   Wilma T. Donahue,
   comp.,   Education for Later Maturity. New York:
   Whiteside and Morrow, 1955. Pp. 145-151.
   A report on programs of evening courses for adults
beyond retirement age of member institutions of the Association of University Evening Colleges. The Boston University Plan of Retirement Scholarships is described as to
students' ages, educational and employment backgrounds,
course preferences and class attendance. Briefer descriptions are given of programs of Hofstra College, Russell
Sage College, Washington University, University of Kansas, City College of New York, Texas Christian University, Brooklyn College, Saint Louis University, University
of Pittsburgh, University of Omaha, Indiana University,
and Cleveland College.   628

Western Reserve University Offers Course for Adults in
   Basic Arts, In School and Society, 68 (September 4, 1948)
   149-150.
   Description of a streamlined program for adults called
"Basic Arts," with the degree of Associate in Philosophy
awarded at completion, initiated in the Fall of 1948 at

230   Wiese, Mildred J.

the School of General Studies, Cleveland College, Western
Reserve University.   629

Wiese, Mildred J.   Equalizing Opportunity Through Adult
Education, In Western College Association, Addresses
on Higher Education for American Democracy.   Spring
Meeting, April 10, 1948, University of California, Los
Angeles, California. Pp. 33-38.
    The Report of the President's Commission on Higher
Education makes a strong case for an expanded program
of adult education by colleges and universities. It emphasizes the responsibility of institutions of higher education
to individuals and to society through adult education.   In
California adult education offerings include classes in subjects covering the whole range of human interest and all
levels from elementary to postgraduate university study.
However, institutions of higher learning are failing to
measure up to the challenge and responsibility. Neither does
the program outside colleges and universities begin to
meet adult education needs.   In considering possibilities
of success in equalizing opportunity through adult education, five questions are considered, all concerned with
the role of higher education in the current stage of development of adult education in California: (1) How can
university extension best serve needs of adult education?
(2) What is the responsibility of colleges and universities
for adequate preparation of teachers of adults?   (3) What
are the most hopeful areas of experimentation with newer
media and techniques of adult education and how can colleges help develop them?   (4) Can institutions of higher
education help in the solution of the problem of coordination or community organization for adult education? (5)
What is the responsibility of these institutions for showing
the way to all adults toward better human relations?
California's adult education programs are ripe for the
leadership and service from higher education recommended
by the Report of the President's Commission.   630

Williams, J. D. Adult Education Activities in Liberal Arts
Colleges, In Institute for Administrative Officers of Higher Institutions Proceedings, 1945. Vol. 17, Emergent
Responsibilities in Higher Education.   Chicago: University of Chicago Press [c1946]. Pp. 68-77.
    In the larger sense there has always been adult educa-
tion by liberal arts colleges, but acceptance of responsibility for meeting educational needs of adults by any considerable number of liberal arts colleges is new.   The

concept behind acceptance of such responsibility is that
the liberal arts college is an institution of society whose
function is to improve the quality of living of the segment
of the society it serves by increasing the understanding
of the people, the understanding of all that affects them,
and by helping people to develop keener appreciation of
moral and spiritual values.   Once this concept is accepted by a college, it has the obvious social responsibility to undertake a positive adult education program
whose boundaries are limited only by the vision of those
responsible for the work of the college.   Illustrations are
given of varying adult education activities to show the
wide variety that exists in what liberal arts colleges are
doing, the wide range of techniques used, and values that
appear to be realized by the faculty, campus students,
and the public.   Some suggestions that have developed
from emerging practices in college programs of adult education are described.   631

Wilson, Howard E.   "Universities and World Affairs."
New York: Carnegie Endowment for International Peace,
1951.   "Off Campus Services of Universities," pp. 59-64.
     In an exploratory survey of universities, the assump-
tion was made that the university has a responsibility for
the education of the adult public beyond the university
campus.   As an agent of general adult education, the university may operate at several levels such as participation of faculty members in civic affairs, organized groups
within the university taking the initiative in projects of
beyond-the-campus education, enterprises directly sponsored by the university or by an agency designated by the
university administration.   The survey showed that a key
factor in determining the role of a university as an agency
of adult education is the determination of the specific audience it desires to reach or is capable of reaching.   The
survey indicated a lack of certainty in the role of the university in adult education arising from lack of clarified
policies and adequate precedents, and a need for careful
analysis of theory and practice before commitment to policy
and action.   632

Wood, William R.   Emerging Patterns of Higher Education
at the Community Level, In National Conference on Higher
Education, Addresses on Current Issues in Higher Education, 1951.   Addresses of the Sixth Annual National Conference on Higher Education, Chicago, Illinois, April 2-4,
1951.   Washington, D. C.:   National Education Association,

232   Wood, William R.

Department of Higher Education [c1951]. Pp. 126-130.
   Contributing to the expansion of adult education activities has been a gradual bringing together of college and
community interests. As the college becomes the heart
of the educational, cultural, and social improvement activity of the community, its destiny becomes one with
that of the community. The college administrator who
has not accepted wholeheartedly the role of the community's college is torn between the desire to preserve so-
called academic standards and the desire to preserve his
institution. By re-examining the mission of his institution and by stating it in broad and flexible terms de-
manded by today's conditions, he can fulfill both desires
and much else of greater importance. If it is assumed
that higher education is concerned only with development
of academic competencies, new efforts in adult education
may be largely wasted, but if the belief is accepted that
the academic is only one of several kinds of ability and
aptitude, opportunities for education are unlimited. Difficulties involved in further extension of educational opportunity to adults are: (1) The academic calendar. (2)
Lack of belief in the necessity of continued education for
all persons in a democracy. (3) The problem of operational control. (4) Selection, preparation, and continued
improvement of professional personnel. (5) Financial
support.   633

Wood, William R. A New Dimension in Higher Education,
   In Junior College Journal, 25 (April, 1955) 430-432.
   In the last twenty-five years the junior college, especially the community junior college has brought a new dimension to higher education, which is breadth, --breadth
of purpose, opportunity, program and service. Traditional machinery of higher education can no longer handle the
total job. Through junior colleges, decentralization of
higher education can be effected. The community junior
college, more than other institutions of higher learning,
is responsive to change at the community level. It recognizes that new kinds of abilities are required today and
explores ways of developing them educationally. Its special function is to make higher education a continuing and
essential feature of everyday life for the millions. It
maintains a flexible program of instruction and service for
part time students of all ages and educational levels. It
has broadened the base of higher education in response
to an upwelling of social and economic pressures from the
community, state and nation. The influence of its efforts

Woods, Baldwin M.   233

permeates the entire higher education structure, as evi-
denced by awareness of colleges and universities of importance and educability of many kinds of abilities, which
is reflected in growth of programs of less than the bachelor's degree length, and in programs of continuing education for adults.   634

Woods, B aldwin M.   University and Its Services to the Professions, In National University Extension Association Proceedings. Thirty-Third Annual Meeting, Chicago, 1948.
Vol. 31. Pp. 31-41. Same condensed in: School and Society, 69 (May 28, 1949) 377-380.
    It is impossible to provide all the education a man
needs while he is in college both because of the volume of
material and because of changes in knowledge.   University extension can serve as an agency to provide educational opportunities in given professions with the sponsorship of the university faculty in those fields. Professional
men also have vital interest as citizens; borrowings from
one program to another are useful to counteract narrow-
ing influence of purely professional training.   University
extension also has an obligation to aid the professions in
developing and applying a sense of values to services
which they render society.   635

Woods, Baldwin M. and Helen V. Hammarberg. "University Extension Education in the United States of America,"
In UNESCO, Universities in Adult Education, Problems in
Education, 4. Paris: UNESCO, 1952. Pp. 128-168.
    Includes: Historical Survey; Present Administrative
Structure--the place of university extension in the adult
education movement, scope and function of extension,
place of university extension in the university, relation of
university extension to schools, to government departments, and to voluntary organizations, finances, recruit-
ment, and training of administrative and teaching staff, the
public served; Analysis of Principles and Methods--phi-
losophy of adult education, methods and media, extension
centers, services to professions, industrial relations,
promotion, publicity and public relations; Results and
Prospects, with a list of problems requiring further study,
analysis, and improved solutions.   636

Wright, Madeline B.   Alumni Answer the Classroom Call,
In Food for Thought, 12 (January, 1952) 26-30.
    Describes two American experiments in extension of
extension.   In the early 1930's alumni colleges in the

United States experienced a phenomenal growth, beneficial
both to alumni and to college and alumni associations.
Trail blazers in this form of adult education were Lafa-
yette College (Easton, Pa.), which established an alumni
college in 1929, and University of Michigan, which originated its Alumni University in 1930.   The idea immediately took hold and other colleges followed.   The motivating idea of these programs was that alumni education
is valuable because it interests certain alumni who would
not return for the normal commencement program; that
it acquaints older alumni with current members of the
faculty; that it enriches lives of students individually and
as members of the community.   Alumni colleges were
suspended during the war and resumed in the post war
period.   Some of the recent programs are described.
The alumni college, whether short or long in duration,
resident or traveling, is recognized as a means to good
alumni relations.   637

Zehmer, George B.   Adult Education in Virginia, In State
    Government, 29 (April, 1956) 60-61, 75.
        Traces adult education in Virginia to the ideas of
    Thomas Jefferson who advocated "a system of general
    instruction that shall reach every description of our citi-
    zens from the highest to the poorest." Also mentioned
    is the influence on the development of adult education of
    former presidents of the University of Virginia.   Examples
    of adult extension work now under way are given.   Ap-
    proximately five hundred study groups were conducted in
    the state in 1956 covering a wide range of subjects.   Prac-
    tically every profession, vocation, cultural and special in-
    terest is represented by participants. In most instances
    the only admission requirements are interest and ability.
    In more formal extension courses for credit toward de-
    grees, candidates must satisfy the University's resident
    requirements for admission.   Recently a broadened con-
    ception of the function of extension education has emerged
    in the establishing of branches of the University in outly-
    ing communities.   Their purposes are to bring two years
    of college work and of professional work in certain fields
    to those who cannot continue studies elsewhere, to help
    meet the need for additional facilities for higher educa-
    tion, and to offer one and two year terminal programs in
    general, technical, and professional education.   A continu-
    ing increase is expected in requests for off-campus educa-
    tional opportunities and in the number of adults taking ad-
    vantage of them.   638

Zehmer, George B.   235

Zehmer, George B. The Development of University Exten-
    sion Services in the United States, In Institute for Ad-
    ministrative Officers of Higher Institutions Proceedings,
    1945. Vol. 17, Emergent Responsibilities in Higher Ed-
    ucation. Chicago: University of Chicago Press [c1946].
    Pp. 50-67.
    The paper is concerned with the role of the larger uni-
versities in the field of general extension education. The
term "university extension" is defined as educational activities of the university beyond traditional functions of
teaching students in residence and maintaining libraries
and laboratories for scholarly research. The history of
university extension is traced from its origins in England
in the early nineteenth century, through significant facts
or stages in growth and development in this country. The
early history of university extension in the United States
is described including work of individuals and of universities that pioneered in this field. The National University Extension Association held its first annual conference
in 1915. By 1925 extension work had been established in
almost all the state universities and several large private
universities. The smaller colleges and municipal universities took up the work in the 1920's and 1930's. The
idea, originally imported from England, had to be adapted
to conditions, circumstances and needs peculiar to this
country. The character of university extension work today shows that, for the most part, subjects and particular
services that were considered earlier are still receiving
most attention. There are too few new ideas and programs. Effects of standardization procedures of the first
two decades of the twentieth century are still in evidence.
However, there are several significant innovations and developments underway. Some of the more important and
promising new ventures are described in a series of
studies published by N. U. E. A.   639

Zehmer, George B. The Off-Campus and Evening College
    Responsibilities of Institutions of Higher Education, In As-
    sociation for Higher Education, Current Issues in Higher
    Education, 1953. Proceedings of the Eighth Annual Na-
    tional Conference on Higher Education, Chicago, Illinois,
    March 5-7, 1953. Edited by Francis H. Horn. Wash-
    ington, D. C.: National Education Association, Associa-
    tion for Higher Education [c1953]. Pp. 129-135.
    There are differences of opinion as to scope and char-
acter of off-campus responsibilities. Running through the
literature on the philosophy and function of university off-

campus work is the thought that publicly controlled and supported institutions have a more direct and inescapable responsibility in extension than do church and privately operated institutions. Opportunities in the field of extension education are so numerous, poignant and significant for a democratic society as to present a new challenge to all concerned with the future role of institutions of higher education. Some off-campus responsibilities deserving careful consideration are summarized: (1) The fact that many able students do not go to college is a double-barreled challenge. Institutions of higher education have the responsibility for closer working relationships with homes and schools for seeing that barriers do not prevent gifted students from entering colleges, and the responsibility for extending opportunities for further education to able students who do not enter institutions of higher education for regular study. (2) The question is raised as to whether work given in off-campus and evening college programs is comparable to that given in residence in respect to subject matter and academic requirements, and whether there is in extension work adequate consultative and advisory services, controls and directives for study, and minimum sequence and continuity essential for sound education and for guaranteeing degrees of educational growth and maturity. (3) Closely related is the problem of quality of instruction, involving abilities of teachers, library and laboratory facilities, and length and frequency of class meetings. (4) More thought should be given to providing extra-curricular and recreational activities for extension students. (5) Programs and procedures developed for resident students are generally not the best ones to serve needs of off-campus and evening college students because of differences in interests, motives, habits and experiences of the adult clientele. Institutions of higher education should supplement extension education with more investigation and basic research. (6) A final problem is the university's responsibility in the area of controversial social, economic, and political problems.   640

Cameron, Donald   237

B. Canada

Cameron, Donald. The Work at the University of Alberta
and the Provincial University in Relation to Extension
Work, In National Conference of Canadian Universities
Proceedings, Twenty-Ninth Meeting, June 8-10, 1953, St.
Francis Xavier University.   Pp. 23-30.

Describes the historical development of extension work
at the University of Alberta from its beginnings with itin-
erant lecture service around 1908 and organization of a
formal extension department in 1912, and the complex organization of the present.   The extension program of a
provincial university is concerned with the whole life of
the individual and his relationships in the community.   It
is the function of the extension department of a university
to mobilize the educational resources of its constituency
for meeting needs of the people.   The success of the extension worker is in direct proportion to the degree in
which he is able to mobilize and develop leaders in the
field.   The modern provincial university has a responsibility to the people who support it and will thrive in direct proportion to the degree in which it is closely associated with the life and work of the people it serves.
Through its extension activities the University of Alberta
is intimately associated with the economic, social and cultural development of hundreds of communities which other-
wise would have little connection with or interest in the
University.   Both the University and community are en-
riched and strengthened.   641

Coady, M. M. Extra-Mural University Adult Education, In
National Conference of Canadian Universities Proceedings,
Twenty-Ninth Meeting, June 8-10, 1953, St. Francis Xa-
vier University.   Pp. 17-22.

Universities can carry out their mission in two ways,
by training students on the campus in arts and sciences
for leadership, and by educating the masses through extra-
mural adult education.   The main reason for the time lag
in developing extra-mural work of universities is the false
philosophy of academic isolationism.   Universities in cooperation with other social and educational institutions,
can give a liberal education to the rank and file of the
people of the world to prepare them for economic, social
and cultural development.   The basic technique by which
the masses of people can be organized to get knowledge
for solution of their problems is the discussion circle, a
procedure applicable to the level of all types of intelli-

gence and all degrees of education. Group action, as
well as personal efficiency, is necessary for the good society. This kind of adult education in addition to passing
on our cultural heritage, also changes society to a fuller
and better democracy. The writer advocates a realistic,
concrete, positive type of education which will result in
external social and economic action.   642

Corbett, Edward A. University Extension Education in
   Canada, In UNESCO, In Universities in Adult Education,
   Problems in Education, 4. Paris: UNESCO, 1952. Pp.
   62-127.
   Traces historical development of university extension
services in Canadian institutions; discusses two types of
university extension programs: traditional, academic
courses for extra-mural students, and the program catering to activities and interests of people outside the university and in its immediate community; responsibility of the
provinces for education, and the work of voluntary agencies in adult education; and purposes Canadian universities
seek to serve through extension activities: (1) meeting individual needs for fellowship, vocational skills, problems
of family life, (2) group action for responsibilities of citizenship, (3) desire for wider knowledge, experience, or
understanding. The article is followed by detailed reports
on extension services of Canadian colleges and universities, arranged by province, and a concluding statement of
the tasks and responsibilities of adult education.   643

Coulter, J. R. Credit and Certificate Courses, In National
   Conference of Canadian Universities Proceedings, Thirty-
   Second Meeting, June 14-15, 1956, University of Montreal.
   Pp. 61-64.
   The most common course offered to adults is the general course leading to a B.A. degree, providing a general,
liberal education. Most educators who have helped formulate policy for extension courses have accepted the philosophy of general education and in so doing have insisted
that daytime standards be maintained. The writer suggests
that each of several universities might experiment with
one new arts course that would differ from the general
course for adults. It is also desirable to consider degree
courses related to other faculties besides the faculty of
arts. The problem in certificate and diploma courses is
how far universities should lean in the direction of non-
degree work and still give sanction in the form of an official document. If suitable standards are to be main-

tained, some questions to be considered are those concerning number of subjects to be studied, number of
hours of lecturing spent on each subject, whether lectures
should be drawn from other professionals as well as
staff members, and ways of equating the standards of examination with day-time undergraduate or graduate examinations. In the area of correspondence courses conducted
by universities in cooperation with professional or semi-
professional associations, there is the problem of convincing these associations that the university does not exist merely as a convenience for their short term needs
and to give them prestige. A certain percent of the
course should be of university subjects. The whole question of education by correspondence needs to be investigated.   644

Friesen, J. K. Non-Credit Services and Community Development, In National Conference of Canadian Universities
Proceedings, Thirty-Second Meeting, June 14-15, 1956
University of Montreal.   Pp. 65-68.
      The question of how the university can parallel the ex-
pansion of credit courses in day classes with a pressing
non-credit program of adult education is considered.   Perhaps the greatest opportunity of the university to make its
influence felt is through offering liberal studies to at least
three constituencies: the general citizenry, select groups
in the business and professional world, and students and
staff of the university.   We need to question whether the
university takes its non-credit program seriously enough
by offering every assistance so that liberal education may
assume a position of priority in extension offerings. Little
regard has been given in Canada to the social area of community development.   In this type of adult education the
university can accept responsibility for carefully selected
pilot programs which it is uniquely qualified to conduct.
Another problem is the role of the extension department
within the administrative structure of the university, the
status of the extension head, and the extent and nature of
his authority.   A final administrative question is that of
releasing adequate staff for both the credit and non-credit
programs of extension.   There is need of more financial
support and facilities with which to conduct an imaginative
extension program.   The trend toward residential centres
is one of the most promising new directions in adult education.   Success in utilizing television for adult education
will be dependent upon direct organizational effort universities are willing to make.   Universities should be con-

cerned with the experimental and the difficult and leave
other programs to mass agencies better organized for
wide dissemination of services.   The university has a
unique role in helping to coordinate effort and to stimulate, train and lead.   645

Kidd, James Roby.   "Adult Education in the Canadian University."   Toronto: Canadian Association for Adult Education, 1956.   137 pp.
      Presents a report on an inquiry into the role of the
   university in adult education, based on a study of the literature, interviews, correspondence, conference discussions, and questionnaires.   Chapter I discusses the role
   of the university in adult education in Canada, Great Britain, and the United States.   Chapter II presents conflicting views on the subject of the responsibility of the university for the education of adults.   Chapter III traces
   historical development of university adult education in
   Great Britain, United States and Canada.   Chapter IV discusses objectives, varieties of adult education activity provided by Canadian universities, support of the university,
   relationship of adult services to the university, staff, e-
   quipment, finance, relationships outside the university,
   demonstration and withdrawal from activities.   Chapter V
   looks at courses and services presently offered, considers
   some developments in university programmes, and gives
   examples of variety in subject matter and method, effects
   of adult education work, and a summary of trends.   Chapter VI examines some problems and developments of the
   future, including increase in enrollment, new institutions,
   liberal adult education, community development, and educational television.   Chapter VII evaluates the achievement
   and opportunities of adult education work in Canadian universities.   The appendix consists of charts from the Universities of British Columbia, Alberta, and Toronto illus-
   trating complexity of services, variety of courses, and
   relationships of this work to other parts of the university.
   A selective bibliography is appended.   646

Kidd, James Roby.   Report of the Special Survey Conducted
   in Canada During the Past Two Years, In National Conference of Canadian Universities Proceedings, Thirty-Second
   Meeting, June 14-15, 1956, University of Montreal, Pp.
   54-60.
      A report of the survey of adult education in Canadian
   universities, published in 1956 by the Canadian Association
   for Adult Education as "Adult Education in the Canadian

University." (See No. 646). Explains the planning of
the study and methods used, and gives a summary of the
contents including statements of views for and against
university adult education, trends, general observations
and conclusions.   647

Laidlaw, Alexander F. "The Campus and the Community."
Ed. D. Dissertation. University of Toronto, Ontario College of Education, 1956.   648

Le Blanc, N. The Training of Leaders, In National Conference of Canadian Universities Proceedings, Thirty-
Second Meeting, June 14-15, 1956, University of Montreal.
Pp. 69-72.
    The recent expansion of adult education is such that it
is becoming a new sector of our educational system. A-
mong the tasks for which the university has unique qualifications are two which seem fundamental to the adult education movement: (1) to contribute through research to
a better understanding of adult behavior in the social and
cultural context of today, and (2) to train dynamic leaders.
Leadership in adult education is shared by individuals at
different operational levels. At the base are the volun-
teers, the leaders of study groups, committees, citizenship councils, various social, economic and religious
groups. At the intermediate level are those who contribute directly to adult education while performing other professional duties. At the top are professional adult educators, most of whom have received training outside Canada. The trend toward increase in the number at the top
level will continue as organizations and institutions become more conscious of the importance of the role of professional adult educators. The university must contribute
to the adult education movement not only general information and background knowledge but genuine leadership training. Adult education requires specialists equipped not only
with skills but with a real insight of the problems and understanding of the people they deal with. The university
is the only agency that can provide training for this type
of top-level leadership.   649

Peers, Frank. University Extension in Canada, In Food for
Thought, 9 (February, 1949) 21-25.
    Most Canadian universities have developed extension
programs, but there is great variation in extent of their
services and in kinds of programs emphasized. There
are two main types of university extension programs. The

first stems directly from the traditional course-giving
function of the university. The second type is built on
existing activities and interests of people outside the universities. The programs of the University of Toronto
and of the University of British Columbia are illustrative
of the two types. In the University of Toronto, the program is related more closely to the fields of study pursued within the University, and methods are likely to be
the lecture or seminar. In the University of British Columbia, the program has been developed in relation to
needs of communities with special attention to remote
areas, and social considerations. This was natural in a
province with few other institutions ready to provide educational services. The University of Toronto Extension
Department shares the adult education field in Ontario with
other institutions and agencies. The success of each university's program is the best proof that it has grown in
the direction in which it can give most service.   650

Sheffield, Edward F.   Shaping University Extension Policy,
    In Food for Thought, 11 (March, 1951) 31-33.
        Extension services of Carleton College in Ottawa, Can-
    ada have from the beginning been related to the basic col-
    lege program. Courses are limited as a rule to those
    meriting sponsorship of regular departments of the college,
    and the institutional department assumes responsibility for
    content, leadership, and a share of planning for promotion.
    A faculty committee acts as a policy making body and co-
    ordinating agent. The College frequently offers an exten-
    sion program in collaboration with a special interest group
    or organization in the community. In case of programs
    not worthy of college support, rental of college accommo-
    dations to the sponsoring group is an alternative to co-
    sponsorship. The College provides only programs which
    serve the purpose both of the university and of adult edu-
    cation, and which it can operate uniquely well. Charac-
    teristics of the community suggest direction in course
    planning. The extension program is not treated as a
    money-maker for the College. Extension programs offer
    opportunities for experiment in content and method.   652

Stearn, Charles H.   The Extent of Extension, In National
    Conference of Canadian Universities Proceedings, Twenty-
    Ninth Meeting, June 8-10, 1953, St. Francis Xavier Uni-
    versity. Pp. 31-35.
        Preservation of standards in degree work of extension
    departments should be no more difficult and no easier than

in intra-mural courses, assuming that credit courses are
parallel in content to those of regular classes and that instruction is given by equally qualified lecturers.   Summer
sessions compensate in part for the handicaps of non-
residence of extension students.   The work of university
extension should be an actual extension of the work of the
university.   The extension department's first duty is to
awaken and increase intellectual interest in a subject.   In
the case of requests from the business community, the extension department should have some criteria by which to
determine which courses are the legitimate interest of a
university.   The writer condemns the forces which would
remove all boundaries from the activities of departments
of university extension.   652

UNESCO.   "Universities in Adult Education." See No. 620.
                                                            653

                        C. Great Britain

Brown, Andrew M.   The First Year at Burton Manor, In
    Adult Education (London), 21 (June, 1949) 194-199.
        Description of Burton Manor, a residential college, in-
    cluding the developing pattern of courses; cooperation with
    industry and commerce, with the armed services and the
    police, and with other bodies; problems of staffing, or-
    ganization and administration.   654

Brown, Andrew M.   The Organization and Administration of
    a New Residential College, In Adult Education (London),
    23 (September, 1950) 122-127.
        Deals with practical problems of running such a college
    --general organization and administration, the college of-
    fice, staff, recruitment of students, publicity, etc.   655

Campbell, C. A. C.   Scottish Universities and Adult Educa-
    tion, In Adult Education (London), 20 (December, 1947)
    66-69.
        Synopsis of an address by the Chairman of Glasgow Uni-
    versity Extra-Mural Committee.   Reasons why Scottish uni-
    versities should play a part in adult education are: (1)
    Universities were pioneers in this field and have accumu-
    lated years of valuable experience.   (2) Universities are
    accustomed to dealing with adult students.   (3) Universi-
    ties enjoy a high prestige with the clientele of adult educa-

tion. (4) The most important reason is that subjects
which attract serious adult students are university subjects, especially the philosophical and social sciences.
As to what role universities should play in adult education, they should devote themselves to longer, more systematic courses in university type subjects. The three-
year tutorial class has always been considered the province of the universities. The need for multiplying tutorial classes is one reason why universities should maintain
permanent staffs of full-time adult education tutors. Little
of this has been done in Scotland because of lack of funds.
One solution is for Local Education Authorities with access to government grants to appoint universities as their
agents to administer types of classes for which universities are specially qualified. Cooperation on the basis of
agreed differentiation of functions between L.E.A., W.E.
A. and the university is the key to future progress of a-
dult education in Scotland.   656

Carey, R. M. Residential Education for Young Factory
    Workers, In Journal of Education (London), 79 (May,
    1947) 250, 252.
        Report on an experimental course held at Rugby School
    in August, 1945 and repeated August, 1946. The curricu-
    lum included poetry, classical music, art, and civilization
    of ancient Greece. A combination of lecture and discus-
    sion group methods were used. Students' comments and
    reactions indicated the courses were highly successful.
                                                     657

Collins, P. A. W. Mr. Wiltshire's Great Tradition: Some
    Disagreements, In Adult Education (London), 29 (Winter,
    1956) 167-173.
        Criticizes the conservative point of view of H. C. Wilt-
    shire (see No. 693) on four points: (1) examinations and
    certificates, (2) concern with an educational elite, (3)
    compatibility of the traditional and the new activities, (4)
    alleged replacement of an adult education movement by
    an educational service.   658

Coulson, S. J. ...and Long-Term Non-Residential Centres,
    In Adult Education (London), 24 (Autumn, 1951) 140-142.
        A reply to Guy Hunter's article, "Short-Term Residen-
    tial Colleges--Toward a Definition." (See No. 669.) De-
    fends the non-residential school against the assumption
    that the residential college is capable of an educational ef-
    fect of more power and value and that it conducts work of

a higher standard. The non-residential centre takes a
longer time to accomplish changes in thinking, living habits and character essential to an individual to be able to
make permanent and profitable use of the educational tradition.   The same work cannot be done in a shorter period at a residential college.   Suggests that the original
sponsors of the residential colleges might have created a
centre to be used both for residential and non-residential
work.   659

Down, Wilfred. 'Night School' and 'Boarding School,' In A-
  dult Education (London), 24 (Autumn, 1951) 135-139.
     Discusses resident and non-resident adult education, the
advantages of each, and concludes that the longer term
study at the evening class or institute and the short, in-
tense experience of the residential college are complementary.   660

Elvin, Lionel. Ruskin College, 1899-1949, In Adult Education (London, 21 (June, 1949) 189-193.
     History of Ruskin College in Oxford, England, a pio-
neer residential college for workers, with description of
its growth, relations with the university, students, and
curriculum.   661

Everett, Samuel. England's Village Colleges, In School Executive, 75 (October, 1955) 66-67.
     Describes the Village Colleges which carry out the com-
munity school idea in England.   Five such schools are now
functioning and five more are projected.   Each of the existing schools combines secondary and adult education in
both day and evening programs, serving several small communities.   The idea for Village Colleges was conceived by
Henry Morris in the middle 1920's to combat the influence of industrialism.   He was convinced that Village Colleges might restore a meaningful rural life to many districts of England.   They were planned to become the educational and social centers for adults as well as children,
and their programs were designed to enrich the life of
each area, furnish stimulus for economic revival, and become significant centers of local culture and learning.
They have inspired the development of similar institutions
in other countries.   Close touch with adult needs is guar-
anteed through a student council with representatives from
adult classes and organizations.   The Colleges are characterized by beauty of spacious grounds and buildings, quality
of staff and varied and rich programs.   662

Fairless, T. A. A. Blackburn People's College, In Adult Education (London), 22 (December, 1949) 134-140.

Blackburn People's College, established in 1946, was the first of its kind to result from the 1944 Education Act. It follows a middle course between the residential college and the community center and offers a wide variety of courses and also informal activities. Early history, organization and achievements of the College are discussed.

663

Flower, F. D. Adult Education in a Technical College, In Adult Education (London), 24 (Autumn, 1951) 107-113.

Over-insistence on the difference between vocational and non-vocational education, or between pure and applied studies is erroneous. In one sense all education can be considered vocational, while on the other hand, almost any course can be liberal education if the teacher approaches the subject in the correct way. A number of non-vocational education courses were added to Hendon Technical College after the war. Relations with the W. E.-A. and Extra Mural Departments of the University have become closer and more organized. Hendon Technical College has tried to combine practical and theoretical work. The technical college is a major establishment of further education and needs to maintain a balanced range of work.   664

Hogan, J. M. The Last Refuge, In Adult Education (London), 29 (Spring, 1957) 246-249.

A criticism of H. C. Wiltshire's article, "The Great Tradition" (see No. 693) as biased. Hogan does not believe there is any single "new policy" in university extramural work, nor that the outmoded purpose of the old tradition can inspire an organization adapted to new requirements. Adult education as a movement was never sustained by people interested solely in a reflective role; a specific sense of purpose is necessary for most students. Wiltshire underestimates the problems and needs of twentieth century industry for technical training. Arts of management require an understanding of the whole character and behavior of man in organized society. The universities can do the most satisfactory job of liberalizing technical education. An important function of an extra-mural department would be not to serve as a last refuge of liberal studies, but to bring influence to bear in all faculties attempting in any way to serve their localities.   665

Hopkinson, D. M. Residential Short Courses--Planning and Method, In Adult Education (London), 24 (Spring, 1952) 294-300.

Residential short courses developed from experience of what residential life could accomplish in personal terms. The Summer School and Residential Conference were their predecessors. Experience of residential schools maintained by the services in war time and also the importance attached to provision of residential facilities by universities, industry, public-services, professional bodies and voluntary societies have contributed to their growth. Considerations affecting program planning are size of college, composition of its teaching staff, location of college, and equipment for practical work. Three functions of the college are to provide general courses open to all without qualifications to arrange special courses for particular groups, and to give hospitality to other bodies holding courses or conferences of their own. Special advantages of the residential course are contact between lecturers and students, exchange of experience and opinion between students, small group discussion or activity.   666

Hughes, H. D. The Long-Term Residential Colleges and the L.E.A.'s, In Adult Education (London), 24 (Autumn, 1951) 143-149.

Describes the work of the small number of colleges which provide residential full-time courses of a year or more in length for adult students and discusses their relationship with Local Education Authorities. They cater primarily for needs of students who left school early and who seek to broaden their knowledge by full-time study in the social sciences. Each of eight colleges is described briefly as to date of establishment, offerings and students. The residential colleges are voluntary bodies, though state and local education authorities have assisted their work according to the 1944 Education Act and Further Education Regulations.   667

Hunter, Guy. "Residential Colleges, Some New Developments in British Adult Education." Occasional Papers, No. 1. New York: Fund for Adult Education [1952]. 77 pp.

The paper is concerned with the development of the short-term residential college for adult education as representing not merely a new method but a new type of education and a new attitude toward it. Underlying themes are the problem of "recasting our conception of the 'humani-

ties' into a mould which contains the scientific and technical content of modern civilization, " which accepts and
redeems the daily occupations of the world; and the problem of clarifying our conception of the transmission of
"culture" in a democracy. The background of adult education is traced from the division of technical or vocation
education and adult education as humane studies for their
own sake; through the weakening of the movement in the
1930's, the new directions developed in the war period,
emphasis on cultural values of hobbies and personal interests, and admiration for the Folk High School of Denmark
and Sweden, and the resulting development of residential
colleges with a diversity of motives. The development of
policy is discussed with regard to length of course and
content, and relation to industrial and social training.
Vocational adult education may well provide the bridge between the technical working life and the heritage of humane culture. Success depends on quality of teaching and
tutors' ability to regard "culture" as the living answer to
living questions, on permeating a whole subject by a humane philosophy. Residential work should break away
from irrelevant standards of tutorial classes. Closer definition is needed of what the new standards are to be, and
some modification of administration to make their achievement possible. The author attempts to relate the residential colleges to other forms of adult education and to
assess their possible field of growth. The essential virtue of the residential course is in the impact on attitudes,
in the revaluation of social, political and personal philosophy which is at the bottom of all cultural life. Appendix 1--"Some Notes on Individual Short Term Colleges." Appendix 2--"Note on Finance."   668

Hunter, Guy. Short-Term Residential Colleges--Toward a
   Definition, In Adult Education (London), 23 (March, 1951)
   285-289.
      Brief description, values, problems and future possi-
   bilities of the short-term residential college. Residential
   colleges fall into two main types: (1) The Cultural Community Center emphasizes hobby and cultural interests
   mainly through weekend courses.   (2) The second type
   runs longer courses on the humanities, especially as related to work. The former widens and enriches ordinary
   cultural opportunities; the latter deepens individual experience and provides a form of political-philosophical
   training which can help to correct the mechanistic tendencies of modern mass society.   669

Hutchinson, E. M. Liberal Education in a Technical Age.
'See No. 367.   670

Kelly, Thomas. The New Approach in University Adult Education, In Adult Education (London), 29 (Winter, 1956)
174-177.
    Criticizes H. C. Wiltshire's conception of the university
tradition of liberal study as too narrow. (See No. 694.)
Kelly believes there will be a continuing need for long-
term study of a non-vocational character open to all without entrance qualifications. However, there are other
needs. Present day schools produce a clientele able to
advance in subjects beyond the range of those produced
earlier with only an elementary education. Another new
approach to liberal study is through the vocational group,
due to increase in technical and professional qualifications, and in number of professional organizations. It is
also appropriate and useful for extra-mural departments to
include high-level vocational courses, especially postgraduate courses presenting recent advances in various
fields of university work.   671

Kelly, Thomas. "Outside the Walls, Sixty Years of University Extension at Manchester, 1886-1946." See No. 343.
                                                         672

Kneller, George F. British Adult Residential College, In
Journal of Higher Education, 21 (January, 1950) 7-10,
55-56.
    British educators have established in recent years a
number of adult residential colleges, inspired by the folk
colleges of Denmark, but adapted to demands of British
life. Adult education in the residential collgge is closely
related to demands of contemporary society. Courses
provide an understanding of national and world problems
and occupational education in its broader aspects. The a-
dult residential colleges feature a variety of study experiences including classes, discussion groups, community activities, and group and individualized experimentation.
Method of teaching is aimed at acquiring knowledge through
active, personal participation. The British adult residential schools flourish because they fulfill a popular demand.
                                                         673

Lee, Christopher. University Standards in Extra-Mural
Work, In Adult Education (London), 22 (September, 1949)
31-37.

Discusses maintaining university standards in extra-
mural work from the point of view of the staff tutor.
The tutor is frustrated because a majority of his students
may not share his interests and outlook, and a class as
a whole may respond on a low level. In determining his
aims and what he should do about standards, the tutor can
build on his students' desires to understand their situation, socially and culturally, his own standards created by
university training and toughened by experience, recognition of the differences of study for adults, and the importance of values and methods. There are several factors in translating the university's values and methods into outside terms: (1) the tutor must be both a general-
ist and a specialist; (2) values and methods can emerge
only from a definite and limited field of study; (3) difficulty of relating various branches of knowledge and activity; (4) the question of priorities in what is offered. The
tutor must work out standards as he goes along, and needs
the collective thinking of his colleagues behind him. 674

Lyle, Edith A.   Reflections on Residential Adult Education,
In Adult Education (London), 26 (Winter, 1953) 190-196.
Adult colleges providing one or two year courses were
founded in the belief they might play a considerable part
in the regeneration of society. But the tendency today is
to think in terms of deficiencies in the student's prior education or of his work life after finishing the course.
The adult colleges, being small enough for their nature
and purpose to be clearly grasped by their members,
have an opportunity of recreating a sense of communion
and social responsibility on a small scale which can be
carried over into the larger community.   Staffs and heads
of such colleges must be conscious of what they are trying to do, and should give a lead to students in favor of
high standards of conduct.   They should present education
in general, and the college in particular, as not merely
an opportunity for the individual to fulfill private ambi-
tions, but as an opportunity to serve purposes transcend-
ing them.   The institutions and customs of the college
community should strike a balance between the claim to
freedom of the individual and his need to perform services as a member of society.   Students should have a
part in discussions and decisions on matters affecting the
community as a whole, and should share communal tasks.
Intellectual standards as high as is compatible with ability
of the students should be maintained.   Students can gain
also in other ways, in quality of spirit, character, and at-

titude. In addition to these functions, the colleges have
a future in continuing to provide periods of retreat for re-
inspiration and re-thinking; they can be among the best
instruments of disinterested culture and learning; and they
can break down class barriers by fostering a new convention appropriate to our time.   675

National Institute of Adult Education. "Liberal Education in
a Technical Age; a Survey of the Relationship of Vocational and Non-Vocational Further Education and Training."
See No. 386.   676

Paice, D. R. Do You Know Hillcroft? In Adult Education
(London), 28 (Spring, 1956) 254-259.
    A description of Hillcroft College, a residential long
term college for women at Surbiton, Surrey, established
in 1920. It is open to any woman over twenty years of
age who has ability to profit from the course. The average age of students is twenty-eight. No examinations are
required for entrance or on leaving. No certificates or
diplomas are awarded. The curriculum provides for the
need of a majority of students for a widening of intellectual and aesthetic experience rather than advanced academic study. The plan of work involves lectures, seminar groups and private tutorials. The writer emphasizes
the fact that too little is known about facilities for further
education, especially so far as residential colleges are
concerned.   677

Philip, W. E. Universities and Adult Education, In Journal of
Education (London), 88 (October, 1956) 439-440.
    The UNESCO Regional European Seminar on "The Uni-
versities and Adult Education," held in Bangor, North
Wales, September 1-14, 1956, was a meeting of representatives of about sixteen countries. The situation in the
English speaking countries was a balancer to the French
view that the university's job is research and teaching
people capable of a genuinely academic type and standard
of work. It was clear that in all countries there are
many members of university staffs individually interested
and taking part in the education of groups of adults. The
question at issue was: "What difference does it make if
a university takes an active and executive part in adult
education, as opposed to merely lending its staff members
as part-time lecturers? There was general agreement
that individual members of a democracy must be given e-
nough knowledge and wisdom to respond intelligently to

rapid developments and changes of the world today. But
there were questions as to how, how much to give, and
to whom. It is already being demonstrated by those continental universities which are attempting to follow the direction of British and American universities, that more is
to be achieved in the early stages by personal friendships
and persuasion, as developed by this seminar, than by
submission of formal statements. The representatives of
many nationalities, realizing the vital importance of adult
education, learned to value what they found in each other,
and may in their different ways and different spheres
bring each other lasting and effective mutual help in their
common undertaking.   678

Raybould, S. G. "A Critical Study of the Organization of
University Extra-Mural Work in England." Ph.D. Dissertation. London University, 1951.   679

Raybould, S. G. "The English Universities and Adult Education." London: Workers' Educational Association, 1951.
169 pp.
A study of the part played by English universities in
the provision and staffing of adult classes. Chapters are
on University Standards, Present Provision and Suggestions for Future Policy, Staffing, Finance, Organization,
Contribution of the Universities to Education in the Armed
Forces. Appendix 1 contains: I. "The Grants Policy of
the Board and Ministry of Education and Its Relation to
Class Provision, " with sections on Extension Lectures,
1873-1924; University Tutorial Classes, 1908-24; The
1924 Adult Education Regulations, with the 1931 and 1938
Revisions ; The Further Education Grant Regulations, 1946;
II. "Factors Affecting Grant Regulations and Class Provision, 1924-49, " with sections on Growth of Adult Education Facilities after 1919; Provision by Approved Voluntary Organizations and Changing Character of Extension
Lecture Courses after 1924; Policy of the New Adult Education and Extra-Mural Departments; Views on University
Standards of the Adult Education Committee of the Ministry of Reconstruction. Appendix 2 is "Statistics of Grant-
Aided Classes Provided by English Universities and University Colleges, 1924-25 to 1948-49 Inclusive. "   680

Raybould, S. G.   University Extra-Mural Education in
Great Britain, In UNESCO,   Universities in Adult Education, Problems in Education, 4. Paris: UNESCO,
1952. Pp. 27-61.

Sections of the study describe the University Extension
Lectures Movement; Workers' Educational Association and
University Tutorial Classes; University Extra-Mural De-
partments--origins, organization, relation to other departments within the university, relation to other adult education organizations, finances, teaching and administrative
staff, programmes and public served; Principles and
Methods; Review and Prospects.   681

Salt, W. E. The Universities and Adult Education, In Universities Review, 23 (September, 1950) 48-55. Summary:
Nature, 167 (January 6, 1951) 1-3.
Describes historical development of university adult education in Great Britain, types and scope of activities,
standards, relation of the department of adult education to
the university as a whole, staff problems for university
extra-mural departments raised by the Education Act of
1944, which places upon Local Authorities the duty of en-
suring provision of adequate facilities for further education.   682

Salt, W. E. Universities and Adult Education, Record of an
Anglo-German Conference, In Adult Education (London),
26 (Summer, 1953) 48-53.
Report on a four-day conference held in December,
1952 at Pembroke College, Oxford, and attended by representatives of adult education in Germany and Great Britain. Subjects of discussion were the different traditions
of British and German universities, contrasting lines of
development in the history of adult education in the two
countries, university standards, objectives, relationships
of organizations engaged in adult education, and administration in adult education. Attention was focused on the
fundamental question of the purpose of a university and
university education. Conclusions were that there were obvious differences between the countries; yet the problems
of adult education were similar, and in both countries
there was a spirit of hopefulness about developments
since 1945.   683

Stephens, Leslie. The Value of Residential Institutions:
England, In UNESCO,   Adult Education Toward Social
and Political Responsibility, edited by Frank W. Jessup.
UNESCO Institute for Education Pub. No. 1.   Hamburg:
UNESCO Institute for Education, 1953. Pp. 103-105.
Adult residential colleges began in Britain about the
same time as the university extension movement and the

Workers' Educational Association. They were originally
planned to provide a year's full time study for working
people. Educational elements in a residential college are:
(1) Liberal studies are a means to understanding of man
in society and the universe. (2) An extension of sympa-
thy and understanding arises from interchange of experience among men from a variety of homes, jobs, and
countries. (3) A year's residence in the college results
in the growth of personal responsibility, developed through
sharing in an organization, and through recognition of
truth in social and political thinking.   684

Thomas, T. W. The Experiment of the Non-Residential
    Summer School, In Adult Education (London), 23 (De-
    cember, 1950) 191-198.
        Discusses values of the non-residential summer school
    in Wales. Sponsored by colleges and the W. E. A., sum-
    mer schools of a week's duration are attended by students
    in the evenings. Tutors are from the University, W. E. A.
    and other bodies. The first schools of this type were
    held in 1942, one in North Wales, and one in South Wales.
    There has been an increase in the number of these
    classes and also in their quality. The writer recommends
    these schools for other areas.   685

UNESCO. "Universities in Adult Education." See No. 620.
                                                686

Verner, Coolie. Some Considerations of Adult Education in
    England, In Teachers College Record, 55 (May, 1954)
    430-437.
        Discusses factors influencing development of adult edu-
    cation in England. Distinguishes between adult and fur-
    ther education. The former includes all educational ac-
    tivities which have evolved under, or are functionally and
    symbolically tied to the universities; the latter includes all
    non-university related educational activities for adults.
    The Workers' Educational Association is the main force be-
    hind British adult education, but it also tends to retard
    the development of newer forms and services. Describes
    the principle methods of university class organization and
    types of activities. Points out the need for reappraising
    traditional forms and the development of newer patterns
    more suited to the changed character of British society,
    and shows implications of British experience to American
    university programs.   687

Vickers, J. O. N. Residential Colleges and Adult Education,
In Adult Education (London), 20 (December, 1947) 70-74.
   The residential college can play a big part in drawing
to adult education people who would not come in any other
way because of its different atmosphere and conditions.
Describes various types of week-end courses, short
courses and long courses. Residential education is an
intrinsic part of adult education as a whole. Residential
colleges have a great contribution to make toward the major tasks of adult education.   688

Waller, Ross D. The English Experience, In Food for
Thought, 17 (December, 1956) 127-133.
   Describes the short-term residential college, which is
primarily a post-war development, although its origins
can be traced in earlier forms of adult education. These
colleges are conducted differently and under different auspices than the older long-term residential colleges. They
also differ among themselves, but some features they have
in common are their beautiful, well-equipped and decor-
ated buildings, located in rural areas; the fact that they
are expensive to set up and conduct; provision of short
courses from a week-end to a fortnight in length; with the
clientele and social-educational effect mainly local. Values of these colleges are the peculiar virtues of residential adult education, in which people live, learn and play
together away from distractions of modern civilization; the
fact that they are more informal and sociable than traditional adult education; and are the best instruments for
development of regional and international relationships.
Their problem is to see that they are truly educational as
well as enjoyable. A list of twenty-five short-term residential colleges is given.   689

Waller, Ross D. "The English Universities' Part in Adult
Education for Political and Social Responsibility, in
UNESCO, In Adult Education Toward Social and Political
Responsibility, edited by Frank W. Jessup. UNESCO Institute for Education Pub. No. 1. Hamburg: UNESCO
Institute for Education, 1953. Pp. 140-143.
   This subject must refer to the entire body of University extra-mural work, including university extension, begun in 1873, whose subject matter was literary, artistic,
scientific, and sometimes historical; university settlements, beginning in 1884 and concerned with social conditions; and the partnership of the Universities with the
Workers' Educational Association through joint committees

and tutorial classes, dating from 1907, in which social,
political and economic subjects predominated from the out-
set. This partnership has helped the universities to feel
rooted in the common life of their areas, and for the
growing political activity of the working class, it has been
a source of knowledge and strength. Although local authorities and voluntary bodies make extensive provision
for adult education, the university is the appropriate center of reference and consultation in English adult education. Universities have now begun to undertake the study
of adult education, its organization, history, psychology,
methods, and training for adult education teachers. The
universities do not accept the social-political aim as the
main objective of adult education, but they carry on their
specialized function as a highly responsible part of society
and discharge their obligations by offering the "fruits of
intellectual freedom," which constitute the heart and core
of a socially responsible democracy.   690

Waller, Ross D.   The Universities and Adult Education, In
    Universities Quarterly, 11 (November, 1956) 43-54.
    Report on the UNESCO European Seminar on Universi-
ties and Adult Education at Bangor, North Wales, September 1-14, 1956. Problems for discussion were: relationship of universities with the community; conditions under which they can properly be concerned; at what levels
and in what ways they should work; relationship of universities in this field with Ministries of Education, Local Education Authorities, trade unions, industry, etc.; difficulties and objections; and minimum administrative apparatus
required for participation by universities in this work.   In
England and other English speaking countries there is
more adult education activity in universities than in continental countries where it is generally not approved as a
function of the university. It was generally agreed, however, that in no country can universities be indifferent to
the social and educational problems involved in adult education, or unwilling to contribute to their solution in appropriate ways.   691

Wilson, R. W. Humane Aspects of Further Education, In
    Adult Education (London) 19 (December, 1946) 92-104.
    Technical education should not be narrowly conceived,
but should be a vehicle for the best kind of general education.   Factors contributing to narrowness of technical
education in the past are: short amount of time available
for study, shortage of space, and misconception of the

real meaning of education.   Discusses four methods by
which humanizing of technical education can be carried
out: (1) development of adult education; (2) drawing in
of existing outside activities; (3) promotion of a corporate
life within the college; (4) humanistic treatment of the vocational syllabus.   Also discusses material needs of physical facilities, environment, and staffing.   692

Wiltshire, H. C.   The Great Tradition in University Adult
   Education, In Adult Education (London), 29 (Autumn,
   1956) 88-97.
      Characteristics of the great tradition in university adult
   education are: (1) It is committed to a liberal curriculum.
   (2) Within this curriculum particular concern is shown for
   social studies and aspects of other studies which illumi-
   nate man as a social being.   (3) It demands from students a non-vocational attitude toward their studies.   (4)
   It rejects selection of students either by examination or
   reference to previous education.   (5) Small tutorial groups
   meeting for guided discussion over a fairly long period is
   its most effective educational technique.   This is no longer
   the central tradition because of changes in the post-war
   period.   Characteristics of the new policy are: (1) Any
   kind of educational provision proper to a university is
   proper to its extra-mural department.   (2) The trend is
   to provide courses for vocational groups and courses leading to examination and awards.   (3) Educational service is
   now addressed to an educational elite.   (4) There is a
   tendency to return to the lecture method and attach less
   importance to tutorial methods and discussion.   The writer
   criticizes the new policy in regard to entry qualifications
   and lack of distinction between liberal and technical, vocational and non-vocational.   The new policy has not provided a new dynamic, new principles, or new purposes.
   It succeeds because it has adapted itself to the new society and new universities.   It is important to the modern
   university to maintain the great tradition in extra-mural
   work as the last refuge of liberal studies.   What is needed
   is a grafting of the vigour and adventurousness of the new
   work upon the stock of the great tradition.   693

Wiltshire, H. C.   The Great Tradition II: A Reply, In Adult
   Education (London), 30 (Summer, 1957) 6-19.
      Mr. Wiltshire clarifies and extends his original case
   for the great tradition in university adult education, and
   answers his critics, P. A. W. Collins (see No. 658),
   Thomas Kelly (see No. 671), and J. M. Hogan (see No. 665),

on several points including selection of students, standards and quality, attitudes toward vocational and non-vocational studies, examinations and awards, distribution of
extra-mural resources, and attitudes toward traditional
work.   694

Wiseman, H. V.   University Extension Work Since 1945, In
Adult Education (London), 24 (Winter, 1951) 180-192.
    This article examines facts and offers viewpoints for
discussion about the horizontal distinction between Extension Work and Joint Committee Work (through which
classes are offered in cooperation with the W.E.A.), and
the vertical distinction between Extension work and work
done by bodies (apart from the W.E.A.) other than the
universities. Statistics on growth of extension work indicate a tendency for extra-mural departments to provide an
increasing number and proportion of short courses, including a variety of facilities from those for small groups
of specialist graduates to provision of lecture courses for
the general public. Two other fields of extension activity
are all courses leading to certificates or diplomas, and
work in which the Extra-Mural Department accepts administrative responsibility for courses in which it does
not provide teaching. It appears almost impossible to discover any real difference between Extension and Joint Committee work in subject matter or type of students. The
problem of vertical distinction is the problem of university standards in adult education. University services
should be only those which are appropriately the province
of the university, and should be only for students at an
appropriate level. In liberal studies for adults the nature
of the course and its demands set the standards. Unless
internal departments of the university cooperate and appreciate the nature and need for extra-mural work, the
latter will be unable adequately to present the university
to the outside world. The university must contribute to
the general welfare of society by training capable minds
through both liberal studies and courses to relate growth
of specialist knowledge to the general purposes of society,
as well as courses aiming at personal rather than social
development. The link between those concerned with research and study of adult education and those engaged in
it as an activity is important.   695

IV. The Roles of Other Agencies

A. Public Schools

1. General

Allion, Helen and Robert A. Luke. Public School Adult Education in the United States; Report of a Survey, In Adult Education, 3 (February, 1953) 69-75. See No. 354 for annotation.   696

American Association of School Administrators. Twenty-Sixth Yearbook. "The Expanding Role of Education." Washington, D. C.: A. A. S. A. [c1948]. Chapter IV, Extension and Enrichment of Education for Adults. Pp. 79-98.   697

Bruntz, George G. Organizing the Adult Curriculum, In Nation's Schools, 39 (February, 1947) 24-25, 32.   698

California State Department of Education. "A Survey of the California Adult Education Program." Sacramento: State Department of Education. June, 1953. 231 pp. See No. 281 for annotation.   699

Clark, Burton R. "Adult Education in Transition: A Study of Institutional Insecurity." Ph. D. Dissertation. University of California, Los Angeles, 1956. Also published as: University of California, Publications in Sociology and Social Institutions, Vol. 1, No. 2, 1956. 202 pp. See No. 357 for annotation.   700

Clark, Clare W. The School as a Centre for Adult Learning, In Food for Thought, 8 (November, 1947) 5-8, 27.   701

Crabtree, Arthur P. "Civic Education, Program for Adults," written for the Curriculum Committee [National Association of Public School Adult Educators] Washington, D. C.: National Association of Public School Adult Educators [c 1956] 64 pp.   702

Dalton, John E.   Adult Education in Small Population Centers, In American School Board Journal, 131 (October, 1955) 28.   703

Enterline, C. G.   Sidelights on a Public Evening High-School Program, In Adult Education Bulletin, 13 (December, 1948) 245-247.   704

Essert, Paul L.   Programs in Adult Education, In School Executive, 75 (January, 1956) 101-102.   705

Finkelstein, Elizabeth.   "A Survey of Adult Education in 296 Public Schools in the U.S.A., 1938-1947 Inclusive." Ph.D. Dissertation.   Temple University, 1950.   706

Hallenbeck, Wilbur C.   New Needs in Adult Education, In Teachers College Record, 48 (May, 1947) 487-493.   707

Hamlin, H. M.   Adult Education in the Rural Schools of the Middle West, In Adult Education Bulletin, 12 (August, 1948) 169-172.   708

Hendrickson, Andrew.   Public School Capstone, In National Education Association Journal, 46 (March, 1957) 199-200.
                                                                   709

Hensarling, Paul R.   "A Study of the Accreditation Standards for Adult Academic Programs in Elementary and Secondary Education in the United States." Ed.D. Dissertation.   University of Houston, 1957.   710

Houle, Cyril O.   Future for Adult Education, In Wisconsin Journal of Education, 79 (September, 1946) 8-10; same: Sierra Educational News, 42 (October, 1946) 25-27; Virginia Journal of Education, 40 (October, 1946) 69-70+; Kentucky School Journal, 25 (December, 1946) 34-37; Ohio Schools, 24 (December, 1946) 404-405; same condensed: Education Digest, 12 (December, 1946) 38-39. See No. 69 for annotation.   711

Houle, Cyril O.   When Are We Really Going to Have Adult Education? In Nation's Schools, 41 (June, 1948) 24-25.
                                                                   712

Kempfer, Homer H.   "Adult Education Activities of the Public Schools; Report of a Survey, 1947-1948." U.S. Office of Education.   Pamphlet 107.   Washington, D.C.:

Government Printing Office, 1949. 21 pp.   See No. 369
for annotation.   713

Kempfer, Homer H.   Adult Education Is Growing, In School
and Society, 68 (September 11, 1948) 171-172.   714

Kempfer, Homer H.   An Adult Education Program For
Smaller Communities, In American School Board Journal,
110 (February, 1945) 19-20.   715

Kempfer, Homer H.   "Checklists for Public School Adult
Education Programs." U.S. Office of Education.   Circular 356. Washington, D.C.: Government Printing Office, 1952. 17 pp. See No. 294 for annotation.   716

Kempfer, Homer H.   How Much Adult Education Do 444
School Programs Provide?, In School and Society, 75
(January 12, 1952) 26-27.   See No. 370 for annotation.
                                                         717

Kempfer, Homer H.   "Identifying Educational Needs   of A-
dults." U.S. Office of Education.   Circular 330.   Washington, D.C.: Government Printing Office, 1951. 64 pp.
Summary: In Adult Education, 2 (October, 1951) 32-36.
See No. 220 for annotation.   718

Kempfer, Homer H. and Grace S. Wright.   "100 Evening
Schools." U.S. Office of Education Bulletin, 1949, No.
4. Washington, D.C.: Government Printing Office, 1949.
71 pp. See No. 371 for annotation.   719

Kendall, Glenn.   Adult Education and the Total Educational
Program, In School Executive, 64 (January, 1945) 59-60.
                                                         720

Kidd, James Roby.   "Adult Education and the School."
Toronto: Canadian Association for Adult Education, 1950.
36 pp.   721

LaSalle, Loy B.   Public School Adult Education, In National
Education Association Journal, 44 (February, 1955) 85.
                                                         722

McClusky, Howard Y.   Adult Education and the Public
Schools, In Michigan University School of Education Bulletin, 16 (February, 1945) 65-69.   723

262 McClusky, Howard Y.

McClusky, Howard Y. The Responsibility of the Public
School for Adult Education, In American Association of
School Administrators, Regional Committee on Adult Education, Now...in Our Town, Emerging Administrative
Practices in Adult Education in Public Schools and Colleges. Washington, D. C.: The Association, 1945. Pp.
1-4.   724

McClusky, Howard Y. School Responsibility for the Education of Adults, In Michigan University School of Education
Bulletin, 22 (April, 1951) 99-102.   725

Martin, Arthur G. and M. Channing Wagner. What Educational Opportunities Can the School Offer to the Adults in
the Community?, In National Association of Secondary
School Principals Bulletin, 40 (April, 1956) 238-242. 726

Mather, Louis K. "The New American School for Adults."
Washington, D. C.: National Education Association, Division of Adult Education Service. [1955] 39 pp. See No.
381 for annotation.   727

Mumma, Richard A. Public School Administrators and Adult
Education, In Adult Education, 1 (October, 1950) 12-18.
See No. 383 for annotation.   728

Mumma, Richard A. Trends in Adult Education Offerings in
Region II, In Adult Education Bulletin, 14 (August, 1950)
180-186. See No. 384 for annotation.   729

National Association of Public School Adult Educators.
"Public School Adult Education, a Guide for Administrators and Teachers." Washington, D. C.: N. A. P. S. A. E.
[c 1956] 156 pp.   730

National Education Association. Division of Adult Education
Service. "A Study of Urban Public School Adult Education
Programs of the United States." Washington, D. C.:
The Division, 1952. 171 pp. See No. 385 for annotation.
                                                          731

Olson, Eva. Adult Education an Integral Part of a School
System, In Adult Education Bulletin, 9 (February, 1945)
78-79.   732

Overstreet, Harry A. Changing Demands on Evening Schools,
In Michigan Education Journal, 23 (December, 1945) 195.

Peterson, Dorothy R.   263

Same condensed in: School Management, 15 (March, 1946) 402.   733

Peterson, Dorothy R. Adult Education in Evening High Schools, In Wilson Library Bulletin, 23 (February, 1949) 436-437.   734

Rabe, Henrietta F. Educational Programing; Public Schools-Adult Education, In Wilma T. Donahue, comp., Education for Later Maturity. New York: Whiteside and Morrow, 1955. Pp. 98-108.   735

Reals, Willis H. Adult Education--the School's Concern, In Journal of Education, 137 (April, 1955) 7-8, 20, 28. 736

Redd, George N. Adult Education for Negroes under Public School Auspices, In Journal of Negro Education, 14 (Summer, 1945) 312-321. See No. 396 for annotation.   737

Rosenberger, Homer T. Offerings for Out-of-School Adults, In National Association of Secondary School Principals Bulletin, 40 (February, 1956) 181-193.   738

Schneider, Perry L. Curriculum Development in Adult Education, In Adult Education Bulletin, 12 (October, 1947) 19-21.   739

Sharer, Robert E. Adults Learn to Live Better, In School Executive, 65 (December, 1945) 47-49.   740

Sheats, Paul H. Adult Education--a Responsibility of Public Education, In School Executive, 64 (January, 1945) 52-53.   741

Sheats, Paul H., Clarence D. Jayne, and Ralph B. Spence. "Adult Education, the Community Approach." New York: Dryden Press [c 1953]. Chapter 7, Public Schools. Pp. 144-174.   742

Spinning, Fred. Veterans Are at Home in Adult Evening Schools, In Baltimore Bulletin of Education, 23 (January-February-March, 1946) 108-109.   743

Thaden, John F. Adult Education in the Public School and the Community, (Study of Adult Education in Rural Areas,) In Rural Social Systems and Adult Education, a Committee Report by Charles P. Loomis and others.

[East Lansing] Michigan State College Press, 1953. Pp.
24-51.   744

Van Sant, Thomas A.   Aspects of Public School Adult Education, In Baltimore Bulletin of Education, 33 (June, 1956)
13-25.   745

Van Sant, Thomas A.   Public School Adult Education Programs, In Handbook of Adult Education in the United
States, edited by Mary L. Ely.   New York: Institute of
Adult Education, Teachers College, Columbia University,
1948.   Pp. 196-200; 412-424.   746

Walton, L. A. and others.   Public School's Responsibility for
Postwar Education of Adults, In National Association of
Secondary School Principals Bulletin, 29 (March, 1945)
36-37.   747

Wetzel, Paul W.   What Are We Doing for School Drop-Outs?
In American School Board Journal, 131 (October, 1955)
29-31.   748

Whipple, Caroline A.   Adult Education and the Public
Schools, In Journal of Educational Sociology, 19 (September, 1945) 20-26.   749

2.   State and City Programs.

Bailey, Thomas D. and S. E. Hand.   On Educating Adults in
the Sunshine State, In School Executive, 77 (December,
1957) 52-55.   750

Beamer, Alan L.   Alexandria's Adult Education Program, In
Virginia Journal of Education, 42 (October, 1948) 13, 40.
                                                          751

Brown, Francis J.   A State Serves Its Veterans, In Adult
Education Bulletin, 10 (December, 1945) 45-49.   752

Bruntz, George G.   ...Through Small Community Programs,
In California Journal of Secondary Education, 21 (November, 1946) 313-315.   753

Crabtree, Arthur P.   Adults Keep Up With the Times, In
National Education Association Journal, 43 (February,

Davison, O. W.   265

    1954) 94-95.   754

Davison, O. W. Oklahoma Accepts Public School Responsi-
    bility for Adult Education, In School Executive, 73 (Sep-
    tember, 1953) 56-58.   755

Degroat, Fannie M. "Elements That Seem to Contribute to
    Successful Adult Education Programs in Selected Public
    Schools of the State of New York." Ph. D. Dissertation.
    Cornell University, 1954.   756

Donohue, Francis J. Principles for Post High-School Edu-
    cation in Michigan, In School and Society, 65 (May 10,
    1947) 346.   757

Eddy, Paul. Development of Adult Education for Veterans in
    Florida, In Adult Education Bulletin, 10 (December, 1945)
    40-45.   758

Enyeart, Buel F. and J. A. Howard. ...Through Veterans
    Education, In California Journal of Secondary Education,
    21 (November, 1946) 306-309.   759

Fossum, Oscar and Harold Davey. Development of an Adult
    Education Program, In American School Board Journal,
    118 (June, 1949) 33-34, 80.   760

Frasure, Kenneth J. "Did the 1946-1947 Offerings and
    Practices of Selected Illinois High Schools Outside Cook
    County Meet Standards for Judging Adult Education Pro-
    grams as Suggested in the Literature of Adult Education?"
    Ph. D. Dissertation. University of Illinois, 1948. 761

Getsinger, Joseph W. "The History of Adult Education in
    the Public Schools of California." Ed. D. Dissertation.
    Stanford University, 1949.   762

Getsinger, Joseph W. What Do California Adult Schools
    Teach?, In Adult Education Journal, 8 (October, 1949)
    231-236.   763

Goldman, Edward D. Current Events and Materials in Adult
    Education, In California Journal of Secondary Education,
    31 (April, 1956) 226-229.   764

Graham, Minnie W. Mighty Oaks from Tiny Acorns Grow,
    In Baltimore Bulletin of Education, 23 (June, 1956)

61-64.   765

Graves, Purdue B. Topeka, Kansas Goes to Night School,
    In Adult Education Bulletin, 9 (February, 1945) 79-80.
                                                            766

Johnson, Janet. Adults Enjoyed Evening Literature, In
    Clearing House, 23 (March, 1949) 414-416.   767

Kempfer, Homer H. State Programs of General Adult Edu-
    cation, In Adult Education Journal, 7 (April, 1948) 75-81.
                                                            768

Kettler, A. J. Indianapolis Public Schools Organize School
    Adult Forums on Peace Problems, In School and Society,
    61 (June 9, 1945) 374.   769

King, Nancy. New Horizons; Adult Education Offers
    Courses in Hobbies, Trades, Commercial, and Cultural
    Subjects, In Virginia Journal of Education, 43 (November,
    1949) 10-11, 21.   770

Mann, George C. Adult Education During Reconversion, In
    California Journal of Secondary Education, 21 (November,
    1946) 299-302.   771

Maurer, Charles L. Adult Education in a University High
    School, In School Review, 60 (April, 1952) 19-24.   772

Mayfield, Leonard B. "Developing an Adult Education Pro-
    gram in Oregon Public Schools." Curriculum Bulletin,
    No. 146. Eugene, Oregon: University of Oregon, School
    of Education, 1955. 11 pp.   773

Pulling, R. J. The Adult Education Curriculum, Mirror of
    the Community, In National Education Association Journal,
    46 (October, 1957) 461-462.   774

Pulling, R. J. and Presco Anderson. Building a Curriculum
    of Adult Education in New York State, In Adult Leader-
    ship, 5 (December, 1956) 171-173, 196.   775

Sac City's Adult Education Program, In American School
    Board Journal, 116 (February, 1948) 54.   776

Sworder, Stanley E. Adult Education in Its Centennial Year,
    In California Schools, 28 (May, 1957) 199-202.   777

Thomas, Ralph R. "A History of the First Hundred Years of Public School Adult Education in Buffalo, New York." Ed. D. Dissertation. University of Buffalo, 1957.   778

Timken, Joseph E. "A Study to Determine the Adequacy of Three Selected Oklahoma Public School Adult Education Programs." Ph. D. Dissertation. Oklahoma Agricultural and Mechanical College, 1952.   779

Van Auken, Robert A. Ohio Practice in Evening School Offerings, In Ohio Schools, 25 (February, 1947) 66-67. 780

Van Sant, Thomas A. Aspects of Public School Adult Education, In Baltimore Bulletin of Education, 23 (June, 1956) 13-25.   781

Younkman, Harold E. Adult Education in Ohio Public Schools, In Adult Education Bulletin, 13 (April, 1949) 103-105.   782

B. Libraries

United States

American Library Association. "Adult Education Activities in Public Libraries." Chicago, A. L. A., 1954. 96 pp.   783

American Library Association. Adult Education Board. Adult Education Policy for Libraries, In A. L. A. Bulletin, 38 (November, 1944) 451-452. Excerpts: Adult Education Bulletin, 9 (February, 1945) 86.   784

American Library Association. Office for Adult Education. Adult Education Project: Interim Report, July 1953- August 1954. Chicago: A. L. A. [1954] 21 l.   785

American Library Association. Office for Adult Education. "Experimental Projects in Adult Education, A Report of the A. L. A. Adult Education Subgrant Project." Chicago: A. L. A., 1956. 36 pp.   786

A. L. A. Survey of Adult Education, In School and Society, 78 (November 28, 1953) 172.   787

A. L. A. Surveys Library Programs in Adult Education, In
Library Journal, 78 (November 1, 1953) 1896.   788

Anderson, Martin P.   Loan Package Library; A Tool for
Implementing Adult Education in a Democracy, In Library
Quarterly, 20 (April, 1950) 119-126.   789

Barensfeld, Thomas E.   I Am Really Sold on Adult Education, In Library Journal, 73 (October 1, 1948) 1351-
1353.   790

Bausman, Charlotte K. and Lena C. Campbell.   Culture
Without College, In Library Journal, 76 (February 15,
1951) 273-274.   791

Blakely, Robert J.   Library and Liberal Adult Education, In
A. L. A. Bulletin, 48 (April, 1954) 201-205.   792

Can Libraries Contribute to Community Adult Education?, In
Library Journal, 72 (November 1, 1947) 1522.   793

Close, Kathryn.   Librarians, Dealers in Ideas, In Survey,
85 (September, 1949) 470-473.   794

The Community Study, Library-Community Project, In A. L. A.
Bulletin, 51 (January, 1957) 14-16.   795

Cory, John M.   Educational Opportunity of the Library, In
Public Libraries, 7 (May, 1953) 1-5.   796

Cory, John M.   What's the Formula? Library-Sponsored
Group Services, In A. L. A. Bulletin, 48 (April, 1954) 208-
210.   797

Dotson, Elizabeth.   Never Too Old to Learn, In Wilson Library Bulletin, 23 (September, 1948) 64-65.   798

Folkman, Jerome D.   Bricks, Brains, and Books, In Library
Journal, 70 (January 1, 1945) 15-17.   799

Foster, Edith L.   Mountain Against Which to Lean the Eyes,
In A. L. A. Bulletin, 48 (April, 1954) 218-221.   800

Grady, Marion B.   Let's Help Educate America, In Library
Journal, 72 (June 15, 1947) 939-941.   801

Greenaway, Emerson.   Setting the Course for the Next Decade, In Public Libraries, 4 (March, 1950) 9-13.   802

Greenaway, Emerson. What's the Formula? Two Points of
View, In A. L. A. Bulletin, 48 (April, 1954) 214-217. 803

Hamill, Harold L. What's the Formula? Boon or Booby
Trap, In A. L. A. Bulletin, 48 (April, 1954) 210-214. 804

Harrison, Florence L. Connecticut Women's Clubs Consider
Libraries; Experiment in Adult Education, In Library
Journal, 71 (April 1, 1946) 455-457.   805

Hawes, Marion E. "Adult Education Service of the Enoch
Pratt, in UNESCO, In Adult Education; Current Trends
and Practices. Problems in Education, 2. New York:
Columbia University Press, 1949. Pp. 122-131.   806

Hawes, Marion E. Planning and Organizing the Library's
Adult Education Programme, In Cyril O. Houle and
others, Libraries in Adult and Fundamental Education,
The Report of the Malmo Seminar. UNESCO Public Library Manuals, 4. Paris: UNESCO, 1951. Pp. 33-41.
807

Hazard, Leland. Couriers of Culture, In Pennsylvania Library Association Bulletin, 12 (Summer-Fall, 1956) 9-
14.   808

Houle, Cyril O. Adult Education as a Function of the Library, In Cyril O. Houle and others, Libraries in A-
dult and Fundamental Education, The Report of the Malmo
Seminar. UNESCO Public Library Manuals, 4. Paris:
UNESCO, 1951. Pp. 21-28.   809

Houle, Cyril O. Adult Education in the Public Library, In
California Librarian, 18 (October, 1957) 249-255.   810

Houle, Cyril O. Basic Philosophy of Library Service for A-
dult Education, In Library Journal, 71 (November 1,
1946) 1513-17; (November 15, 1946) 1600-04.   811

Houle, Cyril O. Chicago Public Library Staff Studies Adult
Education, In Library Journal, 71 (January 1, 1946) 23-
27, 47.   812

Houle, Cyril O. Social Change, Learning, Adult Education
and Libraries, In American Library Association. Library-

Community Project. News. No. 4 (June, 1957) 1-2. 813

Houle, Cyril O. Strengthening the Influence of the Public
Library, In A. L. A. Bulletin, 51 (November, 1957) 765-
771.   814

Hutchins, Robert M. Public Library; Its Place in Education, In Library Quarterly, 20 (July, 1950) 180-186. 815

Kaplan, Abbott. Librarian As Adult Educator, In California
Librarian, 16 (October, 1954) 36-38.   816

Knowles, Malcolm S. Role of the Librarian in Adult Education, In Michigan Librarian, 18 (December, 1952) 5-6.
                                                        817

Lacy, Dan. The Adult in a Changing Society; Implications
for the Public Library, In Library Quarterly, 27 (October,
1957) 279-293.   818

Leigh, Robert D. "The Public Library in the United States;
The General Report of the Public Library Inquiry." New
York: Columbia University Press, 1950. 272 pp.   819

Library Function as an Educator of the People, In Sidney
H. Ditzion, Arsenals of a Democratic Culture; A So-
cial History of the American Public Library Movement in
New England and the Middle States from 1850 to 1900.
Chicago: A. L. A., 1947. Pp. 77-96.   820

Lindquist, Raymond C. If Not the People's University--Then
What?, In Public Libraries, 4 (March, 1950) 3.   821

Luke, Robert A. Library Rooms Into Classrooms, In Library Journal, 70 (February 15, 1945) 152-154.   822

McDiarmid, Errett W. Crusade for an Educated America,
In A. L. A. Bulletin, 42 (July-August, 1948) 289-293. 823

McPheeters, Annie L. Atlanta Branch Aids Negro Groups,
In Library Journal, 74 (March 1, 1949) 342-344, 350.
                                                        824

Maddox, Vivian. On Cutting Your Coat to Fit Your Cloth,
In Library Journal, 79 (November 15, 1954) 2110-2112.
                                                        825

Martin, Lowell A.   Potential Role of the American Public
Library, In American Library Association, Post-War
Planning Committee,   National Plan for Public Library
Service. Chicago: A. L. A. , 1948. Pp. 1-17. Revised
version: In Public Libraries, 2 (December, 1948) 63-
65.   826

Mathews, Mildred Van Deusen. Education at Their Door-
step; The New York Public Library Shares in Providing
College Extension Courses, In Library Journal, 70 (January 1, 1945) 13-14.   827

Mathews, Mildred Van Deusen. Role as Adult Educators,
In Library Journal, 79 (February 1, 1954) 170-176. 828

Milam, Carl H. Notes on Adult Education, In A. L. A. Bulletin, 40 (June, 1946) 213.   829

Milam, Carl H. Role of the Library in Adult Education, In
California Journal of Secondary Education, 21 (November,
1946) 312.   830

Morrison, Duncan G. "Relation of the Public Library to A-
dult Education in the State of Washington." Ph. D. Dissertation. University of Washington, 1949.   831

Munn, Ralph. New Approaches to the Collection and Services,
In Library Quarterly, 27 (October, 1957) 294-304.   832

Murphy, Lucy L.   Adult Education and the Catholic Reader,
In Brother David Martin, ed. ,   Catholic Library Practice. University of Portland Miscellaneous Publication No.
1. Portland: University of Portland Press, 1947. Pp.
85-93.   833

Norton, Ruth. School Bells Ring at the 'People's University', In Wilson Library Bulletin, 21 (December, 1946)
297-298.   834

O'Brien, Katherine and others. Libraries Get Adult Education Role, In Library Journal, 72 (November 1, 1947)
1517-1521.   835

Overstreet, Harry A. Elusive Thing Called Adult Education,
In A. L. A. Bulletin, 48 (April, 1954) 193-196.   836

O'Reilly, R. N. Library Evangelism and the Educational

Functions of the Public Library, In Library Quarterly,
17 (January, 1947) 18-27.   837

Phinney, Eleanor. A. L. A. Projects Supported by the Fund
for Adult Education, In A. L. A. Bulletin, 50 (October,
1956) 591-595.   838

Phinney, Eleanor. "Library Adult Education in Action,
Five Case Studies." Chicago: American Library Association, 1956. 182 pp.   839

Phinney, Eleanor. Library-Community Project Moves A-
head, In Library Journal, 81 (January 15, 1956) 123-
125.   840

Phinney, Eleanor. Putting the Library-Community Studies
to Work, In A. L. A. Bulletin, 51 (March, 1957) 196-198.
                                                         841

Powell, John W. Join the Community-Risk or Opportunity?,
In A. L. A. Bulletin, 51 (May, 1957) 363-365.   842

Powell, John. One Step Nearer Leadership; Guided Group
Reading as a Library Service, In Library Journal, 71
(April 1, 1946) 443-449.   843

Public Library Shares in Louisville's Neighborhood Colleges,
In Library Journal, 72 (September 15, 1947) 1261.   844

Putnam, Miriam. Books as Tools for Adult Education, In
Library Journal, 82 (June 1, 1957) 1400-1404.   845

Rose, Ernestine. "The Public Library and American Life."
New York: Columbia University Press, 1954. 238 pp.
                                                         846

Sheats, Paul, Clarence D. Jayne, and Ralph B. Spence.
"Adult Education, The Community Approach." New York:
Dryden Press [c 1953]. Chapter 6, Public Libraries.
Pp. 120-143.   847

Shirley, William W. What Happened to Our Adult Education
Hopes, In Library Journal, 72 (November 1, 1947) 1503-
1507.   848

Smith, Helen L. Adult Education Activities in Public Libraries, In Adult Education, 5 (Spring, 1955) 166-171.   849

Smith, Helen L. "Adult Education Activities in Public Libraries; A Report on the A. L. A. Survey of Adult Education Activities in Public Libraries and State Library Extension Agencies in the United States." Chicago: A. L. A., 1954. 128 pp. See No. 402 for annotation. 850

Smith, Helen L. Spotlight on Adult Education; The Story of the A. L. A.'s Current Survey of Adult Education in Public Libraries, In A. L. A. Bulletin, 47 (May, 1953) 191-192, 202-203. 851

Spence, Ralph B. and Katherine L. O'Brien. Library Adult Education Aims, In Adult Education Journal, 6 (October, 1947) 166-170. 852

Stevenson, Grace T. Adult Education, In Library Trends, 3 (January, 1955) 290-298. 853

Stevenson, Grace T. Adult Education Plans, In Library Journal, 79 (February 1, 1954) 161-166. 854

Stevenson, Grace T. A. L. A. Adult Education Projects, In Public Libraries, 7 (September, 1953) 9-11. 855

Stevenson, Grace T. A. L. A.'s New Project, In A. L. A. Bulletin, 45 (October, 1951) 301-303. 856

Stevenson, Grace T. "Role of the Public Library in Adult Reading," in National Society for the Study of Education. Fifty-fifth Yearbook, Part 2, In Adult Reading. Chicago: University of Chicago Press, 1956. Pp. 114-135. 857

Stevenson, Grace T. What is Adult Education?, In A. L. A. Bulletin, 50 (October, 1956) 578-582. 858

Stone, Clarence W. Adult Education and the Public Library, In Library Trends, 1 (April, 1953) 437-453. 859

Tompkins, Miriam D. United States of America, In Carl T. Thomsen, Edward Sydney, Miriam D. Tompkins, Adult Education Activities for Public Libraries. UNESCO Public Library Manuals, 3. Paris: UNESCO, 1950. Pp. 57-102. 860

Trends in Postwar Adult Education; Libraries, In Adult Education Journal, 5 (January, 1946) 16-20. 861

Ulveling, Ralph A.   Library and Adult Education, In A. L. A.
    Bulletin, 48 (April, 1954) 197-200.   862

Ulveling, Ralph A.   Moving Forward as the People's Univer-
    sity, In Public Libraries, 4 (March, 1950) 13-16.   863

Warncke, Ruth E.   Library Community Project, In A. L. A.
    Bulletin, 49 (April, 1955) 171.   864

Warncke, Ruth E.   Library Community Project, In A. L. A.
    Bulletin, 49 (November, 1955) 556-558.   865

Warncke, Ruth E.   "Public Libraries," in Study of Adult Ed-
    ucation in Rural Areas, In Rural Social Systems and Adult
    Education. [East Lansing] Michigan State College Press,
    1953. Pp. 172-196.   866

Williams, Dorothy G.   Adult Education in Public Libraries
    and Museums, In Journal of Negro Education, 14 (Summer,
    1945) 322-330.   867

Canada

Althouse, J. G.   Role of the Library in Continuing Educa-
    tion, In Ontario Library Review, 31 (November, 1947)
    373-375.   868

Cawson, M. E.   County Library Association and the Commu-
    nity, In Ontario Library Review, 29 (August, 1945) 304-
    308.   869

Corbett, E. A.   Library and Adult Education, In Ontario Li-
    brary Review, 37 (August, 1953) 176-177.   870

Dolores, Francis, Sister.   The People's Library, In Food
    for Thought, 5 (May, 1945) 12-17.   871

Dunlop, William J.   Libraries Play an Essential Role in A-
    dult Education Work, In Canadian Library Association
    Bulletin, 13 (October, 1956) 65-66.   872

Farncomb, Dora M.   Library and Adult Education, In Ontario
    Library Review, 31 (May, 1947) 122-124.   873

Morison, Charles K.   Experiments in Regional Library Ser-

Munn, Robert R.   275

vice in British Columbia, In Fundamental and Adult Education, 3 (January, 1951) 3-9.   874

Munn, Robert R. Place of the Public Library in Adult Education Today and Tomorrow, In Ontario Library Review, 33 (August, 1949) 194-198.   875

Ponitz, Henry J. Community Role of the Public Library, In Ontario Library Review, 29 (August, 1945) 285-288. 876

Wilson, L. Roberta. Role of Libraries in Adult Education, In Ontario Library Review, 34 (November, 1950) 255-258.   877

Great Britain

Argles, Michael. The Library in Liberal Education, In Adult Education (London), 28 (Autumn, 1955) 126-132. 878

Brew, J. Macalister. Informal Education Through Books, In Library Review, No. 83 (Autumn, 1947) 292-295. 879

Bryon, John F. W. Shelving the Issue, In Library Association Record, 491 (May, 1947) 116-122.   880

Burton, G. L. Public Libraries and the Education Act of 1944, In Library Association Record, 50 (March, 1948) 65-68.   881

Cowles, Frederick C. I. Making Adult Education Attractive, In Publishers' Circular and Booksellers' Record, 160 (July 6, 1946) 530-531.   882

Ford, A. Clow. Library As a Cultural Centre, In Library Association, London and Home Counties Branch, Area Library Cooperation; Library As a Cultural Centre; Library Service in Outlying Areas. Papers read at the Week-End Conference. October, 1947. Pp. 12-24. 883

Fox, Edward S. Adult Extension Activities at Walton Branch Library, Liverpool Public Libraries, In North Western Newsletter, No. 32 (March, 1955) 3-4.   884

Howarth, Reginald. Library's Cultural Contacts, In Library Review, No. 88 (Winter, 1948) 461-463.   885

Liggett, Mary. Library Service and Adult Education: Reflections From a Smaller Town, In Adult Education (London), 24 (Autumn, 1951) 150-156.   886

Littlefield, Joan. St. Pancras Arts and Civic Council, In Wilson Library Bulletin, 21 (February, 1947) 432.   887

London. National Central Library. Provision of Books to Adult Classes, In Library Association Record, 58 (December, 1956) 471-474.   888

MacIntosh, D. M. Further Education and the Library Service, In Library Association Conference, 1947, Brighton, Papers and Summaries of Discussions at the Brighton Conference. Pp. 29-32.   889

Moore, M. S. Library or Cultural Centre, In Library World, 39 (January, 1947) 91-92.   890

The National Central Library Report on an Inquiry into the Provision of Books to Adult Classes, In Adult Education (London), 29 (Spring, 1957) 288-294.   891

Pritchard, E. P. Libraries and Adult Education, In Library Association Record, 48 (June, 1946) 146-150.   892

Rengert, H. J. "Cultural Activities in Public Libraries, In Library Association, London and Home Counties Branch, Problems in Library Administration... Paper read at the Week-End Conference, October, 1948. Pp. 32-37.893

Sydney, Edward. Adult Education and the Public Library, In Adult Education (London), 19 (December, 1946) 73-82.
                                                         894

Sydney, Edward. Adult Education and the Public Library, In Library Association Record, 48 (November, 1946) 275-279.   895

Sydney, Edward. Library as a Centre of Local Cultural Activity, In Library Association, London and Home Counties Branch, Area Library Cooperation; Library as a Cultural Centre; Library Service in Outlying Areas. Papers read at the Week-End Conference, October, 1947. Pp. 14-17.   896

Sydney, Edward. United Kingdom, In Carl Thomsen,

Wragg, Ethel F. 277

Edward Sydney, and Miriam D. Tompkins, Adult Education Activities for Public Libraries. UNESCO Public Library Manuals, 3. Paris: UNESCO, 1950. Pp. 23-53.   897

Wragg, Ethel F. County Libraries and Further Education, In Library Association Conference, 1947, Brighton, Papers and Summaries of Discussions at the Brighton Conference. Pp. 32-39.   898

C. Business, Industry and Labor

Baltzell, E. Digby. Bell Telephone's Experiment in Education, In Harpers Magazine, 210 (March, 1955) 73-77.899

Barbash, Jack. "Universities and Unions in Workers' Education." New York: Harper, 1955. 206 pp. See No. 479 for annotation.   900

Coit, Eleanor G. Labor Unions Educate Against Racial Discrimination, for Political Action and Social Responsibility, In Progressive Education, 23 (January, 1946) 99-101.901

Coit, Eleanor G. Workers' Education, In Handbook of Adult Education in the United States, edited by Mary L. Ely. New York: Institute of Adult Education, Teachers College, Columbia University [c 1948]. Pp. 30-36, 489-501.   902

Connors, John D. Labor Education Today and Tomorrow, In American Federationist, 63 (October, 1956) 14-17.903

Connors, John D. To Help Us Find Our Way, In American Federationist, 58 (August, 1951) 18-20.   904

Costin, Frank. "The Relationship of Employees' Problems and Various Other Factors to Interest in an Adult Education Program." Ph.D. Dissertation. University of Chicago, 1949.   905

Eby, Kermit. Workers' Education for What?, In Antioch Review, 11 (Summer, 1951) 185-192.   906

Gillen, Wilfred D. The Institute of Humanistic Studies for Executives: an Experiment in Adult Education, In Fund

for Adult Education,   Liberal Adult Education.   White
Plains, N. Y.:   F. A. E. [1956]. Pp. 15-27. See No.
523 for annotation.   907

Goldwin, Robert A., ed. "Toward the Liberally Educated
Executive." White Plains, N. Y.: Fund for Adult Education, 1957. 111 pp. See No. 524 for annotation. 908

Hall, Wiley A. Adult Education Program of Labor Unions
and Other Workers Groups, In Journal of Negro Education, 14 (Summer, 1945) 407-411.   909

Hawkins, Gordon. Labour Education in Canada: Needs and
Possibilities, In Food for Thought, 16 (May-June, 1956)
377-383.   910

Kaplan, Abbott. Liberal Education in A Business Civilization, In Conference on Research Developments in Personnel Management,   Research Developments in Personnel
Management. Proceedings of First Conference, University of California, Los Angeles, June 7-8, 1956. University of California, Institute of Industrial Relations, 1957.
Pp. 1-6.   911

Kidd, James R. Liberal Education for Business Leadership,
In Adult Leadership, 6 (May, 1957) 11-14, 32. Same In
Adult Education (London), 30 (Autumn, 1957) 100-109.
                                                             912

London, Jack. A Reappraisal of Labor Education, In Adult
Education, 7 (Winter, 1957) 103-111.   913

McKeon, Jesse. Leadership Development in Industry, In
Association of University Evening Colleges Proceedings.
Fourteenth Annual Meeting, Atlanta, 1952. Pp. 66-71.
                                                             914

Mathews, J. H. Trade Union Education Today and Tomorrow, In Adult Education (London), 26 (Autumn, 1953) 95-
100.   915

Millar, J. P. M. Forty Years of Independent Working-Class
Education, In Adult Education (London), 21 (June, 1949)
210-215.   916

Mire, Joseph. "Labor Education; a Study Report on Needs,
Programs, and Approaches." Madison: Inter-University

Mire, Joseph   279

Labor Education Committee, University of Wisconsin,
1956.   206 pp.   917

Mire, Joseph. The University and the Union in Workers'
Education, In Adult Education, 5 (Summer, 1955) 232-236.
See No. 572 for annotation.   918

Presgrave, Ralph. Adult Education in Canadian Business,
In Food for Thought, 16 (May-June, 1956) 384-394. 919

Schapiro, Theodore. The Challenge of Workers' Education,
In Adult Education, 1 (February, 1951) 91-94. "Comments on Mr. Schapiro's Article" by Irvine L. H. Kerrison, Arthur A. Elder, Orlie Pell, pp. 95-99.   920

Shanner, William M. Industry and Adult Education, In Elementary School Journal, 50 (December, 1949) 183-187.
See No. 400 for annotation.   921

Starr, Mark. Labor's Concern with Adult Education, In
Institute for Administrative Officers of Higher Institutions
Proceedings, Vol. 20,   The Community Responsibilities
of Institutions of Higher Learning. Chicago: University
of Chicago Press, 1948. Pp. 33-42.   922

Townsend, Willard S. Toward Full Equality; Labor Works
for Democratic Adult Education, In Adult Education Journal, 5 (October, 1946) 162-165. See No. 146 for annotation.   923

Willis, Ivan L.   Industry's Concern With Adult Education,
in Institute for Administrative Officers of Higher Institutions, Proceedings, Vol. 20,   The Community Responsibilities of Institutions of Higher Learning. Chicago: University of Chicago Press, 1948. Pp. 23-32. See No.
411 for annotation.   924

"World Affairs and Your Union Education Program." New
York: American Labor Education Service, 1957. 26 pp.
                                                               925

D. Specialized Agencies

Alter, Forrest. A London Center for Research in Adult Education, In Adult Education, 7 (Summer, 1957) 208-211.
926

Barker, Edwin. Liberal Education and Industrial Management; the Y. M. C. A. New Residential Scheme, In Adult Education (London) 18 (March, 1946) 133-136.   927

Blakely, Robert J. The First Year of the Fund for Adult Education, In Food for Thought, 13 (October, 1952) 19-23.
928

Bullock, Ralph W. The Adult Education Program of the Y. M. C. A. Among Negroes, In Journal of Negro Education, 14 (Summer, 1945) 385-389.   929

Bussiere, Eugene. UNESCO and Adult Education, In Adult Education, 3 (September, 1953) 179-183.   930

'The City Lit.,' In Adult Education (London), 24 (Autumn, 1951) 121-127.   931

Educational Work of the National Council of Y. M. C. A.'s, In Adult Education (London), 23 (March, 1951) 307-309. 932

Edwards, Frances H.   Adult Education in Settlements, In Handbook of Adult Education in the United States, edited by Mary L. Ely. New York: Institute of Adult Education, Teachers College, Columbia University, 1948. Pp. 60-64; 452-456.   933

Fletcher, C. Scott. Program of the Fund for Adult Education, In Adult Education, 2 (December, 1951) 59-66. 934

Freeman, Samuel. "Adult Education in the Jewish Community Center." Ph. D. Dissertation. Columbia University, 1953.   935

Fund for Adult Education. "The Challenge of Lifetime Learning." New York: Fund for Adult Education, 1953. 40 pp.   936

Fund for Adult Education. "The Fund for Adult Education, What It Is and What It Is Doing." New York: F. A. E., 1951. 16 pp.   937

Harper, Paul V.   281

Harper, Paul V. Let the Church Educate, In Christian
    Century, 64 (December 17, 1947) 1552-1554.   938

Height, Dorothy I. The Adult Education Program of the
    Y. W. C. A. Among Negroes, In Journal of Negro Educa-
    tion, 14 (Summer, 1945) 390-395.   939

Hewitt, Dorothy. Adult Education on Its Own; the Advant-
    ages of Independent Schools and Centers, In Handbook of
    Adult Education in the United States, edited by Mary L.
    Ely. New York: Institute of Adult Education, Teachers
    College, Columbia University, 1948. Pp. 240-242; 310-
    320.   940

Hunsaker, Herbert C. UNESCO's Work in Adult Education,
    In Harvard Educational Review, 20 (Summer, 1950) 169-
    175.   941

Kidd, James Roby. UNESCO and Education for International
    Understanding-II, In Adult Education (London) 28 (Summer,
    1955) 14-22. Same in: Food for Thought, 15 (March,
    1955) 13-19.   942

Lawley-Wakelin, David. Adult Education by Mental Hospi-
    tals, In Adult Education (London), 20 (March, 1948) 145-
    151.   943

Lawley-Wakelin, David. The Epsom Experiment, In Adult
    Education (London), 25 (Autumn, 1952) 130-136.   944

Lengrand, Paul. UNESCO and International Understanding-I,
    In Adult Education (London) 28 (Summer, 1955) 7-13.945

Lindsay, Inabel B. Adult Education Programs for Negroes
    in Settlement Houses, In Journal of Negro Education, 14
    (Summer, 1945) 347-352.   946

Longmore, T. Wilson and Frank C. Nall. Service, Profes-
    sional and Other Civic Clubs, In Study of Adult Education
    in Rural Areas, Rural Social Systems and Adult Educa-
    tion, a Committee Report by Charles P. Loomis and
    others. [East Lansing] Michigan State College Press,
    1953. Pp. 122-146.   947

Low, Theodore L. "The Educational Philosophy and Practice
    of Art Museums in the United States." New York: Bureau
    of Publications, Teachers College, Columbia University,

1948.   246 pp.   948

Low, Theodore L.   The Place of the Museum in Adult Education, In Handbook of Adult Education in the United
States, edited by Mary L. Ely.   New York: Institute of
Adult Education, Teachers College, Columbia University,
1948. Pp. 236-239; 390-399.   949

Marshall, James.   UNESCO and Its Program, In Adult Education Journal, 6 (July, 1947) 121-124.   950

Men's and Women's Clubs as Agencies of Adult Education,
In Handbook of Adult Education in the United States, edited by Mary L. Ely.   New York: Institute of Adult Education, Teachers College, Columbia University, 1948.
Pp. 153-158; 383-390.   951

Riviere, G. H.   The Museum and Adult Education, a Report, In UNESCO,   Adult Education, Current Trends
and Practices.   Problems in Education, 2.   Paris:
UNESCO, 1949.   Pp. 132-140.   952

Rose, Hanna T.   Museums in Education, In Adult Education
(London), 25 (Spring, 1953) 297-303.   953

Schad, Edward J.   Catholic-Sponsored Adult Schools, In National Catholic Educational Association Bulletin, 53 (August, 1956) 367-370.   954

Sheats, Paul H.   UNESCO and the A. E. A., In Adult Education, 3 (February, 1953) 91-93.   955

Sheats, Paul H.   UNESCO and World Wide Adult Education,
In Adult Leadership, 6 (November, 1957) 129-130, 134.
                                                         956

Smucker, Orden.   Adult Education in the Rural Church, ''
In Study of Adult Education in Rural Areas,   Rural So-
cial Systems and Adult Education, a Committee Report by
Charles P. Loomis and others.   [East Lansing] Michigan
State College Press, 1953.   Pp. 196-229.   957

Stensland, Per and Carol Stensland.   Community Education
for International Understanding, Part 1-State and Local
UNESCO Councils, In Adult Education, 2 (October, 1951)
17-23.   958

Stensland, Per and Carol Stensland. Community Education
   for International Understanding, Part II-Training for
   World Citizenship, In Adult Education, 2 (February, 1952)
   89-97.   959

UNESCO and Adult Education, In Adult Education Journal, 6
   (October, 1947) 165.   960

UNESCO. "UNESCO and Adult Education." Paris:
   UNESCO, 1948. 15 pp.   961

UNESCO. "Report on the UNESCO La Breviere Seminar on
   Workers' Education," 1952. Edited by G. D. H. Cole and
   Andre Philip. Educational Studies and Documents, No. 1.
   Paris: UNESCO, 1953. 41 pp.   962

UNESCO's Austrian Seminar on Adult Education Methods, In
   Adult Education, 1 (February, 1951) 100-106.   963

Wilhelm, J. O. 100 Years of Adult Education; the Royal
   Canadian Institute, In Food for Thought, 11 (February,
   1951) 13-16.   964

Williamson, C. A. Education in Canada's Prisons, In Food
   for Thought, 10 (January, 1950) 32-36.   965

Wormley, Margaret J. Adult Education in Federal Prisons,
   In Journal of Negro Education, 14 (Summer, 1945) 425-
   430.   966

V. Courses and Curricula

Adams, W. S. The Discipline of History, In Adult Education (London), 19 (March, 1947) 145-155.   967

Anderson, Ida M. Art for All, In California Journal of Secondary Education, 28 (April, 1953) 218-220.   968

Austin, A. E. Adult Students and Foreign Languages, In Further Education, 2 (June-August, 1948) 56-62.   969

Barden, John P. and others. The Theory of the Basic Arts Program, In Adult Education Journal, 8 (October, 1949) 237-243. See No. 480 for annotation.   970

Benezet, L. T. General Education for the Adult in Contemporary Society, In Journal of General Education, 2 (July, 1948) 336-340. See No. 481 for annotation.   971

Bengston, Nels A. Geography as a Vital Element in Adult Education, In Clark University, Graduate School of Geography, Clark Graduate School of Geography; Our First Twenty-Five Years, 1921-1946. Worchester, Mass.: Clark University, 1946. Pp. 34-40.   972

Bland, D. S. Literature and Adult Education, In Cambridge Journal, 4 (December, 1950) 172-180.   973

Brown, Muriel W. Adapting Adult Education Programs to Postwar Needs, In National Society for the Study of Education, Forty-Fourth Yearbook, American Education in the Postwar Period, Part I, Curriculum Construction. Chicago: University of Chicago Press, 1945. Pp. 57-79. See No. 22 for annotation.   974

Bruce, Maurice. Science in Adult Education, Developments in the Sheffield Extra-Mural Programme, In Adult Education (London), 23 (March, 1951) 258-262.   975

Bruntz, George G. Organizing the Adult Curriculum, In Na-

Charlton, D. G.   285

tion's Schools, 39 (February, 1947) 24-25, 32.   976

Charlton, D. G.   French Literature for English Extra-Mural
Students, In Adult Education (London), 25 (Spring, 1953)
280-285.   977

Clifford, M. H.   The Place of Science in Adult Education,
In Adult Education (London), 19 (March, 1947) 134-145.
                                                              978

Clifford, M. H.   Science in Adult Education, In Nature, 159
(April, 1947) 560-562.   979

Clifford, M. H.   Taking Science to the Adult, In Discovery,
7 (September-October, 1946) 279-281, 308-310.   980

Crabtree, Arthur P.   "Civic Education, Program for Adults,"
written for the Curriculum Committee [National Association
of Public School Adult Educators] Curriculum Series, No.
1.   Washington, D. C.:   National Association of Public
School Adult Educators [c 1956]. 64 pp.   981

Crawford, Norman P.   "Speech Courses in the Adult
Schools of New Jersey."   Ph. D. Dissertation.   Columbia
University, Teachers College, 1954.   982

Crossland, R. W.   Science in Adult Education, In Further
Education, 2 (December, 1948-February, 1949) 232-242.
                                                              983

Crossland, R. W.   The Teaching of Biology in Adult Education, In Adult Education (London), 29 (Summer, 1956)
45-53.   984

Dees, Norman. History and the Adult, In Adult Education
(London), 21 (June, 1949) 179-183.   985

Dixon, Cecil.   Science in Adult Education, In Adult Education (London), 21 (March, 1949) 123-127.   986

Dumazedier, J.   Content of Adult Education, In UNESCO,
Adult Education, Current Trends and Practices.   Prob-
lems in Education, 2.   New York: Columbia University
Press, 1949.   Pp. 41-53.   See No. 36 for annotation.
                                                              987

Elsdon, K. T.   Music Appreciation, An Experiment, In Adult Education (London), 30 (Autumn, 1957) 127-134. 988

Elvin, Lionel. A Modern Equivalent for the Classics, In
Adult Education (London), 19 (September, 1946) 18-34.
                                                           989

Farington, Benjamin. Greek, Latin, and Adult Education,
In Adult Education (London), 19 (December, 1946) 86-92.
                                                           990

Getsinger, J. W. What Do California Schools Teach?, In A-
dult Education Journal, 8 (October, 1949) 231-236.   991

Goldman, Edward D. Current Events and Materials in Adult
Education, In California Journal of Secondary Education,
31 (April, 1956) 226-229.   992

Harrison, J. F. C. Toward an Interpretation of International
Relations, In Adult Education (London), 21 (December,
1948) 75-81.   993

Holley, N. M. History for the Adult Student, In Adult Education (London), 20 (December, 1947) 87-94.   994

Houle, Cyril O. and William Bowden. The Content of Adult
Education, In Review of Educational Research, 20 (June,
1950) 198-206. See No. 166 for annotation.   995

Hunsaker, H. C. and S. L. Witman. Teaching World Understanding in Schools for Adults, In School Executive, 66
(January, 1947) 57-58.   996

Hunt, H. K. Classical Studies and Adult Education, In Adult
Education (London), 19 (June, 1947) 208-213.   997

Jessup, Frank W. The Arts and Adult Education, In Adult
Education (London), 21 (March, 1949) 117-122.   998

Johnson, Janet B. Adults Enjoyed Evening Literature, In
Clearing House, 23 (March, 1949) 414-416.   999

Johnston, W. D. Humane Learning: a Comment, In Adult
Education (London) 20 (September, 1947) 27-30.   1000

Jones, H. A. Music and Drama in Adult Education, Some
Experiments in Partnership, In Adult Education (London),
27 (Spring, 1955) 273-279.   1001

King, Nancy. New Horizons; Adult Education Offers Courses in Hobbies, Trades, Commercial, and Cultural Subjects, In Virginia Journal of Education, 43 (November, 1949) 10-11, 21.   1002

Layton, David. A Hope for Science, In Adult Education (London), 25 (Autumn, 1952) 112-118.   1003

Levitt, John. Language in Adult Education, In Adult Education (London) 29 (Summer, 1956) 24-32.   1004

Lovell, Bernard. Science as a Vital Factor in Education, In Adult Education (London), 20 (September, 1947) 5-10.
                                                            1005

Lowenthal, Helen. Education Through Art-For All, In Adult Education (London), 20 (June, 1948) 172-177.   1006

Lucas, Peter G. Philosophy in Adult Education, In Adult Education (London), 18 (June, 1947) 221-228.   1007

Matsukawa, Ernest and Peter C. Russell. Adult Education and Nuclear Physics, In Adult Education (London), 30 (Summer, 1957) 59-63.   1008

Mendelssohn, K. A. G. The Teaching of Physics in Adult Education, In Rewley House Papers, V. 2, No. 10, 1948-49. Pp. 16-21.   1009

Morris, C. R. Aims and Content of Adult Education, In Adult Education (London), 18 (December, 1945) 85-92. See No. 114 for annotation.   1010

Pick, F. W. Problems in the Teaching of 'International Relations', In Adult Education (London), 21 (December, 1948) 81-85.   1011

Pickvance, T. J. The Sciences in the Extra-Mural Work of Universities, In Adult Education (London), 27 (Winter, 1954) 205-213.   1012

Pinette, Mattie A. School and Community Face the Atomic Age, In School Life, 35 (September, 1953) 155.   1013

Potter, E. J. The Curriculum of an Experimental College, In Adult Education (London), 24 (Autumn, 1951) 98-106.
                                                            1014

Preston, Everett C.   Curriculum, Its Nature and Scope, In National Association of Public School Adult Educators, Public School Adult Education, a Guide for /Administrators and Teachers. Washington, D. C. : N. A. P. S. A. E. , 1956. Pp. 12-21.   1015

Pulling, R. J.   The Adult Education Curriculum, Mirror of the Community, In National Education Association Journal, 46 (October, 1957) 461-462.   1016

Pulling, R. J. and Presco Anderson.   Building a Curriculum of Adult Education in New York State, In Adult Leadership, 5 (December, 1956) 171-173, 196.   1017

Rosenberger, Homer T.   Offerings for Out-of-School Adults, In National Association of Secondary School Principals Bulletin, 40 (February, 1956) 181-193.   1018

Schneider, Perry L.   Curriculum Development in Adult Education, In Adult Education Bulletin, 12 (October, 1947) 19-21.   1019

Science in Adult Education, In Nature, 164 (October 8, 1949) 608-609.   1020

Science in the Extra-Mural Work of Universities, In Nature, 174 (July 24, 1954) 166-167.   1021

Seiferth, W. S.   Significance of the Humanities in Adult Education,   In UNESCO, Adult Education Toward Social and Political Responsibility, edited by Frank W. Jessup. UNESCO Institute for Education Publication, No. 1. Hamburg: UNESCO Institute for Education, 1953. Pp. 131-139.   1022

Snowden, F. M.   Classics and Adult Education, In Classical Journal, 45 (May, 1950) 373-378.   1023

Thomas, Trevor.   Art for Adults, In UNESCO, Education and Art; a Symposium, edited by Edwin Ziegfeld. New York: Columbia University Press, 1953. Pp. 93-96.   1024

Tsagos, Zoe G.   The Course in Living Classics at Union Junior College, In Junior College Journal, 21 (January, 1951) 280-282.   1025

Vanstone, D.   Adult Courses in Science, In Times Educational Supplement, 2045 (July 9, 1954) 685.   1026

Williams, Stanley W.   "A Study of the Organization, Administration and Supervision of the Curriculum in Adult Education in the United States."   Ph.D. Dissertation. University of Southern California, 1949.   1027

Author and Title Index

(Note: Titles are listed only for articles, pamphlets, etc., having no authors and entered under title in the bibliography.) Numbers refer to items.

Adam, Thomas R., 1
Adams, W. S., 967
Adler, Mortimer J., 2
Adolfson, Lorentz H., 474
Adult Education and the Universities, 475
Adult Education Association of the U.S.A., 3
Adult Education Association of the U.S.A. Committee on Evaluation, 275, 412
Adult Education Association of the U.S.A. National Commission on Adult Education Finance, 353, 413
Adult Education for a New World, 4
Alexander, W.P., 5
Allion, Helen, 354, 696
Alter, Forrest, 926
Althouse, J. G., 868
American Association of School Administrators, 697
American Educational Research Association, 157, 158, 414, 415
American Library Association, 783
American Library Association. Adult Education Board, 784
American Library Association. Office for Adult Education, 416, 785, 786

A. L. A. Survey of Adult Education, 787
A. L. A. Surveys Library Programs in Adult Education, 788
Anderson, Ida M., 968
Anderson, John E., 181, 202
Anderson, Martin P., 789
Anderson, Presco, 775, 1017
Anikeeff, Alexis M., 239, 476
Argles, Michael, 878
Arnold, James E., 333, 477
Atkins, James A., 417
Austin, A. E., 969
Avril, Edwin F., 262

Bailey, Thomas D., 750
Baltzell, E. Digby, 899
Banta, Clarence O., 276, 478
Barbash, Jack, 479, 900
Barden, John P., 480, 970
Barensfeld, Thomas E., 790
Barker, Edwin, 927
Baron, George, 418
Barron, Howard H., 203
Bausman, Charlotte K., 791
Beamer, Alan L., 751
Benezet, Louis T., 481, 971
Bengston, Nels A., 972
Benne, Kenneth D., 6, 7, 8, 309, 482
Beran, D. L., 483
Besterman, Theodore, 419
Bethel, Lawrence L., 9, 484

Fossum, Oscar, 760
Foster, Edith L., 800
Fox, Edward S., 884
Frank, Lawrence K., 45
Frasure, Kenneth J., 289, 761
Freeman, Samuel D., 290, 366, 935
Friedenberg, Edgar, 46
Friesen, John K., 47, 645
Fund for Adult Education 48, 936, 937

Garber, Leonard, 266
Georgia. West Georgia College, 521
Getsinger, Joseph W., 338, 344, 522, 762, 763, 991
Gillen, Wilfred D., 523, 907
Gilligan, Thomas J., 267
Gold, Milton S., 49
Goldin, Frank S., 190
Goldman, Edward D., 764, 992
Goldwin, Robert A., 524, 908
Gordon, K. W., 50
Gordon, Morton, 525, 526
Gould, Samuel B., 51
Grady, Marion B., 801
Graham, Minnie W., 765
Graney, Maurice, 52, 527
Grant, George, 53
Grattan, C. Hartley, 339
Graves, Perdue B., 214, 766
Great Britain. British Information Service. Reference Division, 431
Great Britain. Ministry of Reconstruction. Adult Education Committee, 54
Green, Ernest, 55, 215
Greenaway, Emerson, 802, 803
Grierson, John, 56
Groombridge, Brian, 57
Gruen, William, 58, 59
Grumman, Russell M., 340, 491, 528
Guehenno, Jean, 60

Guerin, Quinon, 191, 245
Guide to Studies in Adult Education, 438
Guzzeta, D. J., 529

Hall, Wiley A., 909
Hallenbeck, Wilbur C., 61, 62, 707
Hamill, Harold L., 804
Hamlin, H. M., 708
Hammarberg, Helen V., 530, 636
Hand, Samuel E., 162, 246, 268, 432, 750
Handbook of Adult Education, 433
Handlists of Studies in Adult Education, 438
Hansen, Kenneth H., 63
Harper, Paul V., 938
Harris, Albert T., 269
Harrison, Florence L., 805
Harrison, J. F. C., 314, 993
Harrison, James W., 270
Harrison, R. Wendell, 531
Havighurst, Robert J., 216, 217, 315
Hawes, Marion E., 806, 807
Hawkins, Gordon, 910
Haworth, Edward, 218
Hayakawa, S. I., 64
Hazard, Leland, 808
Height, Dorothy I., 939
Hendrickson, Andrew, 163, 322, 434, 709
Hendry, Charles E., 291
Hensarling, Paul R., 292, 710
Henson, Guy, 47
Herring, John W., 65
Hershey, Edna-Jean, 293
Hewitt, Dorothy, 940
Hieronymus, Albert N., 164
Hockabout, Marvin C., 323
Hodgkin, T. L., 66
Hogan, J. M., 665
Holley, N. M., 994
Hopkinson, D. M., 666

for Advancement of Teaching..., 554
Library Function as an Educator of the People, 820
Liggett, Mary, 886
Lindeman, Eduard C., 98, 297
Lindquist, Raymond C., 821
Lindsay, Inabel B., 946
Lipsett, Lawrence, 258, 304, 617
Littlefield, Henry W., 555
Littlefield, Joan, 887
Liveright, Alexander A., 377, 556
Locke, Alain L., 99, 100
London, Jack, 298, 324, 913
London. National Central Library, 888
Longmore, T. Wilson, 947
Loomis, Charles A., 405, 462
Loosley, Elizabeth, 101
Lorge, Irving, 167, 194, 195, 196, 251, 316
Lotze, Heiner, 102
Love, Grady, 221
Love, Robert A., 222, 223, 252, 317, 557
Lovell, Bernard, 1005
Low, Theodore L., 948, 949
Lowenthal, Helen, 1006
Lowry, Sheldon G., 552
Lowy, Louis, 447
Lucas, Peter G., 1007
Luke, Robert A., 354, 448, 696, 822.
Lyle, Edith A., 675

Maaske, Roben J., 103, 318
McClusky, Howard Y., 168, 723, 724, 725
McCoy, Dean H., 558
McDiarmid, Errett W., 823
McGhee, Paul A., 104, 105, 106, 559, 560, 561, 562
McGlothlin, William J., 107
McHugh, Vincent, 108

MacIntosh, D. M., 889
Mack, John A., 224
McKeon, Jesse, 914
McLaughlin, Laurence K., 176, 253
MacLean, Malcolm S., 109
McMahan, Frederick J., 225
McPheeters, Annie L., 824
Maddox, Vivian, 825
Malamud, Daniel I., 378, 563
Maloney, Martin, 226
Mann, George C., 344, 771
Marshall, James, 950
Martin, Arthur G., 726
Martin, Lowell A., 826
Martorana, Sebastian V., 379, 380, 564, 565
Masley, John W., 566
Mather, Louis K., 381, 727
Mathews, J. H., 915
Mathews, Mildred V. D., 567, 827, 828
Matloff, Maurice, 568
Matsukawa, Ernest, 1008
Maud, Sir John, 110
Maurer, Charles L., 772
Mayfield, Leonard B., 773
Mead, Margaret, 569
Meder, Albert E., Jr., 570
Melby, Ernest O., 111
Mendelssohn, K. A. G., 1009
Men's and Women's Clubs as Agencies of Adult Education, 951
Microfilm Abstracts, 426
Milam, Carl H., 829, 830
Millar, J. P. M., 916
Miller, Harry L., 112, 299, 571
Mills, C. Wright, 113
Minnis, Roy B., 227
Mire, Joseph, 572, 917, 918
Montross, Harold W., 219
Moore, M. S., 890
Morison, Charles K., 874
Morris, C. R., 114, 115, 1010
Morrison, Duncan G., 382, 831

295

Subject Index

Adult education - Bibliography, see Bibliography
Adult education - History, see History of adult education
Adult education, Rural, see Rural adult education
Adult Education Association of the U.S.A., 8, 78, 93, 95, 120, 132
Adult education centers, see Centers
Adult education leaders, see Leaders
Adult education research, see Research
Adult educators, 112, 312-332
   see also Leaders; Teacher Training
Adult intelligence, 194
Adult learning, 181-201, 599
   ability and adult learning, 185, 186
   aging and adult learning, 182, 195, 196
   aptitude and adult learning, 189, 244
   conditions for adult learning, 183
   retention and adult learning, 190
   studies in adult learning, 160
Adults, Characteristics of, 167, 192, 239-261
Adults, Middle-aged, see Middle-aged adults
Agencies, Specialized, 926-966
Aging, 45, 57, 137, 588, 735
   Research on, 162, 179, 181, 182, 187, 196, 210, 216, 218, 232, 233, 246, 300, 395
Aims, see Direction finding
Akron, University of, 529
Alberta, University of, 641
Alexandria, Va., 751
Alumni education, 508, 513, 637
American Telephone and Telegraph Co., 523, 899, 907
Anglo-German Conference, 682
Art, 491, 968, 998, 1006, 1024
Atlanta, Ga., 824
Australia, 126

Baltimore Cooperative Survey and Work Survey Conference, 287, 307, 308
Baltimore, Md., 765, 767, 781, 806
Basic Arts Program, 480, 629, 970

300

Bell Telphone Co., see American Telephone and Telegraph
   Co.
Bibliography, 412-473
Biology, 983
Blackburn People's College, 663
British Columbia, 824
Brooklyn College Experiment, 610, 613, 614
Buffalo, N.Y., 349, 778
Burbank, Calif., 358
Burton Manor, 654
Business, 524, 899, 907, 908, 911, 912, 919

California, 233, 262, 281, 338, 342, 344, 351, 357, 358,
   362, 630, 699, 700, 753, 759, 762, 763, 764, 771, 777,
   778, 991
   see also Burbank, Los Angeles, Santa Monica, Sonoma
California, University of, 253, 254, 507, 530
Canada, 47, 53, 56, 87, 88, 101, 375, 701, 721, 910, 919
   see also Libraries - Canada; Universities and colleges -
   Canada
Carleton College, 651
Carnegie Foundation for Advancement of Teaching, 554
Catholic Church, 28, 29, 32, 33, 954
Catholic colleges and universities, 499, 576, 580, 611
Center for the Study of Liberal Education for Adults 497,
   556, 606
Centers, 218, 262, 355, 372, 926
   see also Jewish community centers
Certificate programs, 374, 550, 644
Characteristics of adults, see Adults, Characteristics of
Chicago, Ill., 352, 812
Chicago, University of, 530, 542, 549
Church of Jesus Christ of Latter Day Saints, 334
Churches, 28, 29, 32, 33, 290, 334, 336, 350, 366, 399, 935,
   938, 954, 957
Citizenship education, 30, 56, 65, 74, 98, 125, 168, 363, 702,
   981
City College of New York, 567
City Lit, 931
Classical studies, 990, 997, 1023, 1025
Clubs, 805, 947, 951
"College in the Country," 521, 586
Colleges, see Universities and colleges
Colorado, 267
Columbia University, 43, 335, 364, 493, 518
Community centered adult education, 58, 104
Community colleges, 496, 512, 516, 546, 547, 566, 584, 633,
   634

Group study, 122, 219
Groups, Characteristics of, 159

Higher education, see Universities and colleges
Highland Park, Michigan, 283
Hillcroft College, 677
Historical studies, 333-352
History, 967, 985, 994
History of adult education, 314, 339
Hospitals, Mental, 943, 944
Humanities, 1022

Illinois, 289, 761
  see also Chicago
Independent schools and centers, 940
Indiana, 21
  see also Gary; Indianapolis
Indianapolis, Indiana, 769
Industry, 206, 400, 411, 524, 899, 905, 907, 908, 914, 921,
  924, 927
Institute of Humanistic Studies for Executives, 523, 899, 907
Intelligence, see Adult intelligence
Interests, see Students, Adult - Interests
International education, 1, 20, 84, 111, 145, 148, 150, 401,
  492, 533, 538, 584, 632, 942, 958, 959, 993, 996, 1011
International Harvester, 921, 924
Interview, 310
Iowa, 186, 207, 225, 227
  see also Sac City
Ithaca, N. Y. , 224

Jewish adult education, 290, 336, 350, 366, 935
Jewish community centers, 290, 935
Junior colleges, 9, 211, 302, 379, 380, 478, 484, 492, 555,
  564, 565, 592, 634

Kansas, see Topeka
Kansas, University of, 348, 615
Kentucky, see Louisville

Labor unions, 146, 376, 479, 572, 900, 901, 902, 903, 904,
  906, 909, 910, 913, 915, 917, 918, 922, 923, 925
Languages, 969, 1004
  see also Greek; Latin
Latin, 990
Leaders, 41, 67, 328, 329, 331, 332, 355, 377, 536, 649
Learning, see Adult Learning

Liberal arts colleges, 360, 503, 548, 581, 631
Libraries and adult education, 783-898
    Canada, 868-877
    Great Britain, 878-898
    United States, 783-867
    Catholics, 833
    Negroes, 824, 867
    Philosophy of, 811
    Surveys and research studies, 382, 402, 786, 787, 788,
        795, 819, 831, 839, 840, 841, 849, 850, 851, 855, 856,
        864, 865
    Trends, 813, 818, 820, 859, 861
Literary institutes, 931
Literature, 973, 999
Literature, French, 977
Liverpool, England, 884
London Center for Research, 926
London. National Central Library, 888, 891
Los Angeles, 342, 700
Louisville, Ky., 844

Manchester University, 259, 343, 672
Maryland, see Baltimore
Methods, 176, 238, 321
Merchandizing adult education, 105, 106
Michigan, 212, 757
    see also Highland Park
Middle-aged adults, 217, 315
Minnesota, 410
Motivation, see Students - Motives
Motivation research, 223, 317
Mount Union College, 548
Museums, 948, 949, 952, 953
Municipal universities, see Universities, Municipal
Music, 988, 1001

National Central Library, 888, 891
National Education Association. Division of Adult Education
    Services, 18
Needs, see Students, Adult - Needs
Negro colleges and universities, 359, 365, 392, 501, 520
Negro history, 999
Negroes, 99, 269, 277, 359, 392, 396, 737, 824, 929, 939,
    946
    see also Libraries and adult education - Negroes
    see also Negro colleges and universities
New Jersey, 982

New York (state), 86, 265, 273, 350, 754, 756, 774, 775
   see also Buffalo, Ithaca, Pleasantville, New York City
New York City, 827
New York.   City College of New York, 567
New York University,   Division of General Education, 489
Newport News, Va., 770
Night Schools, see Evening colleges; Public schools
Non-residential centers, 659, 660, 685
North Carolina, see Greensboro
North Carolina, University of, 340
Nuclear physics, 1008

Objectives, see Direction-finding
Ohio, 204, 397, 404, 780, 782
Ohio State University, 403, 609
Oklahoma, 305, 755, 779
Older adults, see Aging
Orange Coast College, 492
Oregon, 773

Pennsylvania, see Philadelphia
Pennsylvania State College, 530
Pennsylvania.   University Institute of Humanistic Studies for
   Executives, 523, 899, 907
People's colleges, see Community colleges
Philadelphia, Pa., 772
Philosophy, 1007
Philosophy of adult education, 1-156
Physics, 1008, 1009
Pleasantville, N.Y., 760
Presbyterian Church, 399
Prisons, 278, 965, 966
Program evaluation, 232, 275-308
Program planning, 262-274
Providence, R.I., 236
Psychology, 213
Psychology of adult learning, see Adult learning
Public Libraries, see Libraries
Public schools, 696-782
   general programs, 696-749
   state and city programs, 750-782
   accreditation, 710
   evaluation, 283, 289, 292, 294, 295, 305, 306
   philosophy, 34, 69, 86, 117
   surveys and research studies, 265, 283, 289, 305, 337,
      338, 342, 349, 354, 369, 370, 371, 381, 383, 384, 385,
      391, 394, 699, 700, 706, 710, 713, 716, 717, 718, 719,

728, 729, 731, 737, 756, 761, 763, 778, 779
trends, 69, 116, 384, 697, 711, 729

Reading skills, 191, 201, 245, 857
Religious organizations, see Churches, Y. M. C. A. , Y. W. C. A.
Research in adult education, 157-411
  centers, 926
  needs and methods, 309-320
  reviews of, 157-180
  see also special subjects, e.g. , Aging; Public schools,
    etc.
Residential colleges, 585, 595, 605, 606, 607, 608, 654, 655,
  657, 660, 661, 666, 667, 668, 669, 673, 675, 677, 684, 688
Retirement, 137
Reviews of research, see Research - reviews of
Rochester Institute of Technology, 258
Royal Canadian Institute, 964
Rural adult education, 264, 404, 405,. 708, 754, 866, 957
Ruskin College, 661
Rutgers University, 506, 570

Sac City, Iowa, 776
San Bernardino Valley College, 545
San Quentin Prison, 278
Santa Monica, Calif. , 233
Schools, see Public schools
Science, 213, 975, 978, 979, 980, 983, 984, 986, 1003, 1005,
  1008, 1012, 1020, 1021, 1026
Settlements, 933, 946
Short-term training, 296, 361, 375
Sonoma, Calif. , 362
Specialized agencies, see Agencies, Specialized
Speech courses, 982
Standards in extra-mural work, 674
State teachers colleges, 368
Students, Adult
  ability, 185, 186, 207
  aptitude, 189
  characteristics, 239-261
  intelligence, 194, 251
  interests, 103, 202-238
  motives, 202-238
  needs, 202-238
Summer schools, 685
Surveys, see Research in adult education

Teacher training, 188, 288, 321-332